The Innkeepers' REGISTER

Country Inns of North America
1995

Edited by Kathryn Kinney

INDEPENDENT INNKEEPERS' ASSOCIATION
Marshall, Michigan
Founded in 1972 by Norman T. Simpson

ENDORSED PROVIDER PROGRAM

The Independent Innkeepers' Association is developing an Endorsed Provider Program to serve both our member inns and their guests. Companies selected by the Association to be Endorsed Providers offer superior products that are important to innkeepers and their guests. In many cases, guests will be able to see and enjoy these products as part of their experience at Association inns. We also envision that the special relation between the Association and the Endorsed Provider will prove advantageous to our guests in their acquisition of these products for their homes.

The first Endorsed Provider selected by the Association is Thomasville Furniture Company for its Country Inns and Back Roads furniture collection. Many of the items in this collection are reproduced from originals in Association inns. An illustration of Thomasville's CIBR collection appears inside the front cover of the *Register*. For more information, please contact Country Inns and Back Roads Home Furnishings Collection, Route 202, Box 10, Hollicong, PA 18928. Telephone: 800-500-CIBR (2427)

Photo Credits:
G. E. Arnold
  Madewood Plantation House
Patricia Brabant
  Carter House, Carter Hotel, Eureka, CA
George W. Gardner; all © copyrighted
  Cover Photo—Moose Mountain Lodge, Etna, NH
  Boulder Inn, The, New Preston, CT
  Glasbern, Fogelsville, PA
  Orchard Inn, The, Saluda, NC
  Sea Crest by the Sea, Spring Lake, NJ
  Settlers Inn, The, Hawley, PA
  White Inn, The, Fredonia, NY
  White Oak Inn, The, Danville, OH
Denny Goodman
  LaCorsette Maison Inn, Newton, IA
Stewart Hopkins
  Johnson House, The, Florence, OR
Dave Monaghan
  Montague Inn, Saginaw, MI
Bruce Muncy
  Oak Bed & Breakfast Inn, The, Christianburg, VA
M. P. Myers Photography, Cape May, NJ
  Mainstay, The, Cape May, NJ
  Manor House, The, Cape May, NJ
  Queen Victoria, The, Cape May, NJ
David Schwartz
  Bell Grae Inn, The, Staunton, VA
Mort Tucker Photography, Cleveland, Ohio
  Inn at Honey Run, The, Millersburg, OH

Cover Photo—Moose Mountain Lodge, Etna, NH
Cover Design by Judy Lenz
Commentary by Kathryn Kinney

1995 The Innkeepers' Register

For further information, call Independent Innkeepers' Association,

800-344-5244

616-789-0393

Contents

CANADA

UNITED KINGDOM

INTRODUCTION

We are exceedingly proud to present to our inn-traveling guests this full color edition of *The Innkeepers' Register.* It was only seven years ago that we printed our first *Register,* an off-shoot of Norman T. Simpson's well-read *Country Inns and Back Roads* travel book. During that time our *Register* has developed into a highly respected source for country inn accommodations across America as well as in Canada and Great Britain. With the recent addition of color, the pictures of the Inns provide a more pleasant experience for the traveler who is selecting that special destination. As further assistance for that process, this year we have added another *aid for identification* for all of our Inns, our *Style, Location, and Type Descriptors.* At the end of the paragraph which describes the individual inn, you will find (in parentheses) three single-word descriptors. These words are a universal and concise *key to the Style, Location, and Type of Inn* depicted by the information about that Inn. Additionally, we have included the year in which that Inn first became a member of our Association. All of this information will hopefully help guide you to the accommodations you want.

Charles M. Dedman, President
Beaumont Inn, Harrodsburg, Kentucky

Norman D. Kinney,
Executive Director
Independent Innkeepers' Association
Marshall, Michigan

As you peruse the information about the 296 Inns in this directory, we encourage you to take notice of the special "offerings" at the various places. Wonderful facilities for small-group meetings have been developed at some Inns. Special barrier-free and smoke-free accommodations are noted, and frequently, mention is made of area attractions and recreational facilities. The information in this guide is updated every year; we want you to know our latest and best.

Once again, we invite you to "spend a few days" when you can. Our inns are located in beautiful and interesting villages, towns, cities, and countrysides. Many offer gastronomic adventures and delights. And, most importantly, the innkeepers at IIA Inns are delighted to welcome you and assist in every way to make your stay pleasant and memorable. We like to brag that we are "... the best at what we do."

PREFACE

We are an association of independent innkeepers dedicated to providing our guests with a unique hospitality experience by being the best at what we do . . . individually and collectively.

Through mutual involvement, we work together to educate, promote, and support each other in our continuing efforts to set standards for our profession. —IIA MISSION STATEMENT

These are the goals and objectives of the Independent Innkeepers' Association, which has evolved from the tiny group gathered together in 1966 by Norman T. Simpson. Renowned as the "father of country inns," his book, *Country Inns and Back Roads*, was the first of its kind in contemporary times. He held informal dinners for the innkeepers who were featured in the first early editions. Then, as the number of inns grew, it became clear that country innkeepers felt isolated and out of contact with like-minded people in the hospitality industry. Hotel and motel organizations offered little of value to keepers of country inns. Their appreciation and need for gathering together with other innkeepers was immediately obvious.

The opportunity to discuss mutual problems and find solutions, and the discovery that their failures and triumphs were shared by others, gave rise to the idea of a network of fine country inns in which was implicit the sense of responsibility to each other and their shared values and standards in serving the public.

At first there were annual meetings, which would take place at one or another of the inns in this book. Then, the need for smaller, more focused sessions resulted in several regional meetings in various parts of the country throughout the year.

By 1972, Norman formally established this loose collection of inns as the Independent Innkeepers' Association. The innkeepers in this group came from all walks of life, many of them having left successful careers and lucrative opportunities to experience the joys and tribulations of innkeeping. An important quality in each of them was not only a deep sense of commitment to their inns, but also an enthusiasm and desire to be involved with other innkeepers who shared their goals and standards and who wanted to work together for the common good.

The feeling of fellowship and family is a strong bond rooted in the shared purpose of maintaining what is finest and best in the true tradition and spirit of American innkeeping.

Today, seven years after Norman Simpson's death, the board of directors and the membership are continuing and expanding the work he began. In this ever-increasingly competitive arena, we will hold to the standards of personal hospitality, which he defined and which are so important to us and our many guests who look for both professional excellence and a genuine feeling of friendly welcome.

Accreditation Program

In accordance with our stated purpose of maintaining the highest standards of innkeeping, the Independent Innkeepers' Association requires member participation in a quality assurance program. This program provides for mandatory periodic inspection of every inn by Quality Consultants, Inc., of Greenwich, Rhode Island, specialists who have been retained to give an impartial evaluation of each inn.

Staff members of Quality Consultants are personally trained to provide thorough, unbiased and honest evaluations and do so in an unobtrusive and timely manner. The evaluation visit is for two consecutive nights, whenever possible, to permit the evaluator to get a full picture of the operation of the inn. The visits, of course, are unannounced.

The evaluation begins with the first telephone call placed by the consultants who subsequently visit the facility and report on both the highlights of their stay and any areas which may be of concern. Only upon completion of the checkout procedure do they identify themselves and go over the rough draft of their findings. A formal typed report is mailed to the innkeeper and to the Independent Innkeepers' Association office for follow-up.

Following are a few of the many issues on which member inns are rated:

Basic Requirements

- Warm welcome by innkeepers or staff
- Architecturally attractive facility
- Buildings (inside & out) well maintained
- Safety of guests insured (inside & out)
- Sitting room for guests only
- Impeccable housekeeping throughout inn
- A pleasant dining experience or fine dining available nearby
- Excellent lighting in guest rooms
- Bathrooms well furnished with large, quality towels and adequate shelf space, clothes hooks, etc.

Special Or Personal Touches

- Fresh cut flowers or well-tended houseplants
- Soft music in dining and common rooms
- Quality paintings, artwork, artifacts or memorabilia
- Historical references or other material of interest
- Comfortable, well-maintained outdoor seating
- Books, area maps, magazines, games, bulletin boards and various other materials for guests' amusement
- Quality amenities, refreshments

Another important and valuable adjunct to our accreditation program involves our encouragement of guest evaluations, through card inserts in the back of our book. We are interested in hearing from our guests and will appreciate receiving evaluations of the Independent Innkeepers' Association inns you have visited.

The Independent Innkeepers' Association continues to work with members to support and encourage them in improving their properties and maintaining the high standards which make our members the leaders in their field.

Some Criteria For Membership In The Indepent Innkeepers' Association

These are a few of the criteria used in evaluating the eligibility of an inn for membership in the Independent Innkeepers' Association. Other more stringent criteria are also used; however, these are the most basic requirements.

- Inn is owner-operated or the innkeeper/manager is highly committed to the spirit of personal hospitality. Staff shows genuine interest toward guests.

- The innkeeper has owned/run the inn for a minimum of three years, or, if from a background of successful innkeeping, two years.

- Inn building is architecturally interesting and attractive with appropriately groomed grounds, tasteful, comfortable and inviting interior furnishings and at least one common room for houseguests only. Guest rooms are attractively and completely furnished for comfort of guests.

- Housekeeping and maintenance are excellent, with immaculate guest rooms and bathrooms.

- Breakfast and dinner should be a pleasant eating experience. If the evening meal is not provided on the premises, fine dining must be readily available in the immediate area (preferably within walking distance).

The Beacon of Hospitality Now Lights a Path Beyond Our Door!

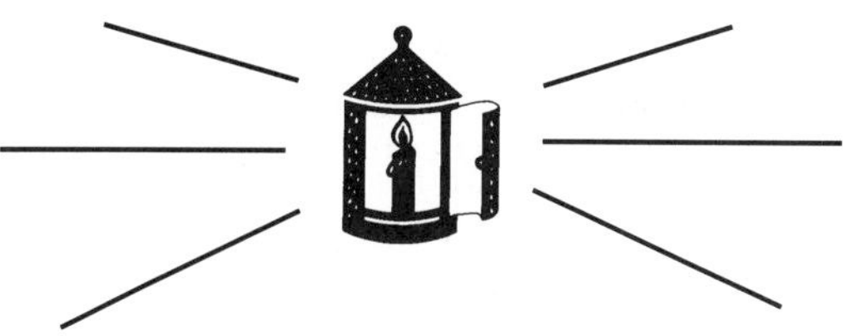

The **Independent Inkeepers' Association** has resolved to pledge our organization to **charitable work** and to help those less fortunate than ourselves.

Our Innkeepers have initiated, on a voluntary basis, the **Quarters for Quarters** campaign to **help build houses** for those in need.

In the spirit of the Independent Innkeepers' Association member inns' welcoming of all people, regardless of Faith, Race, Sex and Culture, we join together to assist and empower people to develop self-sufficiency and life with dignity.

To this end the **Quarters for Quarters** campaign will this year be dedicated to support the work of **Habitat For Humanity International.**

The Independent Innkeepers' Association supports Habitat for Humanity because Habitat challenges people of compassion to provide support—through tax-deductible donations, no-interest loans and volunteer labor—to build or renovate simple, decent houses for the inadequately sheltered. Construction is a partnership venture between volunteers for future homeowners. Houses are sold at no profit and with a no-interest mortgage repaid over a 15 to 25 year period. House payments are recycled into a Fund for Humanity used to build more houses.

Please ask participating Innkeepers for information about Habitat for Humanity and how

Quarters For Quarters Can Help Build Houses

Habitat for Humanity International
121 Habitat St, Americus, GA 31709-3498

STYLE, LOCATION, AND TYPE DESCRIPTORS

At the end of each Inn's "write-up" beneath its picture, you will find (in parentheses) three words chosen from the categories below. The innkeepers at these inns have selected their "descriptors" from these lists in order to uniformly and concisely convey information to the traveler concerning the Location, Style and Type accommodation found at that particular Inn. We hope these *descriptors* will help you select just the right place for you.

STYLE

Decor and Ambiance

Elegant - Emphasis on high style (and cost) furniture, fixtures, furnishings and service.

Traditional - Eclectric but comfortable and well appointed guest rooms and common areas. Furniture and furnishing often from several periods. Attentive but relatively informal service.

Rustic - Emphasis on naturalness, solidity, and straightforward presentation in buildings, furniture and furnishings, and service, and an ambiance of informal comfort. (Rustic at our inns does not mean spare or primitive.)

Contemporary - Modern-to-striking furniture, furnishings and decor. Service tone may range from stylish to relatively informal.

Architecture

Georgian or Colonial, Federal, Greek Revival, Victorian, Western or Southwestern, Contemporary

LOCATION

In Town - Larger town or city, with the range of cultural and other facilities expected in such locations. Properties in smaller towns may offer access to natural attractions as well.

Village - Smaller community of a few hundred to a few thousand people. The smallest may be relatively isolated. Many offer historic, natural, or specialized cultural attractions.

Country - Rural setting, with the conveniences of population centers several-to-many miles away. May offer access to recreation opportunities such as fishing, skiing, bird watching.

Mountain - Country, with "topographical irregularities".

Waterside - River-, lake-, or ocean-side, with related recreational opportunities. May or may not be near population centers.

TYPE

Hotel - Generally fifty rooms or more, with the range of amenities and services traditionally associated with hotels.

Inn - Generally ten to thirty or forty rooms, with an emphasis on personal but professional hospitality from owner and staff. Inns will offer breakfast daily and dinner (to guests only, or to guests and public) four or more nights a week, and furnishings will vary substantially in type among rooms.

Breakfast Inn - Typically five to ten or fifteen rooms offering full morning meals. Decorations, furnishings and hospitality comparable to Inns.

Ranch - An inn, often multiple buildings, located in a ranch setting, with the recreational opportunities associated with that kind of operation. Ranches most often will be in a country location but may be mountain or seaside.

Retreat/Lodge - A property at which the guests' personal and physical privacy is emphasized. The setting most often is one of solitude. Recreational opportunities may include hiking, nature exploration, hunting or fishing, and the like.

Resort - A hotel or inn offering on its own or adjacent grounds, a variety of organized recreational activities such as golf, tennis, racquetball, riding, health and fitness facilities, etc.

KEY TO SYMBOLS

	English	French	German	Japanese	Spanish
	number of rooms; rates and rate plan for 2 people number of suites; rates and rate plan for 2 people credit cards accepted	nombre de chambres, les prix pour deux personnes, plan de repas; nombre d'apparte-ments, les prix pour deux personnes, plan de repas les cartes de crédit acceptées	Anzahl der Zimmer; Tarif-und Tarifplan Anzahl der Zimmerflüchte; Tarif-und Tarifplan Kreditkarten angenommen	部屋数：宿泊料金と料金別プラン スイート数：宿泊料金と料金別プラン クレジットカード通用	número de habitaciones; tarifas y tablas de tarifas para dos personas número de apartamentos; tarifas y tablas de tarifas para dos personas tarjetas de crédito que aceptamos
	baths—private/shared	salle de bains et WC privés ou communs	Bäder privat/geteilt	バス付／共同バス	habitaciones con baño / sin baño
	open/close	période de fermeture ou ouverture	offen: geschlossen	営業中／休業ーシーズン	temporado—fecha en que se abre / fecha en que se cirerra
	children and pets acceptability, inquire for rates	les enfants admis? chiens admis? renseignez-vous sur les tarifs	Kinder und Haustiere erlaubt; nach Tarifen erkundigen	子供とペット可、別料金	reglamentos para niños y animales domésticos (pīdase tarifas)
R	recreation and attractions on premises or in area	les sports et les divertissements à l'hôtel ou l'environs	Erhohlung und Sehenswürdigkeiten; an Ort und Stelle oder in der Gegend	当地のレクレーション・催し物	atracciones y diversiones / en los terrenos o cercanos
	meals available; wine & liquor available	repas offerts et bar sur place	Mahlzeiten und Spirituosen erhältlich	食事と飲食可	comida y licores en venta / no se venden
	smoking acceptability	zone fumeur ou non fumeur	Rauchen erlaubt/ begrenzt/verboten	喫煙可	se puede fumar / no se puede fumar
	wheelchair access	accés pour fauteuil roulant	Fuer Koerperbehin-derte Geeignet	車イス出入口	a notar: acceso para sillas de ruedas
	conference facilities	capacité pour séminaires	Konferenzräume	特別施設　会議室	facilidades para conferencias

MAP	Modified American Plan	Breakfast & dinner included in rate demi-pension Frühstück und Abendessen im Preis einbegriffen 特別アメリカプランー朝・夕食付 la tarifa incluye cena y desayuno
AP	American Plan	3 meals included in rate pension complète (3) drei Mahlzeiten im Preis einbegriffen アメリカプランー３食付 la tarifa comprende desayuno, almuerzo y cena
EP	European Plan	no meals included in rate les repas ne sont pas compris Keine Mahlzeiten im Preis einbegriffen ヨーロッパプランー食事なし la tarifa no incluye comida alguna
B&B	Bed & Breakfast	Breakfast included in rate le petit déjeuner est compris Frühstück einbegriffen 朝食付 la tarifa incluye el desayuno

Reservation and Rate Information

Rates listed herein represent a general range of rates for two people for one night at each inn, and should not be considered firm quotations. The rates cover both high and low seasons; tax and gratuities are usually not included. It is well to inquire as to the availabilty of various special plans and packages. Please be aware that reservation and cancellation policies vary from inn to inn. Listed recreation and attractions are either on the premises or nearby. For more detailed information, ask for inn brochure.

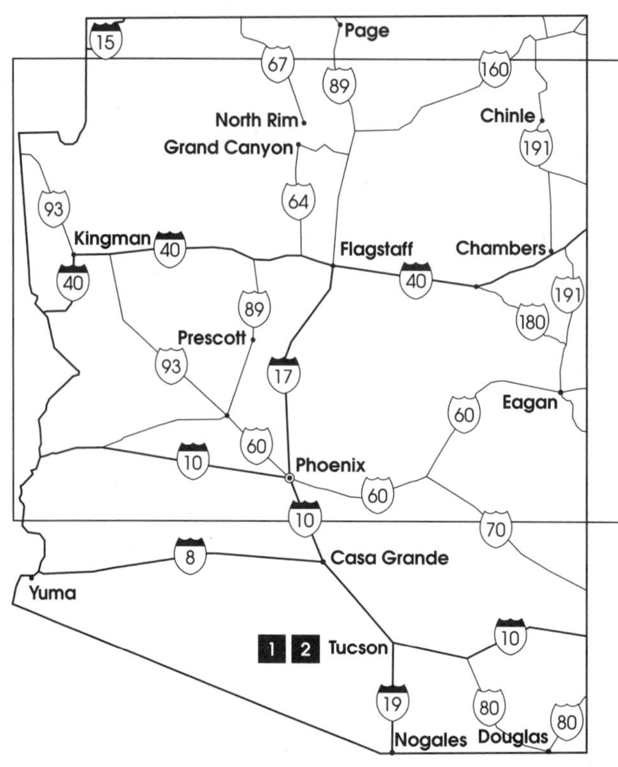

1. Lodge on the Desert, Tucson
2. Tanque Verde, Tucson

THE LODGE ON THE DESERT

33 Rooms, $58/$133 B&B
7 Suites $72/$177 B&B
Visa, MC, Amex, Diners, CB, Discov.
All Private Baths
Open year-round
Children Welcome
Pets by prior arrangement
Heated Swimming Pool, Croquet, Golf, Tennis, Racquet ball, Shuffleboard, Ping-pong
Continental Breakfast, Lunch, Dinner; AP & MAP available 11/1-6/1
Wine & Liquor available
Smoking accepted
Conference Facilities (40)
Wheelchair Access (7 Rooms)

The feeling of old Mexico and of the Southwest is everywhere in the adobe-colored casas grouped around intimate patios at this Mexican hacienda-style resort-inn. Magnificent mountain and desert views, spacious lawns, and colorful gardens belie the proximity of fine residences and nearby downtown Tucson, with all its cultural and recreational attractions.

(*Traditional, In-town, Inn. Member since 1976*)

From I-10 take Speedway exit, 5 mi. (E) to R. turn (S) at Alvernon Way. .8 mi. to Lodge on L. bet. 5th & Broadway.

TEL 602-325-3366 or 800-456-5634; FAX 602-327-5834
306 N. Alvernon Way,
P.O. Box 42500
Tucson, AZ 85733
Schuyler & Helen Lininger, Innkeepers

TANQUE VERDE RANCH

In Tucson, take Speedway Blvd. (E) to dead end at ranch.

TEL. 602-296-6275
FAX 602-721-9426
14301 E. Speedway Blvd.,
Tucson, AZ 85748

Robert Cote, Innkeeper

In a spectacular setting of desert and mountains, this 125-year-old ranch evokes the spirit of the Old West. Horseback riding, guided nature hikes, bird study programs, as well as a modern health spa, tennis, indoor and outdoor pools, selective menus, and a casual, relaxed atmosphere mean good times for lucky guests. It has a 4-star rating by Mobil. (*Western, Country, Ranch. Member since 1970*)

SELECTING "YOUR" INN

Perhaps the first image conjured up by the term "Country Inn" is a beautifully-appointed and cozy guest room located in an architecturally attractive (perhaps historic) structure with inviting gardens and surroundings. Standing in the doorway of this attractive structure is the smiling, gregarious innkeeper extending a warm greeting. Mentally continuing into the apparition, the experienced Inn-traveler will immediately begin to contemplate the special, appetizing fare which has become so much a part of country inn hospitality. Thoughts of a weekend getaway with this ambiance, innkeeper, and cuisine have become an energizing force which helps get some workingpeople through the work-week.

Folks who become acquainted with and enjoy Country Inns very often select one that especially appeals to them. They enjoy returning often to "their" place, revisiting "their" special shops and restaurants, and regaling other, newer guests with a voice of knowing familiarity about such things. That kind of individual selection of an inn can bring personal peace and solace to some inn-travelers. Their inn becomes a pampering home away from home. Their selection becomes, for them, "ownership" in that inn.

Other inn-travelers are into it for the adventure. They appreciate the differences in ambiance, innkeepers, and cuisine, and they want to try them all. One lady from New England says that, over the years, she has visited 128 of the Inns in this guidebook. Certainly this inveterate soul has probably become something of an authority on what it takes to make an inn appeal to the guest.

Selection of an Inn is a personal choice with many variables. Perhaps that is what makes Inn-traveling so appealing in the first place. Just as people and tastes vary, happily so do Country Inns and the manner in which innkeepers manifest their own versions of hospitality. Rest assured, each is unique and ready to be adopted as "your" place or enjoyed as part of "your adventure".

CALIFORNIA

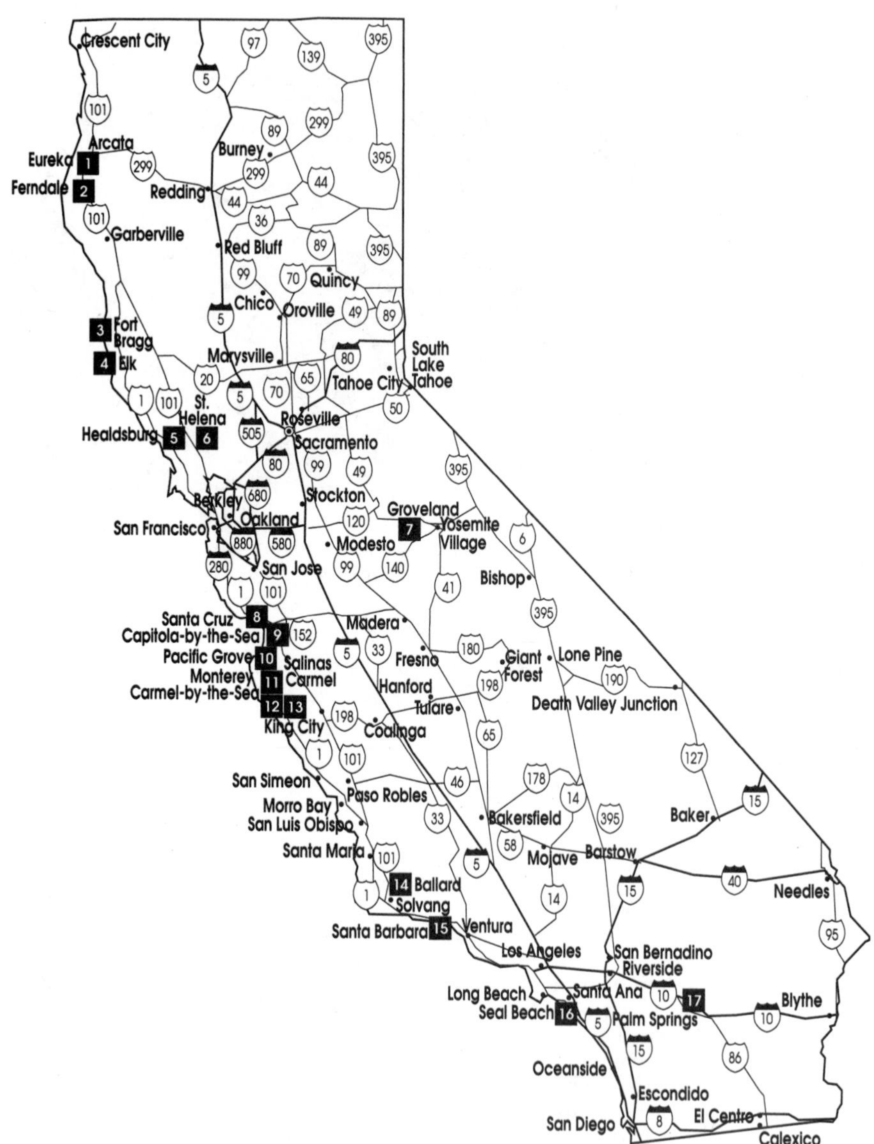

1. Carter House, Eureka
2. The Gingerbread Mansion, Ferndale
3. Grey Whale Inn, Fort Bragg
4. Harbor House Inn by the Sea, Elk
5. Madrona Manor, Healdsburg
6. Wine Country Inn, St. Helena
7. Groveland Hotel, Groveland
8. The Babbling Brook, Santa Cruz
9. The Inn at Depot Hill, Capitola-by-the-Sea
10. The Martine Inn, Pacific Grove
11. Old Monterey Inn, Monterey
12. Sandpiper Inn at-the-Beach, Carmel-by-the-Sea
13. Vagabond's House, Carmel
14. Ballard Inn, Ballard
15. Simpson House, Santa Barbara
16. Seal Beach Inn and Gardens, Seal Beach
17. Villa Royale Inn, Palm Springs

THE BABBLING BROOK

12 Rooms, $85/$165 B&B
Visa, MC, Amex, Carte Bl, Discov
All Private Baths; 4 Jet Baths (2 are enlarged baths for 2)
Open Year-round
Children, with restrictions; No Pets in rooms
Near Tennis, Golf, Fishing, Boating, Beaches, Parks, Redwoods, Narrow-guage Railroad, Wineries, Shopping, Local Artists, Climate year around 50º–80º
Breakfast, Afternoon Tea, Mrs King's Cookies, Wine & Cheese Evenings
No Smoking
Conf. Facilities (12-15)
Wheelchair Access (2 rm., dining rm. & conf. fac.)

From Hwy. 17 take Half Moon Bay exit to Hwy. 1 (N). Continue on Mission St. to L. on Laurel at signal, 1 1/2 blks. down hill on R. From (S) on Hwy. 1, turn L. on Laurel, 1 1/2 blks. on R. From (N) on Hwy. 1 turn R. on Laurel St.

TEL. 408-427-2437; 800-866-1131; FAX 408-427-2457
1025 Laurel St.
Santa Cruz, CA 95060
Helen King, Innkeeper

8 Historic waterwheel, falls and brook in an acre of redwoods and pines surround this secluded inn. Built in 1909 on the foundation of a 1790 gristmill and 2000-year-old Indian fishing village, it's on the National Register of Historic Places. Rooms in French decor with four jet bathtubs, private entrances, decks overlooking the gardens, most have fireplaces. Gazebo is popular for weddings. Top Inn Award, *Country-Inn Magazine*, 1994.
(Traditional, Waterside, Breakfast Inn. Member since 1990)

BALLARD INN

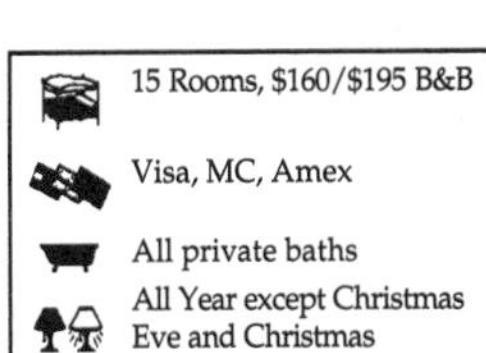

15 Rooms, $160/$195 B&B
Visa, MC, Amex
All private baths
All Year except Christmas Eve and Christmas
No Pets, Well-behaved Parents with Children
Wineries, Golf, Art Galleries, Biking, Hiking, Shopping, Antiques, Glider Rides, Horseback Riding, Horse Ranches
Dinner served, Wed.–Sun. at Cafe Chardonnay
Beer & Wine Available
Smoking permitted on the veranda outside
Conference Facilities (30)
Wheelchair Access (1 rm., dining rm. & conf. fac.)

From Highway 101, take Solvang Exit. Follow Route 246 E. through Solvang to Alamo Pintado Road; turn left. Drive 3 miles to Baseline Ave., turn right and Inn is 50 yards on the right.

TEL. 805-688-7770,
1-800-638-2466
FAX 805-688-9560
2436 Baseline Ave
Ballard, CA 93463
Kelly Robinson, Innkeeper

14 Comfortably elegant accommodations in the heart of the Santa Barbara wine country. Just 40 minutes from Santa Barbara, yet nestled in a country neighborhood of orchards and vineyards, the Ballard Inn offers an intimate retreat. Each of the 15 guest rooms possesses its own special charm and character reflecting local history. All feature individual controlled heating and air conditioning, as well as private baths. AAA◆◆◆◆.
(Traditional, Country, Inn. Member since 1993)

CARTER HOUSE/HOTEL CARTER

19 Rooms, $95/$155 B&B
11 Suites $145/$255 B&B

Visa, MC, Amex, Discover

All Private Baths; 16 Jacuzzis

Open Year-round

No Pets/Appropriate for Children over 8

Golf, Beaches, Tennis, Horseback Riding, Swimming, Redwood Forests, Camping, Hiking, Birdwatching, Kayaking

Breakfast; Dinner; Wine & Cordials available

No Smoking

Conference Facilities

Wheelchair Access (21 Rms., dining rm. & conf. fac.)

1 A remarkably detailed re-creation of an 1884 San Francisco mansion, the inn sits at the gateway to Eureka's historic district. It offers guests exquisite decor, unrivaled hospitality, and what has been called "the best breakfast in California." Hotel Carter next door, another marvelous replica, offers more rooms, a fine restaurant, and conference facilities. The recently restored "Belle House" next to the Inn has three suites with jacuzzi and fireplaces, cable TV, VCRs, and a large common kitchen perfect for groups. (*Contemporary, In-Town, Inn. Member since 1988*)

From Hwy. 101 (N) (5th St.) turn L. on "L" St. From Hwy. 101 (S) (4th St.) turn R. on "L" St. Inn is at 3rd & "L" Sts.

TEL. 707-444-8062
800-404-1390
FAX. 707-444-8067
301 L. Street
Eureka, CA 95501

Mark & Christi Carter, Innkeepers

THE GINGERBREAD MANSION

 5 Rooms, $90/$145 B&B
4 Suites, $120/$185 B&B

 Visa, MC, Amex

 All Private Baths

 Open Year-round

 Appropriate for Children over 10; No Pets

  Games, Library, Bicycles, English Garden, Redwood Parks, Beach, Fishing, Galleries, Unique Shops

 Breakfast, Afternoon Tea with homemade cookies, cakes, candies, and bars

 No Smoking

 N/A

2 Exquisitely turreted and gabled, the Gingerbread Mansion Inn is truly a visual masterpiece. Located in the Victorian village of Ferndale, the inn is surrounded by lush English gardens. The nine romantic guest rooms all offer private baths; some have old-fashioned tubs and fireplaces, for fireside bubble baths. Amenities include a morning tray service, full breakfast, afternoon tea, turn-down service with bedside chocolates, bathrobes, and use of the garden and bicycles. AAA ♦♦♦♦
(*Elegant, Victorian, Village, Breakfast Inn. Member since 1988*)

Hwy. 101, 15 mi. south of Eureka, take Ferndale exit. Continue over bridge 5 mi. to Main St. Turn L. at Bank of America bldg. Go 1 block.

TEL. 707-786-4000
800-952-4136
400 Berding St.,
P.O. Box 40
Ferndale, CA 95536-0040

Ken Torbert, Innkeeper

GREY WHALE INN

 14 Rooms $85/$160 B&B Off seas. 20% less Su.-Th.

 Visa, MC, Discov, Enroute, Amex, JCB

 All Private Baths; 1 Jacuzzi

 Open Year-round

 Appropriate for Children over 12; No Pets

 TV theater with VCR, rec. room with pool table, fishing, hiking, whale-watching. Phones in rms.

 Buffet Breakfast Complimentary sparkling beverages for special occasions

 Non-smoking inn

 Conference Facilities (34)

N/A

Hwy. 101 to Cloverdale, then Hwy. 128 W. to Hwy. 1. Continue (N) to Fort Bragg (3 1/2 hrs. from S.F.). Or Hwy. 1 along the coast (5 hrs. from S.F.)

TEL. 707-964-0640
FAX 707-964-4408
Res. 800-382-7244
615 No. Main Street
Fort Bragg, CA 95437
John & Colette Bailey, Innkps.

3 Mendocino Coast landmark since 1915, and Fort Bragg's premier Bed & Breakfast Inn. Classic revival architecture. Spacious comfort and the utmost in privacy. Ocean, garden or hill views; fireplaces, decks, Jacuzzi. Decor varies: French floral countryside, Traditional elegance, American country comfort, Romantic hideaway. Lavish breakfast buffet includes hot entree, prize-winning coffee cake, fresh fruit. Stroll to ocean, restaurants, shops, galleries, theatre, and Skunk Train. AAA and Mobil approved accommodations.

(Traditional, In-Town, Breakfast Inn. Member since 1980)

GROVELAND HOTEL

 14 Rooms, $85/$105 B&B 3 Suites, $165 B&B

 Visa, MC, Amex, CB, DC, DISC

 All Private Baths

 Year-round

 Children OK; Pets by Arrangement

 Yosemite National Park (23 m.), Golf, Tennis, Hiking, Fishing, Swimming, (Lake w/ 3 beaches), Pool, World-class White Water Rafting

 Continental Breakfast, Afternoon Tea, Wine, Gourmet Restaurant

 No Smoking

Conference Facilities (25)

 Wheelchair Access (6 rms and dining rm)

From Bay Area 3 hours, 80/680 to 580 to 120 at Tracy. From Sacramento & Central Valley, Hwy 5 or 99 to 120 at Manteca. Hotel is located on 120 (18767 Main St.).

TEL 209-962-4000;
800-273-3314–Reservations
FAX 209-962-6674
18767 Main Street
PO Box 481
Groveland, California 95321
Peggy A. & Grover C. Mosley, Innkeepers

7 The 1849 Adobe and 1914 Queen Anne buildings offer 14 rooms and 3 suites with European antiques, terry robes, down comforters, upscale linens and private baths. Some have private entrances to the verandas where white wicker abounds. Suites have separate sitting rooms, fireplaces, and spa tubs. The parlour has books, games, a fireplace, and television. Listed on National Register of Historic Places. Fall/Winter Calendar of Events.

(Traditional, Victorian, Country, Inn. Member since 1993)

HARBOR HOUSE INN BY THE SEA

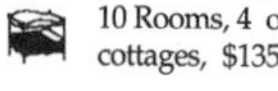
10 Rooms, 4 of which are cottages, $135/$260 MAP

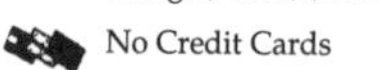
No Credit Cards

All Private Baths

Open Year-round

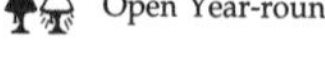

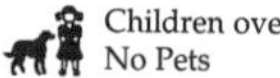
Children over 12
No Pets

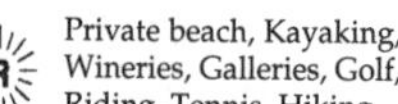
Private beach, Kayaking, Wineries, Galleries, Golf, Riding, Tennis, Hiking

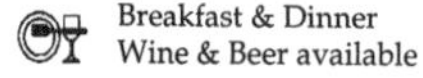
Breakfast & Dinner
Wine & Beer available

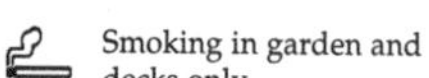
Smoking in garden and decks only

N/A

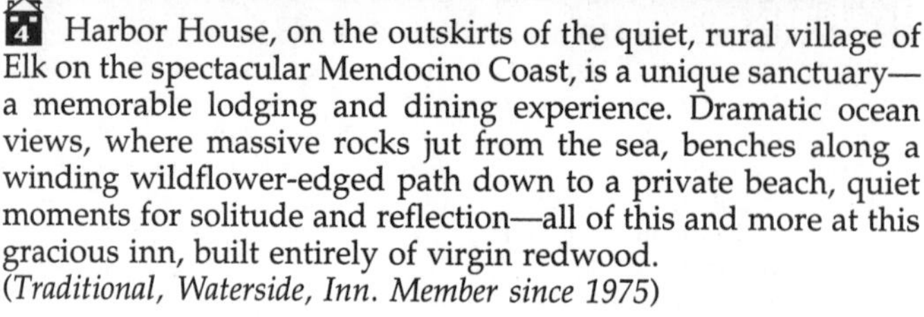

4 Harbor House, on the outskirts of the quiet, rural village of Elk on the spectacular Mendocino Coast, is a unique sanctuary—a memorable lodging and dining experience. Dramatic ocean views, where massive rocks jut from the sea, benches along a winding wildflower-edged path down to a private beach, quiet moments for solitude and reflection—all of this and more at this gracious inn, built entirely of virgin redwood.
(*Traditional, Waterside, Inn. Member since 1975*)

From S.F., 3 hrs. (N) on Hwy. 101. In Cloverdale take Hwy. 128 (W) to Hwy. 1 (S) 5 mi. to Elk.

TEL. 707-877-3203
Box 369
5600 S. Highway One
Elk, CA 95432

Dean & Helen Turner, Innkeepers

THE INN AT DEPOT HILL

4 Rooms, $165/$195 B&B
4 Suites, $210/$250 B&B

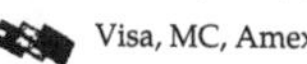
Visa, MC, Amex

All Private Baths, 4 Hot Tubs

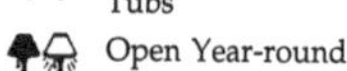
Open Year-round

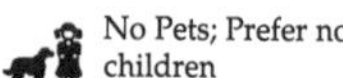
No Pets; Prefer no children

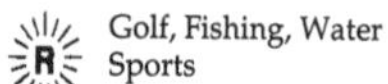
Golf, Fishing, Water Sports

Breakfast
Wine available

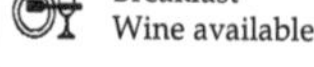
No Smoking

Conference Facilities (16)

Wheelchair Access (1 rm., dining rm. & conf. fac.)

9 Near a sandy beach in a quaint, Mediterranean-style resort, this award-winning inn was named 1 of top 10 inns in the country. A decorator's delight, upscale rooms resemble different parts of the world. All rooms have fireplaces, TV/VCR, stereo systems, phones, modems, robes, featherbeds, and flowers. Most have private hot tubs in private garden patios. Mobil 4 Stars!
(*Elegant, Waterside, Breakfast Inn. Member since 1992*)

From 1 take Park Ave. exit turning towards the ocean for 1 mile. Left on Monterey Ave. and immediately left into our driveway. Look for white columns and international flags.

TEL. (408) 462-3376
800-572-2632
FAX (408) 462-3697
250 Monterey Ave.
Capitola-by-the-Sea, CA 95010
Suzie Lankes, Innkeeper

MADRONA MANOR

18 Rooms, $140/$190 B&B
3 Suites, $190/$235 B&B

Visa, MC, Amex, Discov

All Private Baths

Open Year-round

Children accepted
Leashed Dogs, outer bldgs.

Swimming pool on site, Tennis, Golf, Wine tasting, Canoeing, Balloon Rides nearby

B&B Sun.-Thurs., Full Breakfast; Dinner & Sun. brunch; Wine & Beer available

Smoking in restricted areas

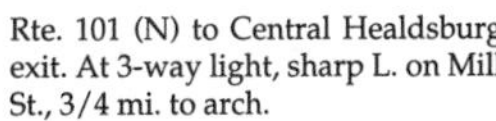
Conference Facilities (40)
Wheelchair Access (1 rm., dining rm. & conf. fac.)

Rte. 101 (N) to Central Healdsburg exit. At 3-way light, sharp L. on Mill St., 3/4 mi. to arch.

TEL. 707-433-4231
FAX 707-433-0703
800-258-4003
101 Westside Rd.
Healdsburg, CA 95448
John & Carol Muir
Innkeepers

This majestic Victorian manor, on the National Register of Historic Places, conveys a sense of homey elegance and gracious hospitality. Guests enjoy thick terry robes, unique and tantalizing cuisine, beautiful mountain views and surrounding Sonoma wine country. Beautiful grounds, eight acres. A new suite, with fireplace & sitting room, boasts a king bed, deck, marble bath and jacuzzi. Internationally acclaimed restaurant serves superb dinners by candlelight. Gold medal wine list. We keep getting better! *(Elegant, Victorian, Country, Inn. Member since 1988)*

WE ASSURE QUALITY

When the innkeeper gave you this Association guidebook, *The Innkeepers' Register*, the intention of his generosity was, 'Here is a guidebook of my fellow innkeepers' Inns. If you liked our Inn, you will probably like the others found in this book. We're all very different, but we hold the same very high standards of excellence.'

The reason this very bold statement can be made is the Quality Assurance Program adopted by the Independent Innkeepers' Association several years ago. The innkeepers so strongly believed that they wanted to continue their quality-protecting role in the industry, that a schedule was established under which every Inn in the Association will be inspected regularly to insure that they do not slip-up in their commitment to being ". . . the best at what we do."

You see, we realize that Inn-traveling has become very popular in recent years. As a matter of fact, so has it become popular to "open an inn." With this rapid growth in our industry, a plethora of guidebooks have become available from which the traveler must select from a plethora of Inns.

In protecting our own quality and the integrity of *The Register* in this growing market, we hopefully will be protecting the true tradition and spirit of American innkeeping. In 1966 Norman T. Simpson started us down the road toward "professional excellence and a genuine feeling of friendly welcome" for our guests. We are constantly aware of our need to protect our leadership position in the Country Inn industry as well as the integrity of *The Innkeepers' Register*. If you liked one of the Inns in this guidebook, we want to assure that you will like them all.

THE MARTINE INN

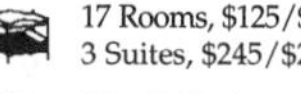 17 Rooms, $125/$230 B&B
3 Suites, $245/$280 B&B

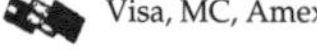 Visa, MC, Amex

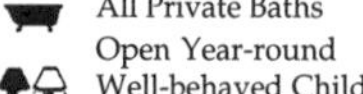 All Private Baths
Open Year-round

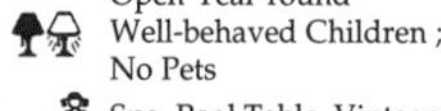 Well-behaved Children ; No Pets

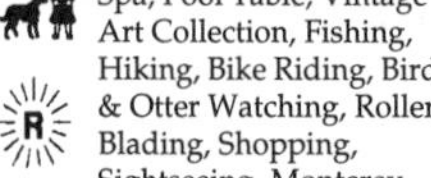 Spa, Pool Table, Vintage Art Collection, Fishing, Hiking, Bike Riding, Bird & Otter Watching, Roller Blading, Shopping, Sightseeing, Monterey Bay Aquarium

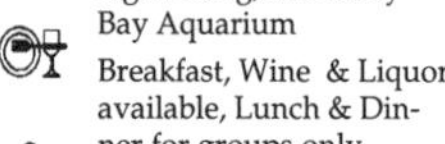 Breakfast, Wine & Liquor available, Lunch & Dinner for groups only

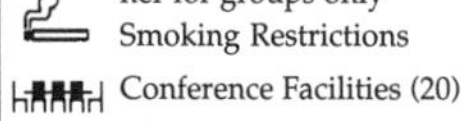 Smoking Restrictions

Conference Facilities (20)

Wheelchair Access (1 rm., dining rm. & conf. rm.)

10 Come relax & enjoy breathtaking views of the Monterey Bay where seals, otters, and whales can be seen while staying at this romantic cliffside mansion. Your room may have a view of the crashing surf or a woodburning fireplace to snuggle up to that special person. Awake to a sumptuous breakfast awaiting you in the parlor. Relish the fine collection of museum quality American antiques in every room.
(*Elegant, Victorian, Waterside, Breakfast Inn. Member since 1992*)

Hwy. 1 to Pebble-Beach-Pacific Grove Turnoff to Hwy. 68 to Pacific Grove. R on Ocean View Blvd. R at 255.

TEL. 408-373-3388
or 800-852-5588
FAX: 408-373-3896
255 Oceanview Blvd.
Pacific Grove, CA 93950
Marion & Don Martine & Tracy Harris, Innkeepers

OLD MONTEREY INN

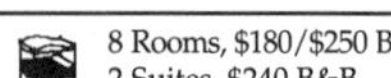 8 Rooms, $180/$250 B&B
2 Suites, $240 B&B

 Visa, MC

 All Private Baths

 Closed Dec. 24-25

 No Pets; not suitable for small children

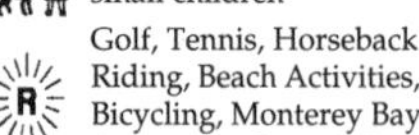 Golf, Tennis, Horseback Riding, Beach Activities, Bicycling, Monterey Bay Aquarium, Carmel, Big Sur coast near by

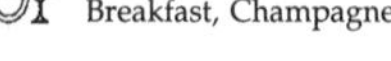 Breakfast, Champagne

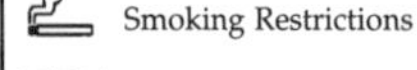 Smoking Restrictions

N/A

11 Surrounded by over an acre of English gardens, Old Monterey Inn offers an exclusive retreat hidden among the trees in the heart of Monterey. This award winning 1929 Tudor mansion, furnished with antiques, has all the modern comforts—private baths with amenities, comfortable sitting areas, wood burning fireplaces, jacuzzi, gourmet breakfasts and hors d'oeuvres, full concierge service for restaurant reservations, golf, tennis, bay cruises, hist. tours and tickets to the Monterey Bay Aquarium. Mobile 4 Stars.
(*Traditional, In-Town, Breakfast Inn. Member since 1993*)

From Hwy 1 take Munras Ave. exit. Make an immediate left to Soledad Dr. then right on Pacific St. Proceed 1/2 a mile to Martin St. on your left.

408-375-8284
1-800-350-2344
FAX 408-375-6730
500 Martin St.
Monterey, CA 93940

Ann & Gene Swett, Innkeepers

SANDPIPER INN AT-THE-BEACH

13 Rooms, $95/$185 B&B
3 Cottage rooms, $95/$150 B&B

Visa, MC, Amex

All Private Bathrooms

Open Year-around

Appropriate for Children Over 12; No Pets

Pebble Beach , 17-Mile Drive, Famous Golf Courses, Big Sur Coast & Point Lobos Reserve, Carmel Mission Basilica (1771).

Continental Buffet Breakfast, Five O'clock Sherry

Smoking in restricted areas

Conference Facilities (15)

N/A

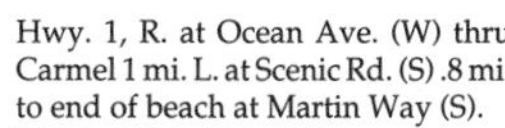

Hwy. 1, R. at Ocean Ave. (W) thru Carmel 1 mi. L. at Scenic Rd. (S) .8 mi. to end of beach at Martin Way (S).

TEL. 408-624-6433;
800-633-6433
FAX 408-624-5964
2408 Bay View Ave.
Carmel by-the-sea, CA 93923

Graeme & Irene Mackenzie
Innkeepers

12 Just 100 yds. from Carmel's white beaches, with unique ocean views across the bay to Pebble Beach. Early California architecture is complemented by country antiques, gardens & patios. Comfortable lounge has a cathedral ceiling & fireplace. Rooms are individually decorated, and some have fireplaces. A romantic getaway in a beautiful, quiet residential area with warm, restful ambiance.
(*Traditional, Ocean-Side, Breakfast Inn. Member since 1981*)

THE SEAL BEACH INN AND GARDENS

10 Rooms, $118/$155 B&B
13 Suites, $185/$255 B&B

Visa, MC, Amex, Diners, Discovery, JCB

All Private Baths, some Jacuzzis/Fireplaces

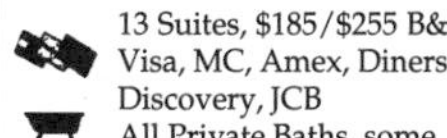
Open Year-round

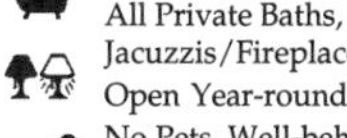
No Pets, Well-behaved children accepted

Beach, Beach Sports, Sailing, Surfing, Wind Surfing, Scuba, Jet Ski, Water Ski, Boating, Onsite Swimming Pool, Golf, Tennis, Racquetball, Handball Nearby

Breakfast, Evening Social Hour, Catered Meals by request, Liquor nearby

No Smoking Inside

Conference Facilities (24)

Wheelchair Access (ding rm and conf fac.)

Hwy. 405 Fwy., Seal Beach Blvd. exit, turn L. for 2.7 mi. R. on Pacific Coast Hwy. for .7 mi. L. on 5th St.

TEL. 310-493-2416; (Reservations only) **1-800-HIDE-AWAY**
FAX 310-799-0483
212 5th Street
Seal Beach, CA 90740

Marjorie Bettenhausen Schmaehl & Harty Schmaehl, Innkeepers

16 The Seal Beach Inn and Gardens is an elegant, historic inn one block from the Pacific Ocean. The Inn sits in lavish colorful flowering gardens in a charming urban seaside village setting. Exquisitely detailed rooms and suites, library, tea room, pool, and accommodations artfully provide a soothing welcome and capture this area's culture and history. Our caring staff look forward to serving you in the Old World tradition of warmth and hospitality.
(*Elegant, Village, Inn. Member since 1981*)

SIMPSON HOUSE

7 Rooms, $105/$175 B&B
4 Suites, 3 Cottages, $205/$275 B&B
Visa, MC, Amex, Disc

All Private Baths

Open Year-round

No pets and no facilities for children

Lawn Croquet, Bicycles, Picnic Baskets, Beach Equipment

Breakfast, Wine Available

Smoking Restrictions

Conference Facilities (20–25)

Wheelchair Access (1 rm., dining rm. and conf. fac.)

Awarded Grand Hotels Award by travel writers and editors—best bed and breakfast in Southern California. The 1874 Victorian, historic landmark estate, secluded in an acre of beautiful English gardens, is elegantly decorated with European antiques, oriental carpets, and fine art. Guest rooms with handprinted Victorian reproduction papers, luxurious suites, and private cottages. Seclusion and luxury within walking distance to downtown. (*Elegant, Victorian, Breakfast Inn. Member since 1993*)

From north on 101, exit on Mission St, go left, at Anacapa St right and at Arrellaga St left. From south on 101, exit Laguna-Garden St. Right on Garden St., at Gutierrez St. left, then right on S. Barbara St. At Arrellaga St. left.

TEL 805-963-7067; 1-800-676-1280; FAX 805-564-4811
121 East Arrellaga St.
Santa Barbara, CA 93101
Linda Davies, Glyn Davies, Gillean Wilson, Innkps.

VAGABOND'S HOUSE INN

11 Rooms, $85/$145 B&B
Suites, $220 B&B

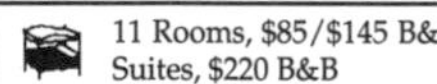
Visa, MC, Amex

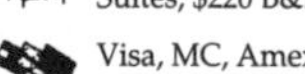
All Private Baths

Open Year-round

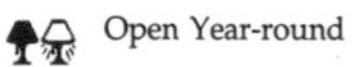
Appropriate for Children over 11; Pets accepted

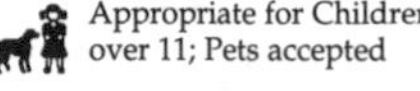
Carmel Beach, 17-Mile Drive, Golf, Tennis, Big Sur, Monterey Bay Aquarium

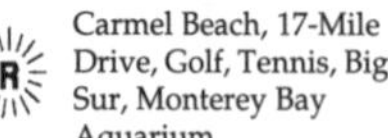
Breakfast; Cream Sherry

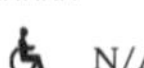

N/A

The stone courtyard here is an almost magical experience, with the great oak and cascading waterfalls, surrounded by vines, ferns, and gorgeous flowers. Tuffy, the watch cat, suns on a doorstep. Around the courtyard are unique rooms with fireplaces. All the natural beauty and fascinating shops of Carmel are just around the corner. (*Traditional, Village, Breakfast Inn. Member since 1976*)

Turn off Hwy. 1 to Ocean Ave., (W) to town center. R. onto Dolores for 2.5 blocks to inn.

TEL. 408-624-7738 or 800-262-1262
FAX 408-626-1243
P.O. Box 2747
Dolores & 4th
Carmel, CA 93921

Honey Spence, Innkeeper

VILLA ROYALE INN

33 Rooms, $59-75/ $169-200 B&B
Suites, $120-150/ $225-270 B&B
Visa, MC, Amex
All Private Baths

Open Year-round

Adults preferred, no pets

Two pools, jacuzzi

Breakfast, Lunch, and Dinner; Wine & Liquor Available

Smoking Permitted

Conference Facilities

Wheelchair Access, 3 rms & dining rm

From I-10 follow 111 to Palm Springs; 111 becomes Palm Canyon Dr. Follow Palm Canyon Dr. to East Palm Canyon. Go 1/4 miles on East Palm Canyon to Indian Trails.

TEL. 619-327-2314
800-245-2314
FAX 619-322-3794
1620 Indian Trails
Palm Springs, CA 92264

Bob Lee, Innkeeper

17 Situated on 3 1/2 acres, the Villa Royale is a full service country inn with a decided European ambiance. With softly splashing fountains, draping bougainvillea, brick courtyards, column arcades, and tile-roofed buildings, one could easily be in the south of France. There are 33 accommodations, each representing a different country. Many have wood-burning fireplaces and private spas. Europa Restaurant, with its fireplace & terracotta walls, could be considered the most romantic dining in the desert. (*In-Town, Inn. Member since 1993*)

THE WINE COUNTRY INN

21 Rooms, $95/$190 B&B
3 Suites, $180/210 B&B
Visa, MC
All Private Baths
Closed the two weeks prior to Christmas
Children and Pets not encouraged
Pool & Jacuzzi, Wineries, Tennis, Golf, Hiking
Breakfast; Wine & Liquor Soon
Smoking Permitted
Conference Facilities (20)
Wheelchair Access (dining room)

From S.F. take I-80 (N) to Napa exit. Follow Hwy. 29 (N) 18 mi. to St. Helena & 2 mi. beyond to Lodi Lane. Turn R. for 1/3 mi. to inn.

TEL. 707-963-7077
FAX 707-963-9018

1152 Lodi Lane,
St. Helena, CA 94574

Jim Smith, Innkeeper

6 Perched on a small hill, overlooking the manicured vineyards and nearby hills of the Napa Valley, this inn is known for its casual and quiet atmosphere. The intimate rooms boast family-made quilts, private balconies, fireplaces and pine antiques. Famous restaurants and wineries tours round out the Napa Valley experience.
(*Traditional, Country, Inn. Member since 1978*)

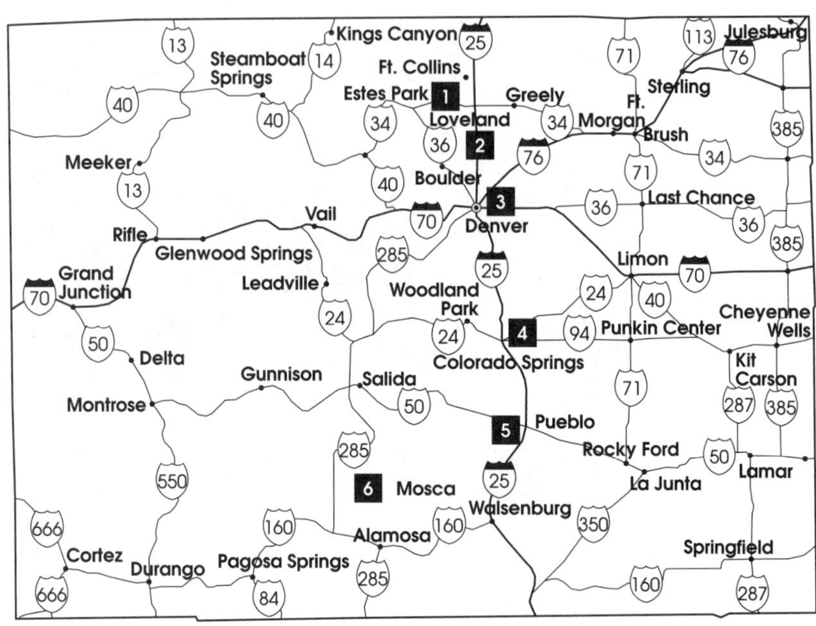

1. River Song, Estes Park
2. The Lovelander Bed & Breakfast Inn, Loveland
3. Castle Marne, Denver
4. Hearthstone Inn, Colorado Springs
5. Abriendo Inn, Pueblo
6. Sand Dune Inn, Mosca

ABRIENDO INN

6 Rooms, $54/$89 B&B
1 Suite, $83 B&B

Visa, MC, Amex, Diners

All Private Baths

Open Year-round

Children over 7 Welcome; No Pets

Museums, Nature, Bike Trails, Historic Walking Tour, Rafting, Fishing, Boutiques, Galleries, Shops

Breakfast, afternoon Cheese & Crackers, and Beverages; BYOB

Smoking permitted on veranda and grounds

N/A

Make this classic mansion your home while visiting Pueblo. Experience the comfortable elegance of the beautiful Foursquare architecture. Feel like you belong here at the Abriendo Inn as you stroll the park-like grounds, view the surrounding neighborhood, and walk through nearby Historic Union Ave. district. From the spiral staircase to the curved stained glass windows and parquet floors, the Inn provides an enchanting ambiance. For your convenience all rooms have the privacy of in-room phones and TV. (*Traditional, Victorian, In-Town, Breakfast Inn. Member since 1992*)

I-25 to Exit 97-B Abriendo Ave. 1 Mile from exit on left side of street

TEL. (719) 544-2703
FAX (719) 542-1806
300 West Abriendo Avenue
Pueblo, CO 81004

Kerrelyn M. Trent,
Innkeeper

CASTLE MARNE

 7 Rooms, $85/$160 B&B
3 Suites, $155/$200 B&B

 Visa, MC, Amex, Discov,

 All Private Baths

 Open Year-round

 Unsuitable for Children Under 10; No Pets

Game Room, City Park w/ Tennis, Running Paths, Golf, Zoo, Museum, Botanic Gardens, Shopping, Historic Sites

 Full Breakfast
Afternoon Tea

 Smoke-Free Inn

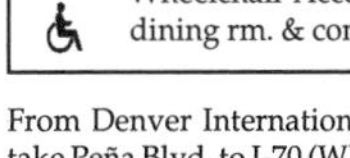 Conference Facility (12)
Wheelchair Access (1 rm., dining rm. & conf. fac.)

From Denver International Airport, take Peña Blvd. to I-70 (W) to Quebec (S) to 17th Ave., right (W) to Esplanade, left (S) one block to 16th Ave., right (W) 4 blocks to Race St.

TEL. 303-331-0621; 800-92-MARNE; FAX 303-331-0623

1572 Race St.,
Denver, CO 80206
Peiker Family, Innkeepers

3 Denver's grandest historic mansion B&B (National and Local Register). Close to Museum of Natural History, Zoo, Botanic Gardens, Cherry Creek Business and Shopping district. Near downtown's 16th Street Mall, Larimer Square, Art Museum, US Mint and Molly Brown's House. Hand rubbed woods, stained glass "Peacock Window," ornate fireplaces blend with period antiques and family heirlooms to create a charming Victorian atmosphere. Game Room and English Garden. Full gourmet breakfast and Afternoon Tea.
(*Elegant, Victorian, In-Town, Breakfast Inn. Member since 1991*)

HEARTHSTONE INN

 20 Rooms, $80/$125 B&B
3 Suites, $125/$140 B&B

Visa, MC, Amex

 All Private Baths

 Open Year-round

 Children Accepted; No Pets

On property—Croquet, Puzzles, Games. Nearby—Walking, Jogging Trail, Golf, Tennis, Pikes Peak, Museums, Rafting, Air Force Academy, Olympic Training Center, Colorado College

 Breakfast; Lunch, groups 20+; Dinner, groups 20+

 No Smoking

 Conference Facilities

 Wheelchair Access (1 rm., dining rm. & conf. fac.)

From I-25, Exit 143 (Uintah St.) (E) away from mountains 3 blocks to Cascade. Turn R. (S) 7 blocks to corner of Cascade & St. Vrain.

TEL. 719-473-4413, 800-521-1885; FAX 719-473-1322

506 No. Cascade Ave.
Colorado Sprgs, CO 80903
Dot Williams, Ruth Williams, Mark Mitchell, Innkeepers

4 Bright Victorian colors of plum, bittersweet, and lilac accent this stunning inn. Antiques throughout, color-coordinated linens, gourmet breakfasts, and friendly, helpful people make this in-town inn a comfortable change of pace. Rooms with working fireplaces are especially popular in the winter while those with open air porches are sought after in the spring and summer. With all the activities of the Pikes Peak Region, you'll find exciting things to see and do for several days!
(*Traditional, In-Town, Breakfast Inn. Member since 1979*)

COLORADO
THE LOVELANDER B&B INN

- 11 Rooms, $84/$125 B&B
- Visa, MC, Amex, Discov
- All Private Baths
- Open Year-round
- Children over 10 welcome; No Pets
- Rocky Mountain Natl. Park, Big Thompson Canyon, Benson Sculpture Park, Galleries
- Breakfast; Beverages & Snacks Available Wine & Liquor available
- No Smoking
- Conference Fac. (15-30)
- Limited Wheelchair Access

2 Combining the essence of Victorian style with contemporary convenience, the Lovelander lies nestled in the Rocky Mountain foothills, a short drive from breathtaking Rocky Mountain National Park. Beautifully appointed rooms, peaceful surroundings, gourmet breakfasts, and old-fashioned hospitality from the heart create a haven for recreational and business travelers alike.
(*Elegant, Victorian, In-Town, Breakfast Inn. Member since 1990*)

I-25, Exit 257B, to U.S. Hwy. 34 (W) for 5 mi. to Garfield Ave. Turn L. 10 blks. to 4th St., then R. to 2nd house on R.

TEL. 303-669-0798
217 W. 4th St.
Loveland, CO 80537

Marilyn & Bob Wiltgen,
Innkeepers

ROMANTIC RIVERSONG

- 2 Rooms, $135/$205 B&B
- 7 Suites, $150/$205 B&B
- Visa, MC
- All Private Baths
- Open Year-round
- No Pets/Children over 12 yrs; only 1 rm. with accommodations for a 3rd person
- Snowshoeing, Cross Country Skiing, Trout Fishing (on property), Hiking, Horseback Riding, Mountain Climbing, Outstanding Wildlife Viewing, Bird Watching, Wonderful Day Trips to Other Mountain Areas. Shopping, Galleries, Antiquing, Golfing
- Breakfast; Dinner; Wine & Liquor available
- No Smoking
- Conference Facilities (16)
- Wheelchair Access, 3 suites

1 Imagine lying in a magnificent antique bed with the glaciers of the Rocky Mountain National Park looming just over the tops of your toes, or seeing the stars through the skylights above your brass bed, or thrill to feeding a gentle fawn outside your door, or being lulled to sleep by a melodious mountain stream. After snow shoeing in the Park, come home to your own romantic fireside jacuzzi. Ahhhh, at River Song, Time seems to stand still.
(*Traditional, Mountain, Retreat/Lodge. Member since 1987*)

Hwy. 36 to Estes Park in Midtown of Estes, Hwy. 36 to Mary's Lake Rd; L. at Mary's Lake Rd; go 1 blk. Cross bridge. Turn R. immediately. Take Country Road following River to the Road End. Road ends at RiverSong.

TEL. 906-586-4666
P.O. Box 1910
Estes Park, CO 80517

Sue & Gary Mansfield,
Innkeepers

GREAT SAND DUNES COUNTRY CLUB AND INN

14 Rooms, $90/$180 B&B
1 Suite, $150/$250 B&B;
Golf pkgs. Available

Visa, MC, Amex, Discov

All Private Baths

Open Year-round except early April & Late Nov.

Children 10 yrs and older Accepted
No pets

18 hole Championship Golf Course, Outdoor Heated Pool, Hot Tub, Fitness Facilities,

Mountain Biking, Hiking, Horseback Riding, Winter Activities

Breakfast, Lunch, Dinner; Wine & Liquor available
No Smoking

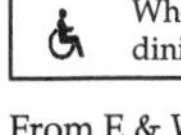
Conference Facilities (35)
Wheelchair Access (1 rm. dining rm. & conf. rm.)

From E & W take US Hwy 160 to State Hwy 150 N 12 mi. Located 4 mi. S of the Great Sand Dunes Nat'l Monument.

TEL. 719-378-2356
or 800-284-9213
FAX: 719-378-2428
5303 Highway 150
Mosca, CO 81146
Oliver Cheng, Innkeeper
Hisa Ota, Owner

"The architecture and setting may evoke the wild west but cowboys never lived this comfortably." Nestled next to the majestic Sangre de Cristo Mountains and the Great Sand Dunes National Monument, this rustic yet luxurious historic inn offers a unique setting where over 2,500 bison roam on the Zapata Ranch. Experience this secluded 15 room property where the amenities include a championship 18 hole golf course, golf school, the cuisine of Chef Sauton and a variety of seasonal workshops. (*Rustic, Country, Retreat. Member since 1994*)

HOSPITALITY

In the late '40's and early '50's as people began to explore the world of hotels and motels, the desire for sequestered namelessness and guaranteed decor during a night away from home was customary. Travelers were comforted by the assurance of not having to deal with an untested, off-brand accommodation. Certainly the last thing that concerned the traveler was the hospitality of the hotel/motel owner. For a quarter century chain hotels and motels reigned supreme. They were new, standardized, plentiful, and everyone was happy.

The needs and desires of the traveling public in the last twenty-five years, however, accompanied by the natural growth and development of the accommodations industry as a whole, have brought about a new emphasis in overnight accommodations. The '80's and 90's have brought a hue and cry for *Hospitality* from the now-experienced traveler, and he has discovered that this ingredient is the essence of the *Country Inn.*

Today's traveler, arriving in his late-model luxury sedan at a present day accommodation for an overnight or weekend, is looking *for an actual person whose purpose in life is to receive and entertain friends or strangers with kindness and generosity.* He wants first and foremost an *experience of Hospitality* in a quality establishment. Listen to what travelers in America brag about after their trips today. The hospitality of the innkeeper and the quality of the accommodation will always be mentioned first.

As the overnight accommodations industry has developed, *Country Inns and Hospitality,* through a natural process, have become good bedfellows: exactly what today's overnight traveler is looking for.

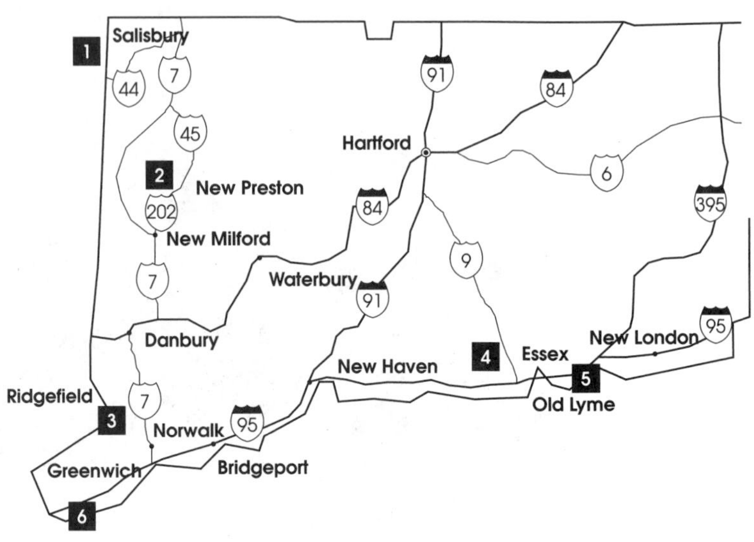

1. Under Mountain Inn, Salisbury
2. Boulders Inn, New Preston
3. West Lane Inn, Ridgefield
4. Griswold Inn, Essex
5. Bee and Thistle Inn, Old Lyme
6. Homestead Inn, Greenwich

BEE AND THISTLE INN

5 In an unspoiled historic village on the Lieutenant River, sits this lovely 1756 inn. Its English gardens, sunlit porches, fireplaces, beautiful, carved staircase, canopied and 4-poster beds, antique quilts and furnishings reflect a gracious lifestyle. Widely commended for its cuisine, it has been voted the most romantic place to dine in Connecticut. (*Traditional, Village, Inn. Member since 1984*)

I-95 (S) Exit 70, turn R. off ramp to inn, 3rd bldg. on L. I-95 (N) Exit 70, turn L. off ramp to 1st light, R. to T in road, then L. to inn. 3rd bldg. on L.

TEL. 203-434-1667; 800-622-4946; FAX 203-434-3402

100 Lyme Street
Old Lyme, CT 06371
Bob & Penny Nelson, Innkeepers

THE BOULDERS INN

17 Rooms, Suites, Guesthouses, $125/$235 B&B; $175/$285 MAP

Visa, MC, Amex
All Private Baths, 5 Whirlpool Baths (Jacuzzis)

Open Year-round

Children Under 12 by special arrangement; No Pets
Tennis, Beach, Boating, Hiking, Bicycles, Downhill & XC Skiing, Antiquing, Golf, Music Festival

Breakfast, Dinner, Wine & Liquor Available
Non-smoking Dining Room

Conference Facilities (20)
Wheelchair Access (guesthouse only)

Rte. 84(E) Exit 7 to Rte. 7(N) to New Milford. Take Rte. 202 to New Preston. L. on E. Shore Rd. (Rte. 45) to Lake Waramaug.

TEL. 203-868-0541
800-55-BOULDERS
East Shore Rd. (Rte. 45)
New Preston, Ct 06777

Ulla & Kees Adema, Innkeepers

2 This 1895 Victorian mansion is located in a spectacular setting at the foot of Pinnacle Mountain, where breathtaking sunsets over Lake Waramaug are enjoyed from the elegantly appointed living room, the glass-enclosed dining room, and most of the guest rooms and guest houses, most of which have fireplaces. The widely-renowned cuisine is also served on the outside terrace in summer.
(*Victorian, Waterside, Inn. Member since 1990*)

THE GRISWOLD INN

14 Rooms, $90 B&B
12 Suites, $95/$175, B&B
Visa, MC, Amex
All Private Baths
Dining Room Closed Christmas Eve/Day
Children Welcome
Pets Accepted
Tennis, Golf, Swimming, Goodspeed Opera, Valley Railroad Steamtrain; Mystic Seaport
Free Continental Breakfast, Lunch, Dinner; Sunday Brunch, Hunt Breakfast; Wine & Liquor Available
Non-smoking areas of restaurant
Conference facilities (up to 75)
Wheelchair Access (1 rm., dining rm. & conf. fac.)

I-91 (S) to Exit 22 (S). Rte. 9 (S) to Exit 3 Essex. I-95 (N&S) to Exit 69 to Rte. 9 (N) to Exit 3 Essex.

TEL. 203-767-1776
FAX 203-767-0481
36 Main St.
Essex, CT 06426

Victoria & William Winterer, Innkeepers

4 A kaleidoscope of nostalgic images delights the eye here: myriad Currier & Ives steamboat prints and Antonio Jacobsen marine art, ship models, firearms, potbellied stove, to name a few. The superb New England cuisine features seafood, prime rib, meat pies, and the Inn's own 1776© sausages. Lucius Beebe considered the Taproom the most handsome bar in America.
(*Traditional, Village, Inn. Member since 1974*)

CONNECTICUT

THE HOMESTEAD INN

17 Rooms, $92/$160
6 Suites, $160/$185
All Major Credit Cards
All Private Baths
Open Year-round
Children Accepted
No Pets
Walking, Running Trails, Parks, Beaches, Shopping, Movies, Theater—all nearby
Breakfast, Lunch, Dinner, Sun. Brunch
Wine & Liquor Available
Smoking Permitted
Conference Facilities (24)
N/A

Gracious, historic elegance with a convivial atmosphere. Exquisitely decorated. Three-star French restaurant under the talented guidance of Parisian chef, Jacques Thiebeult. Described by Fodor's as, ". . . one of the finest lodgings in America." Only 45 minutes from New York City. Unique serene meeting facilities.
(*Elegant, In-Town, Inn. Member since 1969*)

From NYC: I-95 to Greenwich, Exit 3. Turn L. off ramp; from New Haven: turn R. off ramp, then L. at light onto Horseneck Ln. (just before RR overpass), to L. at Field Point Rd. Continue 1/4 mi. to inn on R.

TEL. & FAX 203-869-7500
420 Field Point Rd.
Greenwich, CT 06830
Lessie Davison & Nancy Smith, Innkeepers

FOR YOUR SPECIAL OCCASION

If you are planning a wedding, a birthday, anniversary, rehearsal dinner, shower, or any special celebration and want it to be the most memorable event ever, A Country Inn makes a perfect setting. If you picture a wedding in a lovely Victorian parlor, or beneath an arbor in a formal garden, or maybe beside a mirrored lake, you're holding a book that locates all those places and many more. Even the unique presentation of an engagement ring can become a singular dream for some romantics. By special arrangement at Country Inns, engagement rings have been served under silver domes at the dinner table or hidden in desserts or tied to a bottle of champagne. The special innovative requests made by hopeful grooms somehow spark the romance in all the staff. The event becomes special for everyone.

Innkeepers can make any occasion extraordinary, because most often that event is the primary focus of the entire Inn for that particular day. In planning the event, staff works one-on- one with the client to make sure that everything is exactly the way he or she wants it. The nature and size of Country Inns insures them the time and organization to see that every detail is perfect. Flowers, balloons, a limo, a carriage, a boat, maybe even a horse and sleigh: your request becomes the innkeeper's charge. There are Inns in this book where all of these things, and more, are available. The possibilities are only limited by the combined imaginations and talents of the client and the Innkeeper.

When you have a special occasion coming up, look around your area or thumb through this book, and select a Country Inn for the site. Let your imagination take control. Contact the Innkeeper and plan an event that will live in your memory forever.

UNDER MOUNTAIN INN

 7 Rooms, $160-190 Per Rm. double occ. MAP

 Visa, MC

 All Private Baths

 Open Year-round

 Appropriate for Children over 6; No Pets

Boating, Hiking, Alpine/ Nordic Skiing, Rafting, Antiquing, Music & Theater, Golf, Tennis, Fishing, Horsebk. Riding

 Breakfast, Dinner, Afternoon Tea; Liquor & Wine available

 Limited Smoking; No Pipes or Cigars

Conference Facilities (15)

Wheelchair Access (dining rm.)

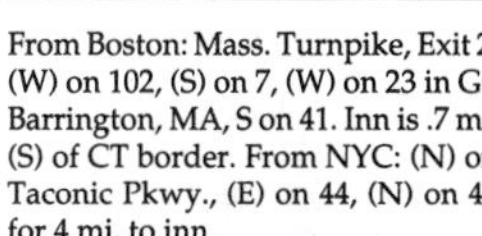
From Boston: Mass. Turnpike, Exit 2, (W) on 102, (S) on 7, (W) on 23 in Gt. Barrington, MA, S on 41. Inn is .7 mi. (S) of CT border. From NYC: (N) on Taconic Pkwy., (E) on 44, (N) on 41 for 4 mi. to inn.

TEL.203-435-0242
FAX 203-435-2379
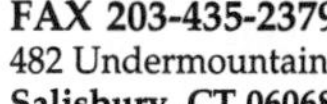
482 Undermountain Road
Salisbury, CT 06068
Peter & Marged Higginson, Innkeepers

1 Enjoy British-flavored hospitality in an 18th century farmhouse, with a proper cup of tea, *The Manchester Guardian*, and a full English breakfast. Dinners could be bangers & mash, steak & kidney pie, or other English specialties cooked up by Manchester-born owner-chef Peter Higginson. A well-stocked library and cozy fireplaces vie with the lure of outdoors and many cultural attractions. *Travel and Leisure* raved, "This is the country getaway we all wish we had."
(*Traditional, Colonial, Mountain, Inn. Member since 1991*)

WEST LANE INN

15 rooms, $110/$165 B&B With Fireplaces st. at $145

Visa, MC, Amex, Diners

All Private Baths

Open Year-round

Children Accepted No Pets

Golf, Tennis, Swimming, Antiques, Boutiques, Shopping

Continental Breakfast

Smoking Permitted

Conference Facilities (25)

N/A

From NYC & Westside Hwy. (N) to Sawmill River Pkwy. & Exit 43 (Katonah). Turn R. on Rte. 35 (E) 10 mi. to Ridgefield. Inn is on L. From Rte 90 & I-84, Exit 3 to Rte. 7 (S) to Rte. 35 and Ridgefield.

TEL. 203-438-7323
FAX 203-438-7325
22 West Lane
Ridgefield, CT 06877
Maureen Mayer, Innkeeper

3 Rich oak paneling, deep pile carpeting, and a cheery fire crackling on the hearth sets the tone of polished refinement at this luxurious inn. Framed by a stand of majestic old maples, a broad lawn, and flowering shrubs, it offers gracious hospitality and a quiet retreat from worldly cares, about an hour north of New York City.
(*Elegant, Colonial, In-Town. Member since 1980*)

1. Chalet Suzanne, Lake Wales
2. Hotel Place St. Michel, Coral Gables
3. The Marquesa Hotel, Key West

CHALET SUZANNE

26 Rooms, \$125/\$185 B&B
4 Suites, \$145/\$195 B&B
Visa, MC, Amex, Discov. DC, Personal Checks
All Private Baths, 5 Jacuzzis
Open Daily except Monday in Summer
Children Welcome
\$20 Per Pet
Swimming, Lawn Games, Jogging, Antiquing, Fishing, Airstrip, Winter Passion Play, Golf, Tennis, Sky Diving, Air Boating, and Lake Cruises nearby.
Breakfast, Lunch, Dinner; Special Packages
Intimate Lounge, Extensive Wine Collection
Non-Smoking in most Dining Rooms
Conference Facilities (50)
Wheelchair Access (2 rms.)

"Fairy tales can come true . . ." A storybook inn with an around-the-world look to its cottages grouped at odd angles, its fountain courtyards, balconies and fascinating furnishings. Winner Uncle Ben's — Ten Best Country Inns of 1991–'92. The Mobil 4-star restaurant is famous for superb fare and caring attention. Chalet Suzanne is AAA 3 diamond Inn and listed on Nat'l Register of Historic Places.
(Traditional, Country, Inn. Member since 1973)

I-4 (W) from Orlando or I-4 (E) from Tampa to U.S. 27 (S), Exit 23 (Cypress Gardens) 18 mi. (S). Turn L. on County Rd. 17A for 1.5 mi. to inn on R.

TEL. 813-676-6011 or 800-433-6011
FAX 813-676-1814
U.S. Hwy 27 & Co. Rd. 17A
3800 Chalet Suzanne Dr.
Lake Wales, FL 33853-7060
Hinshaw family, Innkeepers

HOTEL PLACE ST. MICHEL

24 Rooms, $95/$125 B&B
3 suites, $135/$165 B&B

Visa, MC, Amex, Diners

All Private Baths

Open Year-round

Children—Yes
Pets Not Accepted

Beaches, Golf, Tennis, Coral Rock Swimming Pool, Theaters, Galleries, Shopping, Jogging, Bike Trails, Fitness Ctr.

Nearby
Restaurant, French Deli, Sun. Brunch; Bar-Lounge, Wine & Liquor Available
Non-Smoking Dining Area

Conference Facilities (30)

Wheelchair Access (dining rm.)

I-95 (S), becoming U.S. 1 (S. Dixie Hwy.), continue (S) to Ponce de Leon Blvd., R. to corner of Alcazar Ave. & hotel.

TEL 305-444-1666
800-848-HOTEL
FAX 305-529-0074
162 Alcazar Ave.
Coral Gables, (Miami) FL 33134
Stuart N. Bornstein, Alan H. Potamkin, Innkeepers

2 Filled with antiques, this intimate European-style hotel (ca. 1926) in the heart of Coral Gables, offers superb service and comfort. Welcome baskets of fruit and cheese, complimentary continental breakfast, & the morning paper at your door. One of Florida's "top 10" small hotels, with award-winning restaurant. Major renovations in 1993. (*Elegant, In-Town, Hotel. Member since 1991*)

THE MARQUESA HOTEL

13 Rooms, $120/$225 EP
14 Suites, $160/$280 EP

Visa, MC, Amex, Diners

All Private Baths

Open Year-round

Children – Yes
Pets not Accepted

Heated Pools, nearby Snorkeling, Fishing, Sailing, Historic attractions and homes

Restaurant or Room service for Breakfast, Dinner; Poolside beverage service; Wine & Liquor available
Non-Smoking Cafe

Conference Facilities (25)

Wheelchair Access

U.S. 1, R. on No. Roosevelt Blvd., becomes Truman Ave. Continue to R. on Simonton for 5 blks. to Fleming. Turn R. to front of hotel.

TEL. 305-292-1919; 800-869-4631; FAX 305-294-2121
600 Fleming St.
Key West, FL 33040
Richard Manley,
Erik de Boer, Owners;
Carol Wightman, Manager

3 In the heart of Key West's historic district, the Marquesa Hotel and Cafe is a landmark 111-year-old home, restored to 4-Diamond status in 1988. Floor-to-ceiling windows, large bouquets of flowers, two shimmering pools and lush gardens are Marquesa trademarks. Rooms and suites are luxurious, all with private marble baths. Located within walking distance to Duval Street for galleries, shops, and nightlife. The *Miami Herald* rated it as one of Florida's 10 top inns.
(*Elegant, Greek Revival, In-Town, Hotel. Member since 1991*)

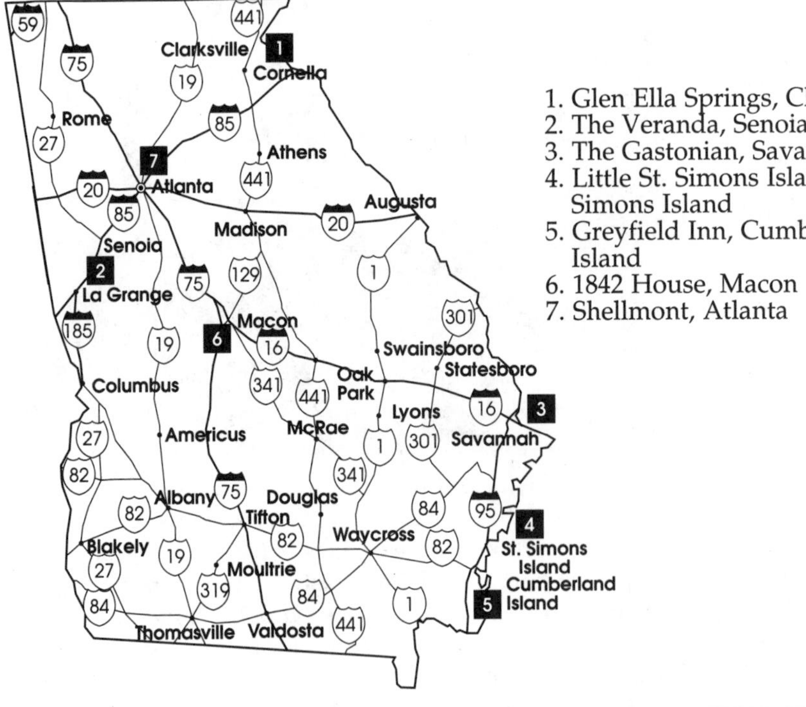

1. Glen Ella Springs, Clarkesville
2. The Veranda, Senoia
3. The Gastonian, Savannah
4. Little St. Simons Island, St. Simons Island
5. Greyfield Inn, Cumberland Island
6. 1842 House, Macon
7. Shellmont, Atlanta

THE GASTONIAN

10 Rooms, $115/$200 B&B
3 Suites, $165/$275 B&B

Visa, MC, Amex

All Private Baths, 6 Jacuzzis

Open Year-round

Appropriate for Children over 12; No Pets

Antiquing, Guided tours, Beaches, Biking, Fine Dining, Galleries, Museums, River Cruise & nearby Golf, Sea Fishing, Tennis

Full Breakfast

Wine Available

No Smoking

Conference Facilities (25)

Wheelchair Access (1 rm.)

3 In the largest Historical Landmark District in the U.S., this 1868 inn is furnished with English antiques, offers beautiful gardens and sundeck with hot tub. Rooms have fireplaces, heat and A/C, Jacuzzi baths, showers, cable TV, fruit and wine — plus nightly turndown with sweets and cordials. Guests feast on a full, hot, sitdown Southern breakfast. Mobil ★★★★, AAA ◆◆◆◆.

(Elegant, In-Town, Breakfast Inn. Member since 1988)

From I-16 exit at W. Martin Luther King Blvd. straight ahead with no turns, which becomes Gaston St. Continue to inn at 220 East Gaston St.

TEL. 912-232-2869;
800-322-6603;
FAX. 912-232-0710
220 E. Gaston St.
Savannah, GA 31401
Hugh & Roberta Lineberger,
Innkeepers

GLEN-ELLA SPRINGS

14 Rooms $80/$150 B&B
2 Suites $150 B&B
Visa, MC, Amex

All Private Baths

Open Year-round; Closed 1 wk. in Jan.

Children 6 yr & older in some rms. No Pets

Walking, Hiking, Bicycle Trails, nearby Whitewater Rafting, Boating on Calmer Waters, Trout Fishing, Horseback, Golf in the area

Breakfast (guests only), Lunch (Sum. & Fall) Dinner (by reservation, days limited in Winter), BYOB
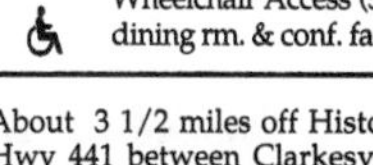
Smoking in some areas
Conference Facility (23)
Wheelchair Access (5 Rms., dining rm. & conf. fac.)

About 3 1/2 miles off Historic Old Hwy 441 between Clarkesville and Clayton; 90 miles north ofAtlanta: I-85 to I-985, (exit 45) becomes US 441, L. on Hardeman Rd. at Turnerville, R. on Old 441 & follow signs.

TEL. 800-552-3479 (except GA); 706-754-7295
FAX 706-754-1560
Bear Gap Rd., Rte 3, Bx 3304
Clarkesville GA 30523
Bobby and Barrie Aycock, Innkps.

Down a country lane at the edge of the Chattahoochee National Forest, this 100-year-old inn on the National Register combines charm of the past with modern comfort. All of the pine paneled guest rooms open onto porches with rocking chairs and lovely views. The 17 acres of grounds contain beautiful perennial, herb, and vegetable gardens, a creek, and a swimming pool. Located just a short 90 miles north of Atlanta, the inn was selected in 1992 as one of Travel and Leisure's top ten resorts.
(*Rustic, Country, Inn. Member since 1990*)

GREYFIELD INN

7 Rooms, 4 Suites, $245/$350 AP

Visa, MC, Pers. Checks

3 Private, 3 Shared Baths

Open Year-round except August

Children 6 years & up No Pets

Birdwatching, Hiking, Swimming, Shelling, Biking, Fishing, Photography

Breakfast, Picnic Lunches, Dinner, Wine & Liquor Available

Smoking only in Bar & Porches

Conference Facilities (22)
N/A

Cumberland Island is accessible only by boat; our ferry service provides transportation to island from Fernandina Beach, FL.

TEL. 912-267-0180
904-261-6408
FAX. 904-261-0964
Cumberland Island, GA
P.O. Box 900
Fernandina Beach, FL 32035-0900
Mitty & Mary Jo Ferguson, Innkps.

This turn-of-the-century mansion is on Cumberland Island, Georgia's largest and southernmost island. Miles of hiking trails traverse the island's unique ecosystems along with a beautiful, endless beach for shelling, swimming, sunning and birdwatching. Fine food, lovely original furnishings, and a peaceful, relaxing environment provide guests with a step back into another era. Overnight rate includes an island outing with our naturalist, bicycles for exploring the island, and roundtrip boat passage on our private ferry.
(*Traditional, Colonial, Waterside, Inn. Member since 1982*)

LITTLE ST. SIMONS ISLAND

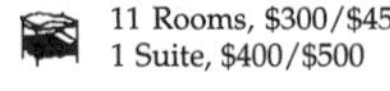

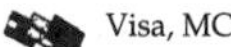

11 Rooms, $300/$450
1 Suite, $400/$500

Visa, MC

All Private Baths

Open Year-Round

No Pets; Children 6 years & up; all ages June–Aug. 15

Canoeing, Hiking, Beachcombing, Fishing, Motorboating, Birding, Naturalist Tours, Horseback Riding, Golf

Breakfast, Lunch, Dinner; Early Light Breakfast, Snacks, Cocktails;Wine & Liquor Available

Smoking Restricted

Conference Facility (3 rms., 24)

N/A

4 Comfortable country inn on 10,000 acre privately-owned island. A visit to this island is a step back in time. Seven miles of beaches, acres of pristine forests and marshes offer the opportunity to explore, hike, birdwatch, canoe, motorboat, and fish. Take a driving tour with a naturalist; enjoy the swimming pool and rocking chairs. Rates include accommodations, meals, and all activities.
(*Rustic, Waterside, Retreat. Member since 1993*)

Two boats daily leaving from Hampton River Club Marina on St. Simons Island.

TEL. 912-638-7472
FAX 912-634-1811
PO Box 21078
St. Simons, Island, GA 31522

Debbie McIntyre, Innkeeper

SHELLMONT BED & BREAKFAST INN

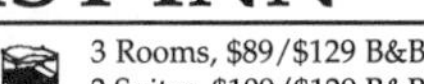

3 Rooms, $89/$129 B&B
2 Suites, $109/$129 B&B

Visa, MC, Amex, DC

All Private Baths

Open Year-round

Children under 12 Carriage house only
No Pets

Botanical Gardens, Art Museums, Theatres, Historic Tours, Galleries, Symphony, Fine Dining, Shopping, GA World Congress Center, Omni, GA Dome, Underground Atlanta

Breakfast

Smoking on Verandas Only

N/A

7 Impeccably restored 1891 National Register mansion located in Midtown-Atlanta's theatre, restaurant and cultural district. A virtual treasure chest of stained, leaded and beveled glass, intricately carved woodwork and hand-painted stenciling. Guest rooms are furnished with antiques, Oriental rugs and period wall treatments. Wicker-laden verandas overlook manicured lawns and gardens—including a Victorian fishpond. The experience is unforgetable. City of Atlanta landmark Building. Recipient of Mayors Award of Excellence for Historic Preservation. AAA ♦♦♦.
(*Traditional, Victorian, In-Town, Breakfast Inn. Member since 1994*)

I-75/85 Northbound, Exit #95A; go N. 1 1/4 mi.; I-75/85 Southbound, Exit N. Ave., (Georgia Tech) Turn L., go to 5th traffic light (Piedmont Ave); Turn L., go 5 blocks to Piedmont & 6th St.

TEL. 404-872-9290
821 Piedmont Ave, N.E.
Atlanta, GA 30308

Ed & Debbie McCord, Innkeepers

THE VERANDA

9 Rooms, $90/$110 B&B

Visa, MC, Amex, Discov

All Private Baths, 1 Whirlpool

Open Year-round; Reservations necessary

Children Accepted (inquire); No Pets

Rare Player Piano/Organ, Extensive Library; nearby: Tennis, Golf, Fishing, Callaway Gardens, Warm Springs, NASCAR Races, Braves Baseball

Full Breakfast; Dinner & Lunch by reservation only

Smoking only on verandah

Conference Facilities (20)

Wheelchair Access (downstairs)

From Atlanta I-85 (S), Exit 12; L.(SE) on Hwy. 74 for 16.7 mi. R.(S) on Rockaway Rd. for 3.3 mi. At light turn L.(E) for 1 block to inn. Ask for brochure/map 9 .

TEL. 404-599-3905
FAX 404-599-0806
252 Seavy St., Box 177
Senoia, GA 30276
Jan & Bobby Boal, Innkeepers

With wrap-around porch and rocking chairs, this elegant turn-of-the century inn on the National Register offers a quiet, relaxed Southern lifestyle just 37 miles south of bustling downtown Atlanta. Guests enjoy fresh flowers, kaleidoscopes, books, games, puzzles, walking canes, and historic memorabilia, plus The Veranda's acclaimed gourmet meals and lavish breakfasts. Local attractions include antiques, historic tours, Riverwood Studios (where movies such as *Fried Green Tomatoes, The War*, etc. were filmed) and The Veranda's unique gift shop. 1990 INN OF THE YEAR. (*Traditional, Village, Inn. Member since 1989*)

1842 INN

Exit 52 on I-75 (Hardeman Ave. Exit), Turn L from N, R from S; Go 2 Lights to College St.; Turn L; Inn is 2 blocks on L.

TEL. 912-741-1842
FAX: 912-741-1842
TEL. 800-336-1842
353 College St.
Macon, GA 31201

Phillip Jenkins & Richard Meils, Innkeepers

With an atmosphere straight from Gone With The Wind, the 1842 Inn in Macon, Georgia blends the amenities of a grand hotel with the ambience of a country inn. The 21 guest rooms and public areas are tastefully designed with English antiques, tapestries and paintings. The Inn's Courtyard Garden is a delightful setting for breakfast and evening cocktails. Amenities include in-room breakfast with morning newspaper, overnight shoe shines, fresh flowers in each guest room, evening turndown service, and access to an exclusive private dining and health club. Some rooms have four-poster beds, working fireplaces and whirlpool tubs. Listed on the National Register of Historic Places the Inn has sustained the coveted Four Diamond Award from AAA for seven years. The Inn is situated in a beautiful historic district within walking distance to restaurants and museum houses. (*Elegant, In-Town, Inn. Member since 1994*)

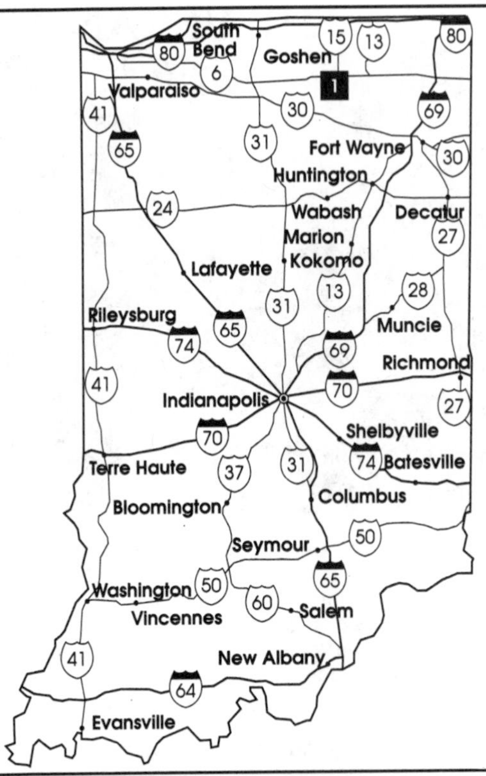

1. The Checkerberry Inn, Goshen

THE CHECKERBERRY INN

11 Rooms, $112/$140 B&B
3 Suites, $160/$325 B&B

Visa, MC, Amex

All Private Baths

Closed January

Children with Restrictions; No Pets

Tennis, Outdoor Pool, Croquet Green; Golf, Lakes nearby

Breakfast; Lunch, (Wed. only); Dinner, Tues.-Sat.; Beer & Wine Available

No Smoking

Conference Facilities (28)

Wheelchair Access (3 rms., dining rm. & conf. fac.)

1 Watch for Amish horses and buggies in this pastoral farmland. On a 100-acre wooded estate, the inn offers breathtaking views of unspoiled rolling countryside from individually decorated rooms. While away the hours enjoying fields of wildflowers, massive Beech trees, miles of country roads, and grazing horses in a nearby pasture. Imaginative meals and fine wines provide memorable dining.
(*Elegant, Georgian, Country, Inn. Member since 1990*)

Exit 107, Ind. toll road, (S) on State Rte. 13 to R. on State Rte. 4 to L. on County Rd. 37; 1 mi. to inn on R.

TEL. 219-642-4445
FAX 219-642-4445
62644 CR 37
Goshen, IN 46526
John & Susan Graff, Innkeepers
Shawna Koehler & Kelly Graff, Asst. Innkeepers

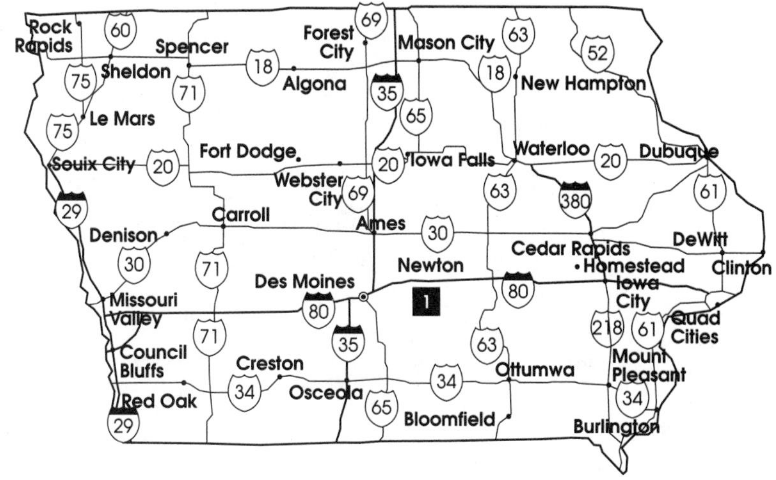

1. LaCorsette Maison Inn, Newton

LACORSETTE MAISON INN

5 Rooms $70/$165, 2 Suites $135

Visa, MC, Amex

All Private Baths

Open Year-round

Children & Pets by Arrangement

Nearby YMCA, Tennis, Swimming, Cross Country Skiing, Parks, Bicycle Trails

Breakfast, Brunch, Dinner Wine Available

No Smoking

Conference Facility (10)

N/A

On I-80 east of Des Moines. 7 blocks east of the city square.

TEL. 515-792-6833
FAX 515-792-6597
629 1st Ave. East
Newton, IA 50208
Kay Owen, Innkeeper

Erected in 1909, LaCorsette Maison Inn is a mission-style mansion. The Inn is elegant, yet comfortable, with cozy nooks and alcoves. It is on the National Historic Register. Kay Owen, the innkeeper, is also a gourmet chef and specializes in Continental food with a French flair. The Inn offers deluxe accommodations and exquisite meals to travelers. (*Traditional, In-Town, Inn. Member since 1993*)

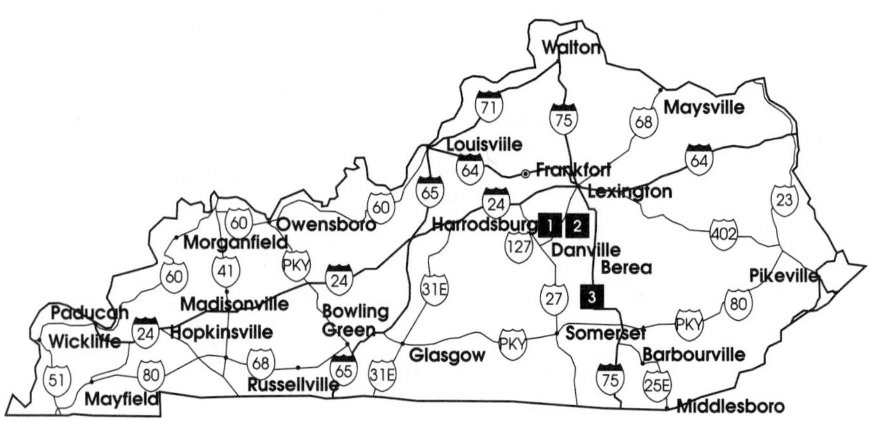

1. Beaumont Inn, Harrodsburg
2. Inn at Pleasant Hill, Harrodsburg
3. Boone Tavern Hotel, Berea

BEAUMONT INN

33 Rooms $75/$100 EP

Visa, MC, Amex, Discov

All Private Baths

Open March–Mid-Dec.

Children Accepted; No Pets

Swimming Pool, Tennis, Shuffle-board, Golf, Fishing, Historic attractions Antique Galleries & Summer Theater

Breakfast, Dinner Daily Lunch, Tues.–Sun.

Non-smoking rms. available, non-smoking dining rm.

Conference Facilities (25)

N/A

Owned and operated by 4 generations of the Dedman family, this country inn, on the National Register of Historic Places, was built in 1845 as a school for young ladies. In the heart of Bluegrass country, it is redolent of Southern history, brimming with beautiful antiques, fascinating memorabilia, and the food is traditional Kentucky fare. Over 30 varieties of trees grace the grounds. The town of Harrodsburg, founded in 1774, is the first permanent English settlement west of the Allegheny Mountains. Located amid numerous historic sites and attractions. (*Traditional, Village, Inn. Member since 1979*)

In Harrodsburg at intersection with U.S. 68, take U.S. 127 (S) to inn, at south end of town on east side of U.S. 127.

TEL. 606-734-3381
800-352-3992
FAX 606-734-6897
638 Beaumont Inn Dr.
Harrodsburg, KY 40330
The Dedman Family, Innkeepers

BOONE TAVERN HOTEL

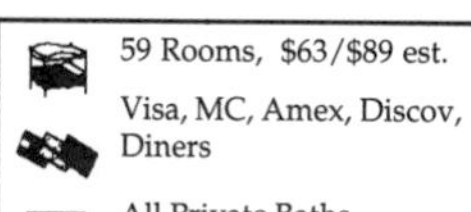

59 Rooms, $63/$89 est.

Visa, MC, Amex, Discov, Diners

All Private Baths

Open Year-round

Children Welcome; No Pets

Campus Tours, Appalachian Museum, Craft & Antique Shops, Danforth Chapel, and Planetarium

Breakfast, Lunch & Dinner served daily; Dress code for Dinner and Sunday Lunch

We Kindly Request No Smoking

Conference Facility

Wheelchair Access (2 rms., dining rm. & conf. fac.)

I-75 S. Lexington approx. 45 mi, Exit 76, L off ramp, follow U.S. 25 to 4th stop light, R. 1 block to Boone Tavern Hotel, or I-75 N. Knoxville, TN to Exit 76, R off ramp, follow U.S. 25 to 4th stop light, R 1 block to Boone Tavern Hotel

TEL. 800-366-9358; 606-986-9358

Main and Prospect Street

Berea, KY 40403

Robert A. Stewart, Innkeeper

2 Historic Boone Tavern Hotel is nestled within and owned by Berea College, which provides tours and attractions to guests. Berea proudly bears the title of "Arts and Crafts Capital of Kentucky" because of its many crafts and antique shops. The Hotel dining and meeting rooms offer superb southern cuisine, charming atmosphere, and friendly student service. Come to Boone Tavern Hotel and experience the true southern hospitality that is always waiting for you.

(*Georgian, Village, Hotel. Member since 1992*)

SHAKER VILLAGE AT PLEASANT HILL

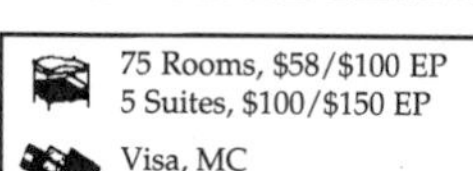

75 Rooms, $58/$100 EP
5 Suites, $100/$150 EP

Visa, MC

All Private Baths

Closed Dec. 24 & 25

Children Accepted
No Pets

Village Touring, Riverboat

Breakfast, Lunch, Dinner

Non-Smoking Dining Rm.

Conference Facilities (75)

N/A

From Lexington, U.S. 68 (W) 25 mi. and R. to village. From Harrodsburg, U.S. 68 (E) 7 mi. Turn L. to village.

TEL. 606-734-5411

3500 Lexington Rd.

Harrodsburg, KY 40330

Christopher Brassfield, Innkeeper

3 Part of a restored Shaker community, originally established in 1805, the inn's rooms are located in 15 of the 33 original buildings clustered along a country road on 2,700 acres in Bluegrass country. Rooms are simply and beautifully furnished with examples of Shaker crafts. Meals are hearty and homemade, and tours, demonstrations, and cultural events abound.

(*Rustic, Country, Inn. Member since 1971*)

1. Madewood Plantation House, Napoleonville

MADEWOOD PLANTATION HOUSE

8 Rooms, $165 MAP
Visa, MC, Amex, Discover
All Private Baths
All year except Thanksgiving, Christmas, and New Year's eve and night.
No Pets; Mature Children
Swamp Tours, Historic Homes
Breakfast & Dinner
Smoking Restrictions
Conference Facility (100)
Wheelchair Access (1 rm., dining rm. & conf. fac.)

The "Queen of the Bayou," Madewood Plantation House offers elegant accommodations in a homelike atmosphere. This National Historic Landmark is lovingly maintained by its long-time staff, who provide the relaxed atmosphere for which Madewood is noted. Guests enjoy antique-filled rooms and canopied beds along with a wine and cheese hour prior to a family style candlelight dinner prepared by Madewood's cooks. One of the top 12 inns of '93 by *Country Inns* magazine.
(Traditional, Greek Revival, Country, Inn. Member since 1993)

75 mi. NW of New Orleans. From New Orleans, I-10 W to Exit 182 (Donaldsonville/Sorrento). Follow "Bayou Plantations" signs. Cross Sunshine Bridge to 70 to Spur 70 to L. onto 308, through Napoleonville, 2 mi. farther on 308.

TEL 504-369-7151
FAX 504-369-9848
4250 Hwy 308
Napoleonville, LA 70390
Keith & Millie Marshall, Innkeepers; David D'Aunoy, Res. Mgr.

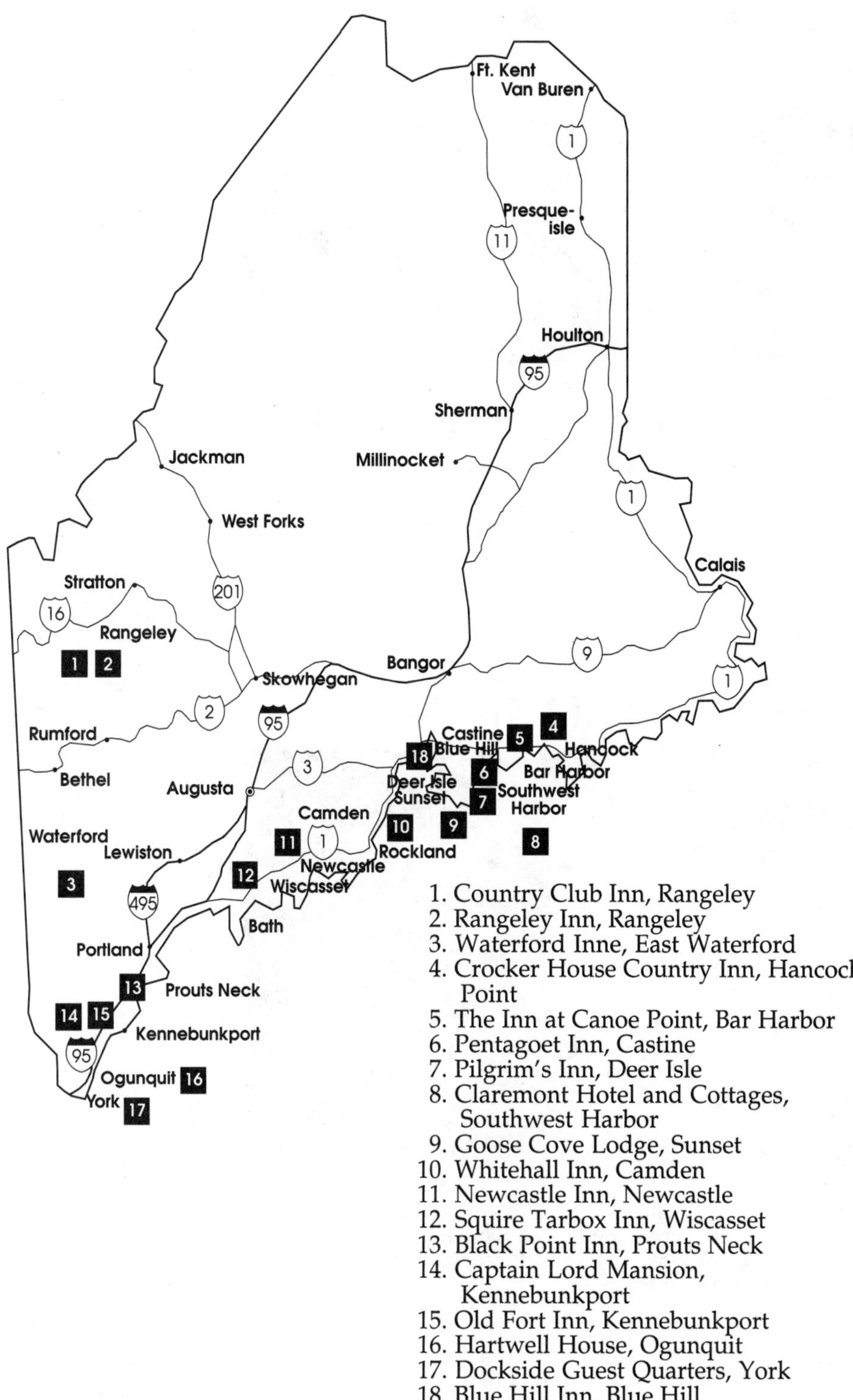

1. Country Club Inn, Rangeley
2. Rangeley Inn, Rangeley
3. Waterford Inne, East Waterford
4. Crocker House Country Inn, Hancock Point
5. The Inn at Canoe Point, Bar Harbor
6. Pentagoet Inn, Castine
7. Pilgrim's Inn, Deer Isle
8. Claremont Hotel and Cottages, Southwest Harbor
9. Goose Cove Lodge, Sunset
10. Whitehall Inn, Camden
11. Newcastle Inn, Newcastle
12. Squire Tarbox Inn, Wiscasset
13. Black Point Inn, Prouts Neck
14. Captain Lord Mansion, Kennebunkport
15. Old Fort Inn, Kennebunkport
16. Hartwell House, Ogunquit
17. Dockside Guest Quarters, York
18. Blue Hill Inn, Blue Hill

BLACK POINT INN

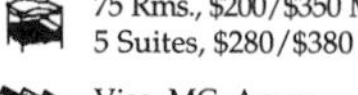

75 Rms., $200/$350 MAP
5 Suites, $280/$380 MAP
Visa, MC, Amex
All Private Baths
Open May 1–Dec. 1
No Children or Pets
Golf, Tennis, 2 Beaches, 2 Pools (1 indoor), 2 Hot Tubs, 1 Sauna, Bird Sanctuary, Fishing, Sailing, Bicycles, Croquet, Volleyball
Breakfast, Lunch, Dinner
AP rates available
Wine & Liquor Available
Smoking Restrictions
Conference Facilities
Wheelchair Access (3 rms, dining rm. & conf. fac.)

13 Quintessentially New England is this seaside resort inn, the favored retreat of generations of guests since the late 1800s. Easy, gracious hospitality and understated, genteel elegance, along with the vast ocean views, bracing salt air, hearty meals, beachcombing, sailing, and more, make this a world-class seaside resort-inn.
(*Elegant, Waterside, Resort. Member since 1969*)

I-95 (Maine Turnpike) to Exit 6, turn left at first light onto Payne Rd. Turn right at next light onto Rt. 114, drive thru next light. Rt. 114 becomes Rt. 207. Drive 4.8 mi. to Inn.

TEL. 207-883-4126
Reserv. 800-258-0003
510 Black Point Rd.
Prouts Neck, ME 04074
Normand H. Dugas, Innkeeper

THE BLUE HILL INN

9 Rooms, $120/$170 MAP
2 Suites, $120/$170 MAP
(15% service + 7% tax additional)
Visa, MC
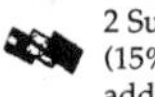
All Private Baths
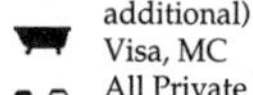
Closed Dec. 1–15 & Jan.
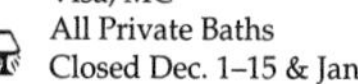
Children over 10
No Pets

Sailing, Hiking, Biking, Kayaking, Chamber Music, Art Galleries
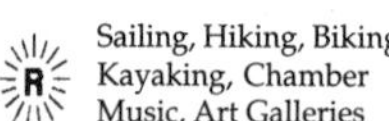
Breakfast, Dinner, Wine & Liquor Available
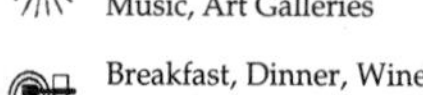
No Smoking
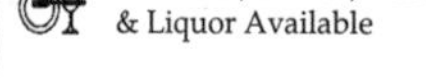
Conference Facilities (15)
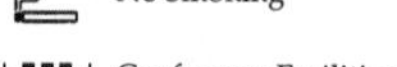
Wheelchair Access (1 rm.)

18 The Village of Blue Hill, with its mountain as backdrop, looks southeast across Blue Hill Bay to the mountains of Acadia National Park. The multichimneyed and clapboarded inn, a short walk from the head of the bay, art galleries, and chamber music, has served as the village hostelry since 1840. Down comforters, fireplaces, hors d'oeuvres hour, candlelight dining, sophisticated cuisine, extensive wine list, and attentive service create an intimate atmosphere for inn guests.
(*Traditional, Village, Inn. Member since 1994*)

I-95 N. to Augusta Rte 3 N. Belfast through Bucksport to Rte 15 S. to Blue Hill to I77. Turn R heading W 1/10th mi.

TEL. 207-374-2844
800-826-7415
FAX: 207-374-2829
Union St.
PO Box 403
Blue Hill, ME 04614
Mary & Don Hartley, Innkeepers

CAPTAIN LORD MANSION

16 Rooms, $125/199 B&B

Visa, MC, Discov

All Private Baths

Open Year-round

Appropriate for Children over 6; No Pets

Antiquing, Shopping, Beaches, Sailing, Whale watching, Tennis, Golf, Fishing, Bicycling

Full Breakfast; BYOB

No Smoking

Conference Facilities (14)

N/A

ME Tpke., Exit 3. L. onto Rte. 35 for 5.5 mi. to Rte. 9 (E). Turn L., go over bridge. R. onto Ocean Ave.; after 3/10 mi., turn L. onto Green St.

TEL. 207-967-3141
FAX 207-967-3172
P.O. Box 800
Kennebunkport, ME 04046-0800
Bev Davis & Rick Litchfield, Innkeepers

14 The beautifully appointed, spacious rooms of this stately 1812 mansion, with its elliptical staircase and imposing cupola, feature period wallpapers, crystal chandeliers, fireplaces and many objects d'art. Superb comfort and gracious hospitality have been rewarded for many years with four diamonds by AAA. Many year-round activities are offered in this charming seacoast village.
(*Elegant, Village, Breakfast Inn. Member since 1975*)

CLAREMONT HOTEL & COTTAGES

30 Rms., $95 BB/$185 MAP
1 Suites, $185/$200 MAP
12 Cotts., $85/$200 EP

All Private Baths

Early May to Late October

Children Accepted; No Pets

Tennis, Croquet, Rowboats, Bikes, Golf, Sailing, Swimming, Acadia Nat'l. Park

Breakfast and Dinner; Lunch late May to late Oct. only. EP off-season; Wine & Liquor Available

No Smoking in Guest Rooms

Conference Facilities (125)

Wheelchair Access (5 rms.; dining rm. & conf. fac.)

ME Tpke., Exit 15 (Augusta), Rte. 3 (E) thru Ellsworth to Mt. Desert Is. Take Rte. 102 to SW Harbor, Follow signs.

TEL. 207-244-5036
FAX 207-244-3512
Box 137,
Southwest Harbor, ME 04679
John Madeira, Jr., Manager

8 The dock and the Boathouse on Somes Sound are the center of much activity at this 110-year-old summer hotel, although croquet and the annual Claremont Classic run them a close second. On the National Register of Historic Places, the Claremont, with its panoramic views of mountains and ocean, offers serene and happy sojourns to its many returning guests.
(*Traditional, Waterside, Hotel. Member since 1974*)

COUNTRY CLUB INN

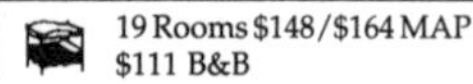

19 Rooms $148/$164 MAP $111 B&B
Visa, MC, Amex
All Private Baths
Open late May.–mid-Oct.; late Dec. – late Mar.
Children Welcome; Pets Allowed, $10 daily
Golf, Swimming Pool, Hiking, Fishing, Lake Swimming, Boating, Lawn Games, Canoeing, Antiquing, X-country & Downhill Skiing, and Snowmobiling
Breakfast & Dinner; Box lunch available; Wine, Beer & Liquor available
No Smoking in Dining Room
Conference facilities (100)
N/A

AN INN FOR ALL SEASONS . . . A sophisticated little resort catering to only 40 guests desiring casual luxury, tranquility, sumptuous meals, and warm hospitality. Few locations offer such beauty and grandeur in all seasons as Rangeley with its wide skies, vast mountain ranges and sparkling lakes. Magnificent scenery can be enjoyed from all guest rooms, dining room, and lounge at nearly 2000 feet in elevation. Public 18-hole golf course adjacent to Inn (golf packages available), Hiking, Boating, Fishing, X-country skiing, downhill skiing, and over 100 miles of snowmobile trails. (*Traditional, Village, Inn. Member since 1981*)

ME Tpke., Exit 12 to Rte. 4. I-91 in VT & NH to St. Johnsbury; (E) on Rte. 2 to Gorham & Rte. 16(N) to Rangeley.

TEL. 207-864-3831
P.O. Box 680
Rangeley, ME 04970

Sue Crory, Margie & Steve Jamison, Innkeepers

CROCKER HOUSE COUNTRY INN

11 Rooms, $80/$115 in season, B&B
$70/$90 off season, B&B
Visa, MC, Amex, Discov
All Private Baths
Closed Jan.1 — Apr. 20; Open Fri. & Sat. only in Nov. & Dec.
Well mannered Children Accepted; Pets with prior permission
Spa, Croquet, Library, Clay Tennis courts, Antiquing, Golf, Acadia Nat'l Park region
Breakfast & Dinner; Sunday brunch Memorial-Labor Day
Smoking & Non-smoking Dining Rooms
Conference Facilities (36)
N/A

Sequestered on Hancock Point, this restored 109-year-old inn is a three minute walk from Frenchman Bay. The carriage house, converted in 1992, adds two spacious guestrooms, an additional common room and a spa. The restaurant, open to the public, continues to draw guests from distant places for its extraordinary cuisine and live jazz piano on Friday and Saturday nights.
(*Traditional, Country, Inn. Member since 1987*)

From Ellsworth go 8 (eight) miles (N) on US Rt. 1, to R on Hancock Pt. Rd. Continue 5 miles to Inn on R.

TEL. 207-422-6806
FAX 207-422-3105
Hancock, ME 04640

Richard Malaby, Innkeeper

DOCKSIDE GUEST QUARTERS

15 Rooms, $59/$102 EP
6 Suites, $98/$145 EP
Off season rates and packages available
Visa, MC, Personal Chks.
19 Private, 2 Shared Baths
Open Year-round
Weekends only Nov-May
Winter apts. available
Children welcome
No Pets
Beaches, Boats, Bicycles, Fishing, Shuffleboard, Badminton, Croquet, Swimming,Golf Tennis, Outlet shopping, Historic sites
Breakfast, Lunch, Dinner, Lounge; Weddings, Group Functions
Wine & Liquor available
Non-smoking Rooms
Conference Facilities (30)
N/A

From I-95 exit to U.S. 1 South. Rte. 1-A thru Old York to Rte. 103. Cross bridge & watch for signs to inn.

TEL. 207-363-2868
1-800-270-1977
FAX 207-363-1977
Harris Island Rd.
P.O. Box 205
York, ME 03909
The David Lusty Family, Innkeepers

17 A small family run resort uniquely situated on a private peninsula in York Harbor. A seacoast inn and multi-unit cottages offer comfortable and attractive guest rooms, most with private decks and water views. Spacious grounds offer privacy and classic Maine scenery. The restaurant is renowned for creative presentations of fresh Maine seafood. Rated 3 diamonds by AAA.
(*Traditional, Country, Inn. Member since 1975*)

GOOSE COVE LODGE

11 Rms., $145/$181 MAP
11 Cotts., $165/$350 MAP

MC, Visa

All Private Baths

Open May 15 to Oct. 15, 1995

Children Welcome; No Pets

Sea Kayaking, Sailing, Beach, Nature Trails, Golf, Tennis, Sailing, Bicycling, Acadia Nat'l. Park

Breakfast & Dinner, May-Oct.; B&B Option in off-season; Wine & Liquor Available

No Smoking in Main Lodge

Conference Facility (25)
Wheelchair Access (1 rm., dining rm. & conf. fac.)

I-95 to Augusta, Rte. 3 to Belfast. Rte. 1 (N), 4 mi. past Bucksport. R. on Rte. 15, in town of Deer Isle R. on Sunset Rd., 3 mi. to inn sign & R. 1.5 mi. to inn.

TEL. 207-348-2508
FAX: 207-348-2624
Deer Isle,
Sunset, ME 04683
Joanne & Dom Parisi, Innkeepers

9 Secluded lodging, sand beaches, moss-covered trails, and magnificent ocean vistas. Cottages have fireplaces, sundecks, kitchenettes and ocean views. Many artists and craftspersons nearby. Pleasant daytrips on land and water. Outstanding cuisine in rustic "Down East" lodge with lobster cookouts on the beach. A Family Inn.
(*Rustic, Ocean Front, Inn/Lodge. Member since 1981*)

HARTWELL HOUSE

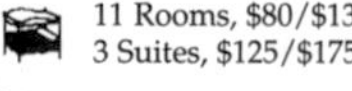
11 Rooms, $80/$135 B&B
3 Suites, $125/$175 B&B

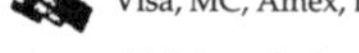
Visa, MC, Amex, Disc.

All Private Baths

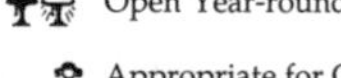
Open Year-round

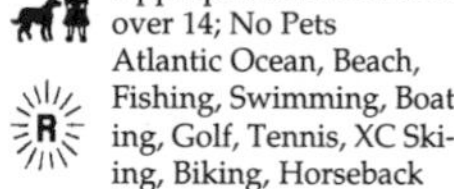
Appropriate for Children over 14; No Pets

Atlantic Ocean, Beach, Fishing, Swimming, Boating, Golf, Tennis, XC Skiing, Biking, Horseback Riding

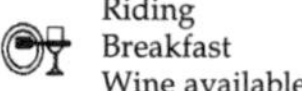
Breakfast
Wine available

No Smoking

Conference facilities (25)

N/A

16 View the sculpted lawn and gardens from your balcony filled with flowers. Unwind with a walk along the breathtaking and nearby marginal way. Early American and English antiques, stunning fabrics, and a delicious gourmet breakfast all add to the ambiance of this elegant country inn. Walking distance to beaches and Perkin's Cove. Seasonal lodging and dining packages available.
(*Elegant, Village, Breakfast Inn. Member since 1981*)

I-95 (N) & York/Ogunquit Exit. L. on Rte. 1 for 4.4 mi. to R. at Pine Hill Rd. L. at Shore Rd. for .2 mi. to inn.

TEL. 207-646-7210
FAX 207-646-6032
118 Shore Rd., P.O. Box 393
Ogunquit, ME 03907

Trish & Jim Hartwell, Renee & Alec Adams, Innkeepers

THE INN AT CANOE POINT

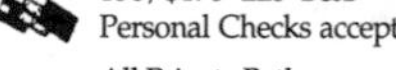
3 Rooms, $80–95/$125–150 B&B; 2 Suites, $120–150/$175–225 B&B

Personal Checks accepted

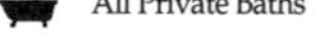
All Private Baths

Open Year-round

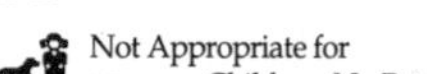
Not Appropriate for younger Children; No Pets

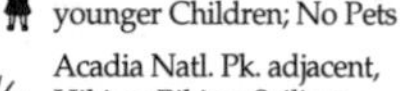
Acadia Natl. Pk. adjacent, Hiking, Biking, Sailing, Mtn. Climbing, XC Skiing

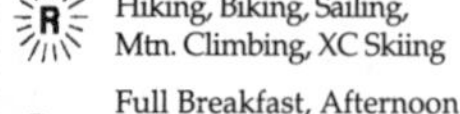
Full Breakfast, Afternoon Refreshments; Port Wine in Rooms; BYOB

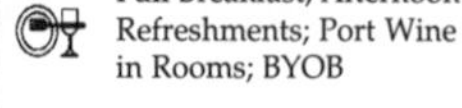
Non-Smokers Preferred

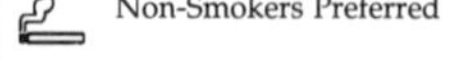
Conference Facilities (20)

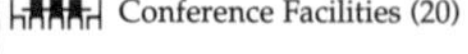
N/A

5 This secluded waterside inn among the pines is only moments away from lively Bar Harbor and next door to the unspoiled natural attractions of Acadia National Park. With views of Frenchman's Bay, mountains, trees, flowers, rocky coast and the ocean, guests will be tempted to laze by the granite fireplace in the ocean room or out on the deck, listening to the rolling surf.
(*Traditional, Waterside, Bed & Breakfast Inn. Member since 1991*)

From Ellsworth, Rte. 3 (NE) approx. 15 mil. toward Bar Harbor, through Hulls Cove Village. Continue past Acadia Natl. Pk. entrance 1/4 mi. to inn on L.

TEL. 207-288-9511
Box 216, Hulls Cove
(Bar Harbor), ME 04644

Don Johnson & Esther Cavagnaro, Innkeepers

THE NEWCASTLE INN

 15 Rooms, $60/$135 B&B
$120/$195 MAP

 Visa, MC

 All Private Baths

 Open Year-around

 Older, well behaved Children; No Pets

 Walking trails, Beaches, Bicycling, Antiquing, Birding, Boating, Touring, XC Skiing

 Breakfast – Guests only
Dinner by Reservation
Wine & Liquor available

 No Smoking

 Conference Facilities (20)

 N/A

Maine Tpke. to Exit 9; I-95 (N) to Brunswick Exit 22, Rte. 1(N); 6 mi.(N) of Wiscasset. Take R. on River Rd. Continue 1/2 mi. to inn on R.

TEL. 207-563-5685
FAX 207-563-1390
800-832-8669
River Road
Newcastle, ME 04553
Ted and Chris Sprague, Innkeepers

11 At the end of your day's travels, a warm greeting, exceptional dining with national acclaim, and a pampering atmosphere await you, overlooking the harbor and lovely flower gardens here by the broad and salty Damariscotta River. Individualized attention is reflected in the details you will find in each of our bedchambers. In one of the midcoast Maine's quintessential villages, with easy access to numerous attractions, the feeling of warmth, friendship, and seclusion make this a retreat where guests may relax and unwind.
(*Traditional, Village, Inn. Member since 1990*)

OLD FORT INN

 16 Rooms $98–$190/
$125–$240 B&B

 Visa, MC, Amex, Discov. Enroute

 All Private Baths;
4 Jacuzzis

 Closed Dec. 10 — April 14

 Appropriate for Children over 12; No Pets

 Tennis Court, Pool, Ocean, Golf, Walking, Jogging

 Breakfast

 Non-smoking

Conference Facilities (32)

 N/A

I-95 Exit 3, turn L. on Rte. 35 for 5 1/2 mi. L. at light at Rte. 9 for 3/10 mi. to Ocean Ave. Go 9/10 mi. to Colony Hotel, then L. & follow signs 3/10 mi. to inn.

TEL. 207-967-5353;
800-828-3678
FAX 207-967-4547
Old Fort Ave., P.O. Box M
Kennebunkport, ME 04046
Sheila & David Aldrich, Innkps.

15 A short walk from the ocean along a country road, this secluded inn in an old seaport town offers rooms with antiques, canopied and 4-poster beds, color TV and phones. Guests find new friends over a buffet breakfast of fresh fruit and homemade breads; a charming antiques shop, fresh-water pool, and private tennis court provide pleasant diversion. The unique combination of yesterday's charm and today's conveniences entice many guests to return to the Inn year after year and recommend it to their friends. AAA Four Diamond Award.
(*Elegant, Waterside, Resort. Member since 1976*)

MAINE

THE PENTAGOET INN

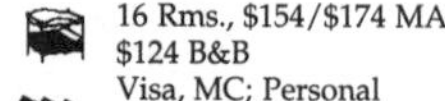 16 Rms., $154/$174 MAP
$124 B&B

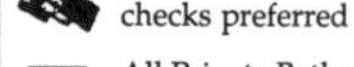 Visa, MC; Personal checks preferred

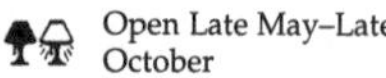 All Private Baths

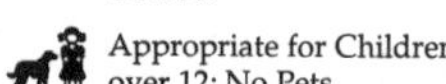 Open Late May–Late October

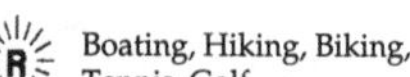 Appropriate for Children over 12; No Pets

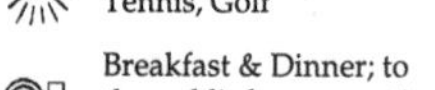 Boating, Hiking, Biking, Tennis, Golf

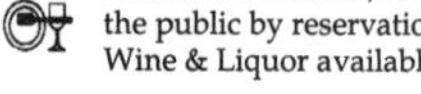 Breakfast & Dinner; to the public by reservation
Wine & Liquor available

 No Smoking

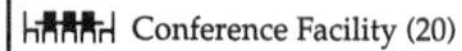 Conference Facility (20)

 N/A

6 Capacious porches, fresh flowers and nightly room freshening are just a few of the "perks" at this lovely old Victorian inn. With its feeling of a private country home, the Pentagoet offers excellent food and an extensive wine list. After a day of exploring or relaxing, join others for cocktails and special chamber music or storytelling preceding dinner. Tiny, historic Castine in Penobscot Bay provides fresh sea air, harbor activities in a tranquil setting. (*Traditional, Village, Inn. Member since 1988*)

I-95 to Augusta & Rte. 3 (E) to Belfast, turn L. (N) on Rte. 1 past Bucksport 3 mi. to R. (S) on Rte. 175. Turn (S) on Rte. 166 to Castine. Inn is on Main St.

TEL. 207-326-8616
800-845-1701
Main St., P.O. Box 4
Castine, ME 04421

Lindsey & Virginia Miller,
Innkeepers

PILGRIM'S INN

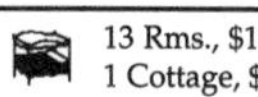 13 Rms., $130/$170 MAP
1 Cottage, $180 MAP

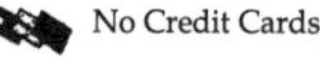 No Credit Cards

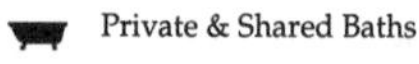 Private & Shared Baths

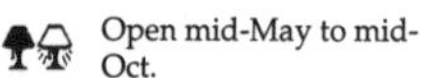 Open mid-May to mid-Oct.

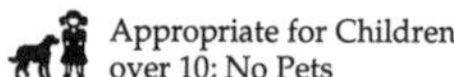 Appropriate for Children over 10; No Pets

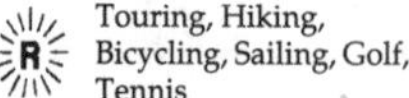 Touring, Hiking, Bicycling, Sailing, Golf, Tennis

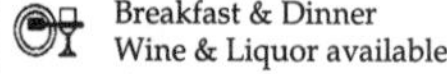 Breakfast & Dinner
Wine & Liquor available

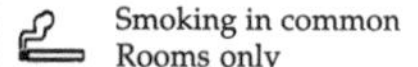 Smoking in common Rooms only

Conference Facilities (35)

N/A

7 Overlooking Northwest Harbor and a picturesque millpond, this 1793 Colonial home is surrounded by the unspoiled beauty of remote Deer Isle in Penobscot Bay. Glowing hearts, soft Colonial colors, pumpkin pine floors, antique furnishings, combined with warm hospitality and gourmet meals in the charming barn dining room, have pleased many happy and contented guests. On the National Register of Historic Places. Easy access to the renowned Haystack School of Crafts and the busy fishing Village of Stonington. (*Traditional, Colonial, Country Inn. Member since 1980*)

I-95 (N) to Augusta. Rte. 3 (N) to Belfast, thru Bucksport to Rte. 15 (S), thru Blue Hill. Over bridge to Deer Isle Village. Turn R., 1 block to inn on left.

TEL. 207-348-6615
Deer Isle, ME 04627

Dud & Jean Hendrick,
Innkeepers

RANGELEY INN

50 Rooms $59–$69/ $97–$107, 1 Suite $89–$99
Visa, MC, Amex, Discov
All Private Baths; Several Whirlpools
Open Year-round
Children Accepted; Pets Discouraged
Skiing at Saddleback & Sugarloaf; x-country & snowmobiling from our backdoor; swimming, sailing, canoeing, hiking near
Breakfast & Dinner; MAP optional; Dining Open Mem. Day–Col. Day & Wint.; Wknds. and for Group Business anytime; Wine & Liquor Available
Smoking Restrictions
Conference Facilities (150)
Wheelchair Access (2 rms., dining rm.)

On Rte. 4 past Farmington 40 mi.to Rangeley. From west take Rte. 16. Inn is on Main St.

TEL. 207-864-3341
1-800-666-3687
FAX 207-864-3634
Box 160, Main St.
Rangeley, ME 04970

Fay & Ed Carpenter,
Innkeepers

2 The big blue clapboard building with the long veranda across the front has that grand old summer hotel look and the homelike, roomy lobby has a bit of an old-fashioned feeling. The elegant dining room is up to the minute with creative, interesting menus. Several acres of lawns and gardens border a bird sanctuary, and the area is a nature-lover's and sportsman's paradise. So return with us now to yesteryear—and visit our mountain & lake resort from our 1907 Inn. We look forward to serving you.
(*Traditional, Village, Inn. Member since 1989*)

THE SQUIRE TARBOX INN

11 Rooms, $85/$166 B&B $139/$220 MAP
Visa, MC, Amex, Discov
All Private Baths
Closed late Oct. to early-May
Appropriate for Older Children; No Pets
Walking path, Rowboat and Bikes on premises, Beaches, Harbors, Antiques nearby
Breakfast for guests only; Dinner to public by reservation; Wine & Liquor available
Smoking in weather protected area
N/A

I-95 to Brunswick, Exit 22, follow Rte. 1 (N) past Bath bridge 7 mi. to Rte. 144. Continue 8.5 mi. on Westport Island.

TEL. 207-882-7693
R.R.2, Box 620, Route 144
Wiscasset, ME 04578

Bill & Karen Mitman,
Innkeepers

12 On a road to nowhere, this comfortable colonial farmhouse on a wooded hillside by a small inlet, is a respected full-service inn offering historical significance, a natural country setting, relaxed comfort, and a diversity of Maine Coast interests. Quiet rural privacy is here for guests who seek moments of personal solitude. Known for its savory fireside dinners and goat cheese from its purebred dairy herd. Built 1763–1820, the Inn is pleasantly removed from tourist crowds, but still near to beaches, harbors, antique shops, museums, lobster shacks, and L. L. Bean. (*Colonial, Country, Inn. Member since 1974*)

THE WATERFORD INNE

9 Rooms, $75/$100 B&B
1 Suite, $100 B&B

Amex

7 Private Baths; 1 Shared Bath

Closed March 15—April 30

Children Accepted; Pets with $10 fee

Library, Parlor Games, Down-hill & XC Skiing, Swimming, Boating, Hiking, Antiquing

Breakfast & Dinner; BYOB

Smoking Discouraged

Conference Facilities (15)

Some Wheelchair Access

3 A 19th-century farmhouse situated on a country lane midst 25 acres of fields and woods, Distinctively different, a *true* country inn offering uniquely decorated guest rooms, a charming blend of two centuries—the warmth of early pine furnishings combined with contemporary comforts. Outside—rolling terrain, a farm pond, an old red barn. Inside—an air of quiet simple elegance, antiques and art, barnboard and brass, pewter and primitives. Country chic cuisine to pamper your palate.
(*Traditional, Colonial, Country, Inn. Member since 1979*)

From Maine Tpke.: Use Exit 11, follow Rte. 26 N. approx. 28 mi. into Norway, then on Rte. 118 W. for 8 mi. to Rte. 37 S. (left). Go 1/2 mi., R. at Springer's Gen. St., up the hill 1/2 mi.

TEL 207-583-4037
FAX 207-583-4037
Box 149 Chadbourne Rd.
Waterford, ME 04088

Rosalie & Barbara Vanderzanden, Innkeepers

WHITEHALL INN

50 Rooms, $130/$165 MAP
Off Season $80/$110 B&B

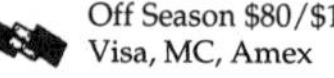

Visa, MC, Amex

Private & Shared Baths

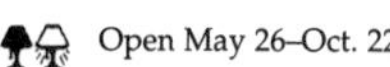

Open May 26–Oct. 22

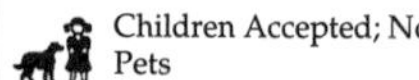

Children Accepted; No Pets

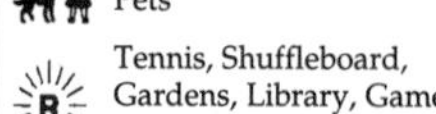

Tennis, Shuffleboard, Gardens, Library, Games, Rocking Chairs, Golf, State Park, Lakes, Sailing

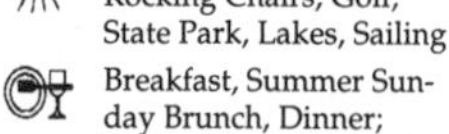

Breakfast, Summer Sunday Brunch, Dinner; Wine & Liquor Available

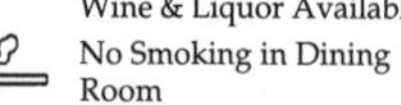

No Smoking in Dining Room

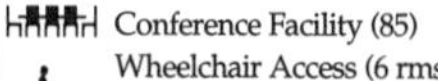

Conference Facility (85)

Wheelchair Access (6 rms, dining rm. & conf. fac.)

10 If ever an inn and a setting were made for each other, this is it—Camden, Maine and the Whitehall Inn. Tree-lined streets, comfortable old homes echo the feeling of old-fashioned friendliness and hospitality in this rambling, homey inn, originally built in 1834, and operating as an inn since 1901. The inn has been run by the Dewing family for 23 years. One of the few remaining authentic coastal summer hotels preserving not only its history and grandness, but the commitment to comfortable accomodations, fine service, and dining excellence.
(*Traditional, Village, Inn. Member since 1973*)

Camden is 2 hrs. north of Portland on Rte. 1. Inn is 1/4 mi. north of village.

TEL. 207-236-3391
1-800-789-6565
FAX 207-236-4427
52 High St., P.O.Box 558
Camden, ME 04843

The Dewing Family, Innkeepers

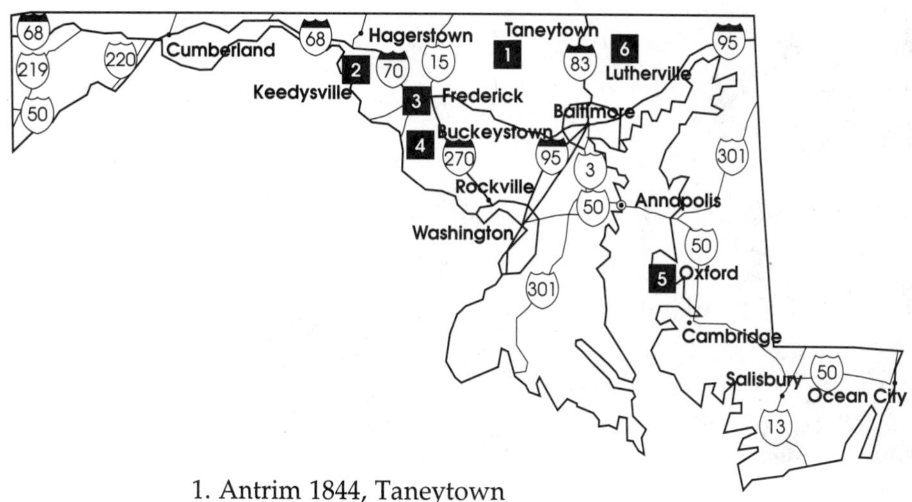

1. Antrim 1844, Taneytown
2. Antietam Overlook Farm, Keedysville
3. Tyler Spite House, Frederick
4. Inn at Buckeystown, Buckeystown
5. Robert Morris Inn, Oxford
6. Twin Gates B&B, Lutherville

ANTIETAM OVERLOOK FARM

Located in the Western Maryland mountains just over one hour west of Baltimore and Washington D.C.—Call for directions and availability

TEL. (800) 878-4241
P.O. Box 30
Keedysville, MD 21756
Barbara & John Dreisch, Innkeepers

2 Our 95-acre mountaintop farm overlooking Antietam National Battlefield has extraordinary views of four states. The hand-hewn timber framing, rough-sawn walls and stone fireplaces juxtaposed to the softly flowered furnishings and fine crystal create a warm, comfortable atmosphere. Spacious suites include fireplaces, queen beds, sumptuous bubble baths, and private screened porches. While our seclusion and tranquillity are unparalleled, many guests also enjoy visiting the neighboring Civil War battlefields at Gettysburg, Bull Run/Manassas, and Harpers Ferry.
(*Traditional, Mountain, Retreat/Lodge. Member since 1992*)

ANTRIM 1844

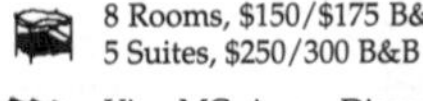
8 Rooms, $150/$175 B&B
5 Suites, $250/300 B&B

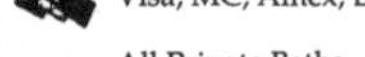
Visa, MC, Amex, Discov

All Private Baths

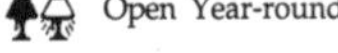
Open Year-round

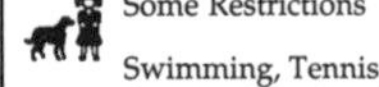
Some Restrictions

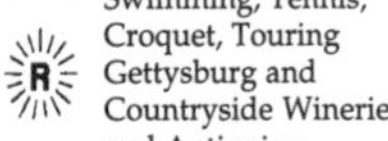
Swimming, Tennis, Croquet, Touring Gettysburg and Countryside Wineries, and Antiquing

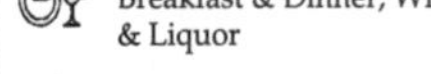
Breakfast & Dinner; Wine & Liquor

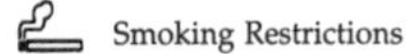
Smoking Restrictions

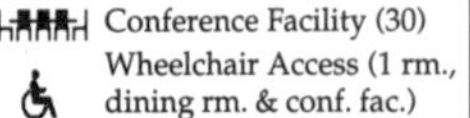
Conference Facility (30)
Wheelchair Access (1 rm., dining rm. & conf. fac.)

One of Maryland's most renowned country inn resorts. Antebellum ambience together with genuine hospitality and acclaimed cuisine has earned Antrim 1844 a place in country inn connoisseurs' hearts. Guestrooms are appointed with elegant decor, roaring fireplaces, and jacuzzis. Relax by the fire in the Pickwick Tavern, Library, Smokehouse, or Drawing Rooms. Turn-down service, tea, cocktail party, and endless amenities spoil even the most discriminating traveler. "A must see" if your are near Washington, D.C. or Baltimore.
(*Elegant, Country, Inn. Member since 1993*)

From Wash., D.C. , 495 to I-270 W; then 15 N and 140 E to Taneytown. Through light and over tracks and then bear right on Trevanion Rd.

TEL. 800-858-1844;
410-756-6812;
FAX 410-756-2744
30 Trevanion Rd
Taneytown, MD 21787
Dort & Richard Mollett,
Innkeepers

THE INN AT BUCKEYSTOWN

3 Rooms, $225 MAP
4 Suites, $250/$300; MAP
1 cottage MAP
(Tax & Service Incl.)

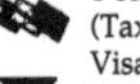
Visa, MC, Amex

7 Private Baths

Open Year-round; Closed some Mondays & Tuesdays

By Reservation Only
Appropriate Mature Teenagers; No Pets

Hiking, Antiquing, Civil War sites

Breakfast & Dinner
Complimentary Wine, Tea & Refreshments

Non Smoking

Conference facilities (20)
Wheelchair Access (dining rm., conf. fac.)

Lovingly restored, this impressive 1897 mansion and 1884 church are in a nostalgic village, on the National Register of Historic Places. Rooms are luxuriously furnished with outstanding antiques and collectibles. A wraparound porch with rockers looks out on park-like grounds. Gourmet dining and the friendly ambiance bring guests back to this award-winning Inn. The changing seasons and all holidays are reasons to celebrate here. In fact, all stays are considered celebrations—a celebration of life!
(*Victorian, Village, Inn. Member since 1987*)

From I-70 or I-270, take Rte. 85(s) to Buckeystown. Inn is on left. (35 mi. from Dulles Airport.)

TEL. 301-874-5755
RES. 800-272-1190
c/o General Delivery
3521 Buckeystown Pike
Buckeystown, MD 21717
Daniel R. Pelz, Chase Barnett,
Rebecca Smith,
Innkeepers

THE ROBERT MORRIS INN

 35 Rooms, $70/$220 EP

 Visa, MC

All Private Baths

Lodging Year-round B&B Dec.-Mid Mar.; Rest. open Mid Mar.-Nov.

 Appropriate for Children over 10; No Pets

Tennis, Biking, Golf, Antiquing, Sailing, Historic Car Ferry, Goose Hunting

 Full Service Wed.-Mon.; Cont. Bkfst. only Tues.; Wine & Liquor available

 All Rooms Non-Smoking

 Executive Conference Facilities (10-20)

Wheelchair Access, 2 rms.

Hwy. 301 to Rte. 50 (E). Turn R. on Rte. 322 for 3.4 mi. Turn R. on Rte. 333 for 9.6 mi. to inn

TEL. 410-226-5111
312 No. Morris St.
P.O. Box 70
Oxford, MD 21654

Wendy & Ken Gibson, Owners
Jay Gibson, Innkeeper

5 Chesapeake Bay and the Tred Avon River play a big part in the life of this Eastern Shore country-romantic 1710 inn. Delicacies from the bay are featured in the nationally acclaimed seafood restaurant and the Tred Avon offers lovely views from many of the rooms and porches. Country furnishings add to the friendly feeling here in the historic waterside village of Oxford. James A. Michener, author of "Chesapeake," rated the Robert Morris Inn's crab cakes the highest of any restaurant on the Eastern Shore." *(Traditional, Waterside, Inn. Member since 1970)*

TWIN GATES B&B INN

 6 Rooms, $85/$135 B&B
1 Suite, $135 B&B

 Visa, MC, Amex

 All Private Baths

 Open Year-round

 Appropriate for Children over 12; No Pets

 Antiquing, Hiking, Bicycling, Birding, Tennis, National Aquarium, Wineries, Ladew Topiary Gardens, Museums, Historic Sites

 Breakfast

 No Smoking

 Conference facilities (10–12)

 N/A

I-695 (Baltimore Beltway) Exit 25 N. R. (eastward) on Bellone Ave. 3 blocks to Morris Ave.

TEL. 800-635-0370
FAX: 410-560-2161
308 Morris Ave.
Lutherville, MD 21093
Gwen & Bob Vaughan, Innkeepers

6 Surrounded by perennial gardens with a romantic wicker gazebo and magnificent trees, Twin Gates is nestled in a Victorian village on the northern edge of Baltimore City. Lutherville, a National Historic District, provides a country setting but is only 15 minutes to the center of Baltimore and all of its attractions. Nearby are good seafood restaurants, free winery tours in Maryland Hunt Country, and the world famous Ladew Topiary Gardens. Soft music, fresh flowers, and decadent but heart–healthy breakfasts punctuate the warm hospitality at Twin Gates B&B.
(Traditional, Victorian, Village, Breakfast Inn. Member since 1994)

TYLER SPITE INN

- 7 Room, $140/$200 B&B
- 2 Suites, $200
- plus 20% Tax & Service
- Visa, MC, Amex
- 3 Private Baths
- Open Year-round
- No Children or Pets
- Swimming Pool, Hiking, Tennis, Biking, Golf; Museum and Performing Arts Theater 3 blocks away
- Breakfast, High Tea at 4:00 P.M., Complimentary Wine & Sherry
- No Smoking
- Conference Facility (30)
- N/A

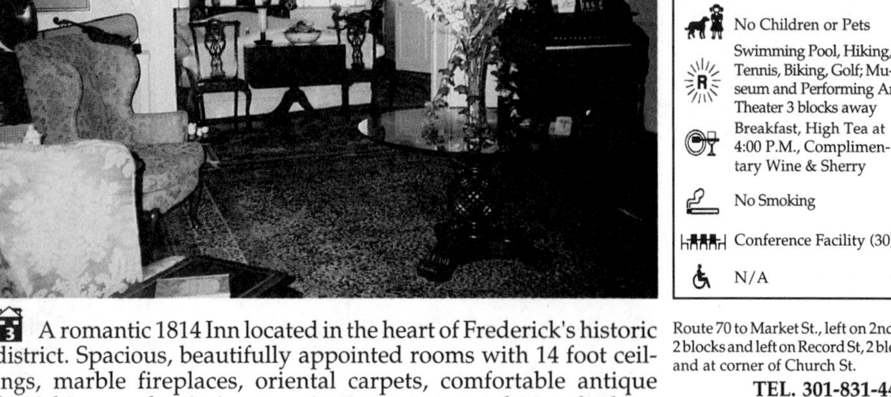

A romantic 1814 Inn located in the heart of Frederick's historic district. Spacious, beautifully appointed rooms with 14 foot ceilings, marble fireplaces, oriental carpets, comfortable antique furnishings and paintings captivate our guests who are looking for the ultimate in romanticism. Walled gardens replete with color entice guests for a leisurely stroll. A stay is complete once you ascend from the carriage block located at the front door for a horse drawn carriage tour through Frederick's quaint city.
(*Elegant, In Town, Breakfast Inn. Member since 1993*)

Route 70 to Market St., left on 2nd St., 2 blocks and left on Record St, 2 blocks and at corner of Church St.

TEL. 301-831-4455
800-417-3264
112 W. Church St
Frederick, MD 21701

Bill & Andrea Myer,
Innkeepers

IT LOOKS SO EASY - LIKE DUCKS ON A POND

Many of our guests aspire to become Innkeepers once they have visited and experienced one our fine Inns. Many of them do indeed follow through and become part of the Innkeeping world. However, many more become discouraged when they sit down with someone who has had several years' experience or visit with a consultant or perhaps attend a seminar on Innkeeping. They are amazed about *everything* that goes into being an Innkeeper

Innkeepers themselves are responsible for the perception that the business is an "easy, fun" way to spend one's time. Guests see them smiling as they greet their guests or pour coffee or chat about the local area while giving directions on interesting things to see and do. Guests never get to see their hosts dealing with leaky pipes, disgruntled employees, late food purveyors, obstinate suppliers, laundry equipment breakdowns, hours of bookwork, government regulations etc., etc. And that is as it should be.

Norm Kinney, the executive director of Independent Innkeepers' Association, always says that Innkeepers make it look too easy. He likens Innkeepers to ducks swimming on a pond. They are gliding along smoothly on the surface and paddling like crazy underneath.

So, is Innkeeping as easy as it looks? NO. Would most Innkeepers do it again? I think the majority of them would tell you, YES. Even with all the breathless paddling, Innkeeping is an exciting, gratifying, challenging, and enviable way to *fully* live each day and *soundly* rest each night.

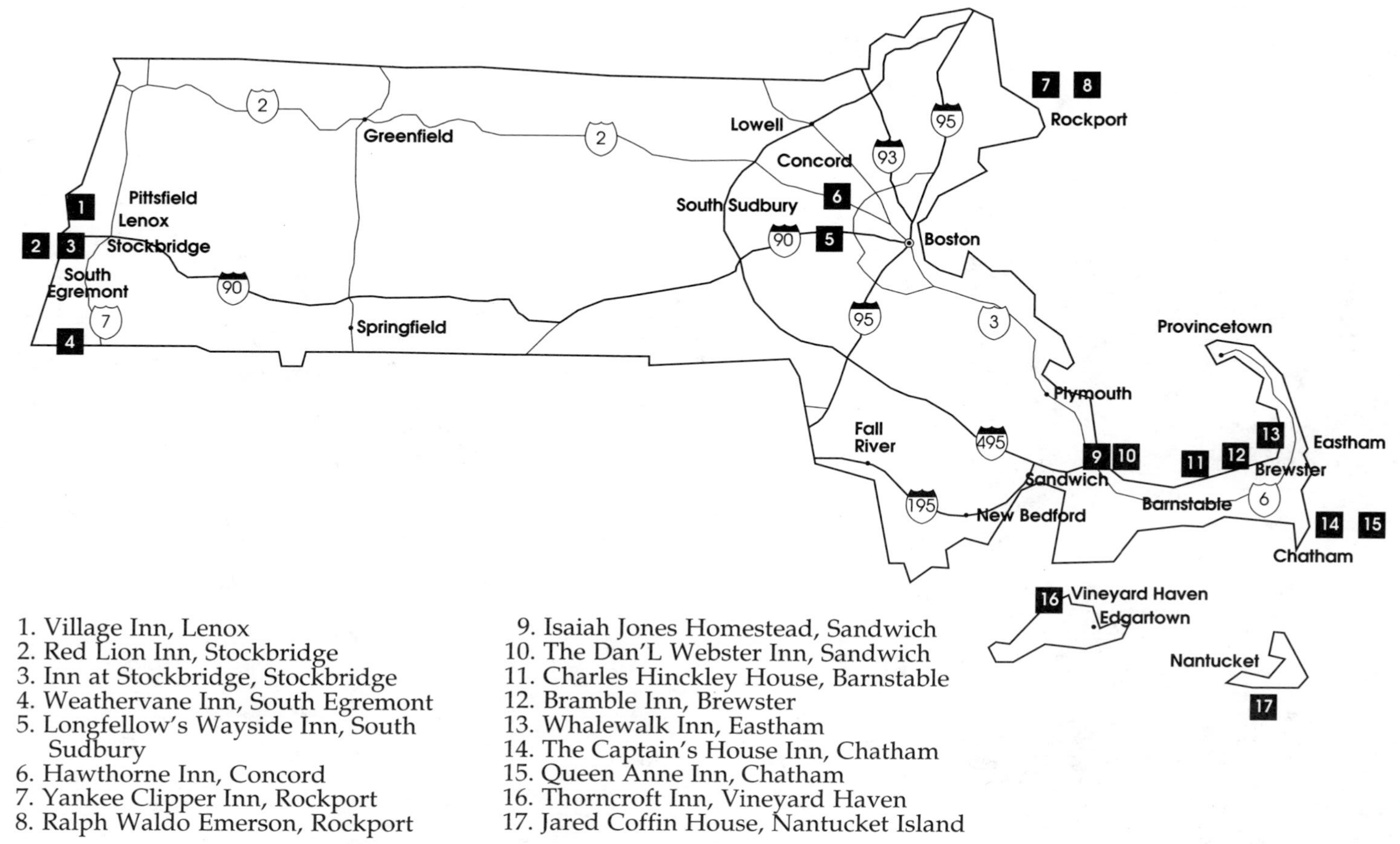
Pittsfield
Lenox
Stockbridge
South Egremont
Greenfield
Springfield
Lowell
Concord
South Sudbury
Boston
Rockport
Plymouth
Fall River
New Bedford
Sandwich
Barnstable
Provincetown
Eastham
Brewster
Chatham
Vineyard Haven
Edgartown
Nantucket
1. Village Inn, Lenox
2. Red Lion Inn, Stockbridge
3. Inn at Stockbridge, Stockbridge
4. Weathervane Inn, South Egremont
5. Longfellow's Wayside Inn, South Sudbury
6. Hawthorne Inn, Concord
7. Yankee Clipper Inn, Rockport
8. Ralph Waldo Emerson, Rockport
9. Isaiah Jones Homestead, Sandwich
10. The Dan'L Webster Inn, Sandwich
11. Charles Hinckley House, Barnstable
12. Bramble Inn, Brewster
13. Whalewalk Inn, Eastham
14. The Captain's House Inn, Chatham
15. Queen Anne Inn, Chatham
16. Thorncroft Inn, Vineyard Haven
17. Jared Coffin House, Nantucket Island

THE BRAMBLE INN AND RESTAURANT

 12 Rooms, $78/$128 B&B
1 Suite, $118/$128 B&B

 Visa, MC, Amex, Discov

 All Private Baths

 Open April 15–Dec. 31

 Appropriate for Children over 8; No Pets

 Tennis, Swimming, Fishing, Bicycling, Horseback, Riding, Whale-watching, Antiquing

 Breakfast, Price-fix Dinner by reservation, Wine & Liquor available

 Smoking restricted

N/A

12 Dine superbly at one of Cape Cod's top three restaurants, where Ruth Manchester creates dishes sought after by *Bon Appetit* and *Gourmet*. Wide pine floors, antiques, and flowered wallpapers adorn the guest rooms in the three 18th and 19th century buildings of this family-owned and operated intimate inn on the historic north side.
(Traditional, Village, Inn. Member since 1977)

Rte. 6, Exit 10 & bear L. on Rte. 124 to R. on Rte. 6A for 1/8 mi. to inn on left.

TEL. 508-896-7644
2019 Main St.
Route 6A, Box 807
Brewster, MA 02631

Cliff & Ruth Manchester, Innkeepers

THE CAPTAIN'S HOUSE INN OF CHATHAM

 15 Rooms, $130/$225 B&B 1 Suite, $150/$200 B&B

 Visa, MC, Amex

 All Private Baths

 Open Year-round

 Doesn't meet needs of Children; No Pets

 Beaches, Tennis, Golf, Boating, Theater, Fishing, Bicycling, Lawn Croquet

 Breakfast, Afternoon Tea

 Non-Smoking Inn

Conference Facilities (16)

N/A

14 A quiet getaway, without television, and cheerful, caring attention are here for guests who choose to stay at this historic, elegant 1839 inn set on two acres, a half-mile from Cape Cod's south shore beaches. The decor is reminiscent of Williamsburg with fine antiques, canopied beds, and fireplaces in warm, inviting guest rooms. This lovely inn has rated the AAA 4-diamond award for past eight years.
(Elegant, Waterside, Inn. Member since 1989)

Rte. 6 (Mid-Cape Hwy.) to Rte. 137, Exit 11 (S) to Rte. 28; left on Rte. 28 to Chatham Center. Continue around rotary on Rte. 28 toward Orleans 1/2 mi. to inn on left.

TEL. 508-945-0127
FAX 508-945-0866
369-377 Old Harbor Rd.
Chatham, Cape Cod, MA 02633
Jan & David McMaster, Innkeepers

CHARLES HINCKLEY HOUSE

2 rooms, $119/$139 B&B
2 suites, $149 B&B
Personal Checks accepted
All Private Baths
Open Year-round except Dec. 22–27
Appropriate for Children 10 & over; No Pets
Antiquing, Beaches, Golf, Tennis, Sailing, Fishing, Museums, Historic Sites
Complimentary Breakfast, Lunch upon request, Dinner on weekends only, Complimentary Sherry
No Smoking
Wheelchair Access (1 room)

Rte. 6 to exit 6, end of ramp stop sign go left onto Rte. 132 to stop sign, turn right onto 6A, 1 1/2 miles on left

TEL. 508-362-9924
FAX 508-362-8861
Olde Kings Hwy., (Rte. 6-A),
P.O. Box 723
Barnstable, MA 02630

Les & Miya Patrick,
Innkeepers

11 An architectural gem listed on the National Register of Historic Places on the Olde Kings Highway is this 1809 Colonial home of an early shipwright. The young innkeepers have lovingly restored and furnished it, polishing the wide pumpkin pine floors, refurbishing the fireplaces, and putting in 4-poster beds. Where no detail is overlooked. The Charles Hinckley House defines elegant simplicity. A small intimate country inn where great expectations are quietly met. The unspoiled natural beauty of Cape Cod Bay is just a stroll away. *(Traditional, Federal, Village, Breakfast Inn. Member since 1988)*

DAN'L WEBSTER INN

46 Rooms, $89/$300

Visa, MC, Amex, Discovr, CB
All Private Baths
Open Year-Round; Closed Christmas
Children welcome, No Pets
Outdoor Pool on Premise; Bicycling, Golfing, Fishing, Ocean, Tennis nearby-Health Club Membership
Breakfast, Lunch, Dinner, & Sun. Brunch; Devil'n Dan Tavern
Smoking restrictions
Conference Facilities (10-200)
Wheelchair Access. (1 rm., dining rm., conf. fac.)

From Boston, MA: Rte. 3 S to Rte 6 (mid-Cape Hwy) to Exit 2. Turn L on Rte. 130. Approx. 2 mi. R at fork. Inn on L.

TEL. 508-888-3622
800-444-3566
FAX: 508-888-5156
149 Main St.
P.O. Box 1849
Sandwich, MA 02563-1785
The Catania Family,
Innkeepers

10 300 years ago, weary travelers found this stage coach stop a rewarding respite. Today, nestled in the quintessential New England Village of Sandwich with its tree-lined streets, old sea captains' homes, duck pond and grist mill, yet only steps from the beaches of Cape Cod Bay, this award-winning historic Inn still offers its guests the same warm and caring hospitality, with today's amenities tucked in. Relax in spacious, yet cozy, individually decorated rooms - some with canopy bed, fireplace, and whirlpool tub. A romantic dinner by the fire in the Heritage Room, or in the beautiful glassed Conservatory, might include, among many other delectable entrees, fresh hybrid striped bass grown in the Inn's own Aquafarm. An informal Gathering Room complete with games, puzzles, and books bids the guest welcome to this "home away from home". *(Traditional, Colonial, Village, Inn. Member since 1994)*

HAWTHORNE INN

On land where Emerson, Alcott, and Hawthorne lived, and among trees planted by these illustrious men, the Hawthorne Inn follows their lead in the cultivation of art and appreciation of the spiritual in life. Friendly, caring innkeepers and nature walks, where land, sky, and water refresh the senses, imbue this winsome, intimate inn with a very special feeling.
(Traditional, Village, Breakfast Inn. Member since 1980)

Rte. 128-95, Exit 30-B (W) (Rte. 2A) for 2.8 mi. Bear R. at fork toward Concord for 1.2 mi. Inn across from Hawthorne's home.

TEL. 508-369-5610
462 Lexington Rd.
Concord, MA 01742

Gregory Burch & Marilyn Mudry, Innkeepers

THE INN AT STOCKBRIDGE

Consummate hospitality and outstanding breakfasts distinguish a visit at this turn-of-the-century Georgian Colonial estate on 12 secluded acres in the heart of the Berkshires. Close to the Norman Rockwell Museum, Tanglewood, Hancock Shaker Village, summer theaters, and four-season recreation. The inn has a gracious, English country house feeling, with two well-appointed living rooms, a formal dining room, and a baby grand piano.
(Elegant, Village, Breakfast Inn. Member since 1986)

Mass. Tpke. Exit 2 & (W) on Rte. 102 to Rte. 7 (N) 1.2 mi. to inn on R. From NYC, Taconic Pkwy. to Rte. 23 (E) & Rte. 7 (N) past Stockbridge 1.2 mi.

TEL 413-298-3337
FAX 413-298-3406
Rte. 7 (North), Box 618
Stockbridge, MA 01262

Lee & Don Weitz, Owners

ISAIAH JONES HOMESTEAD

 5 Rooms, $75-$124 B&B

 Visa, MC, Amex, Discov.

 All Private Baths

 Open Year-round

 Children over 12 accepted; No Pets

Museums, Antiques, Gift Shops, Beach, Fishing, Whale Watching, Tennis, Golf, Biking, Hist. Sites

 Breakfast & Afternoon Tea; Warm Cider by Fireside or Lemonade on Porch. Low Cholesterol Cooking featured

 No Smoking

N/A

Rte. 6 (mid-Cape-Hwy.) Exit 2, L on Rte. 130 and bear R. at fork for 2/10 mi. on L.

TEL. 508-888-9115
or 800-526-1625

165 Main Street
Sandwich, MA 02563

Shirley Jones Sutton, Innkeeper

9 This 1849 Italianate Victorian in the historic village of Sandwich, Cape Cod's oldest town, is within walking distance of most points of interest and fine restaurants. Beautifully furnished with antiques, oriental carpets, and fresh flowers, its quiet elegance harks back to a time when life was tranquil and travelers were pampered. Enjoy the elegant rooms including the master suite with over-sized jacuzzi bath; the Beale Room with fireplace. All rooms have private baths. Breakfast is served by candlelight. (*Victorian, Village, Breakfast Inn. Member since 1989*)

JARED COFFIN HOUSE

60 Rooms, $100/$200 B&B

Visa, MC, Amex, Diners, Discov

All Private Baths

Open Year-round

Children & Pets Accepted with prior approval

Excellent Bike Trail, Conservation Walk, Swimming, Sailing, Fishing (none on premises)

All meals available on premises; Wine & Liquor available

Smoking Restrictions

Conference Facilities (24)

Wheelchair Access (6 rms., dining rm. & conf. fac.)

Flights available from NYC, Boston, New Bedford, & Hyannis. Or take Hyannis ferry, leaving car in Hyannis — cars unnecessary on Nantucket.

TEL. 508-228-2400
Res: 800-248-2405 (M-F, 9-5); FAX 508-325-7752

29 Broad St., P.O. Box 1580
Nantucket, MA 02554-1580

Philip & Margaret Read, Innkeepers

17 A collection of buildings from the mid-1800's tastefully restored to provide today's guest with the feeling of a gentler past. The inn is conveniently located in the Old Historic District near Main Street shops with easy access to island beaches and bike paths. The Tap Room and JARED's offer both casual and more formal dining featuring American cuisine. The inn is open for the Thanksgiving, Christmas, and New Year holidays and offers guests the friendly feeling of a home away from home. (*Historic, Island, Inn. Member since 1969*)

LONGFELLOW'S WAYSIDE INN

10 Rooms, $90

All Major

All Private Baths

Closed Dec. 25th & July 4th

Children Accepted
No Pets

Historic sites, Famous Revolutionary War landmarks

All Meals (overnight guests only); Wine & Liquor available

No Smoking in Public Areas

Conference Facility (50)

Wheelchair Access (dining rm. & conf. fac.)

5 Immortalized in 1863 by Longfellow in his *Tales of a Wayside Inn*, the inn is located off U.S. Rt. 20 on Wayside Inn Road. Next to the inn is a working gristmill, (open April-November); the Red Stone School House of *Mary and Her Little Lamb* fame (open seasonal weather) and the Martha Mary Chapel for weddings. Reservations for lodging and for dining made well in advance.
(*Traditional, Colonial, Country, Inn. Member since 1967*)

Between Boston & Worcester off Rte. 20. 11 mi. (W) of Rte. 128 & 7 mi. (E) off Rte. 495. Sign on R., for Wayside Inn Rd.

TEL. 508-443-1776
FAX 508-443-2312
Wayside Inn Rd. off Rte. 20
South Sudbury, MA 01776

Robert H. Purrington, Innkeeper

THE QUEEN ANNE INN

27 Rooms, $115/$275 B&B; 4 Suites, $242/$300 B&B

Visa, MC, Amex

All Private Baths; 2 Jacuzzis

Open April 1–1/1/96

Children Accepted
Kennel nearby for Pets

Outdoor Swimming Pool; Indoor Spa, 3 Tennis Cts, Bikes, Boating, Scuba Diving, Fishing, Golf

Breakfast, Dinner: May 1st–Oct. 31st
Wine & Liquor Available

No Smoking in Guest rooms & restaurant except Lounge & porch

Conference Facilities (15)

Wheelchair Access (1 rm.), Dining Room, Conference Facilities

15 Spacious guest rooms with tv, antiques, garden views, private balconies, working fireplaces, and private whirlpool baths are a few of the amenities that may be found here on Cape Cod's picturesque south shore. The intimate restaurant features superb cuisine, and pursuits to beguile quiet hours or to engage the energetic are all around.
(*Traditional, Victorian, Village, Inn-Resort. Member since 1981*)

Rte. 6 (E) to Exit 11, R. on Rte. 137 and L. on Rte. 28 for 3.5 mi. to light and R. fork to Queen Anne Rd. and up hill to inn.

TEL. 508-945-0394
RES.800-545-INNS
FAX 508-945-4884
70 Queen Anne Rd.
Chatham, MA 02633
Guenther Weinkopf, Innkeeper

RALPH WALDO EMERSON INN

34 Rooms, $85-$120/$96-$131 EP; 2 suites, $95-$120/$106-$131
Visa, MC, Discov.
All Private Baths
Open May 1–Oct. 31
April & Nov. weekends
Children Accepted
No Pets
Heated Salt Water Pool, Sauna, Whirlpool, Game Room, Theater with Projector TV & VCR, Lawn Games, Boating, Bicycles, Whale Watching, Golf, Sight Seeing nearby
Breakfast & Dinner (July-Labor Day)
Smoking Permitted
Conference Facilities (35)
Wheelchair Access (2 rms., dining rm.)

Rte. 128 (N) to traffic light in Gloucester, left on 127 to our sign in Pigeon Cove (Phillips Ave.)

TEL. 508-546-6321
FAX 508-546-7043
Phillips Ave., Box 2369
Rockport, MA 01966

Gary & Diane Wemyss, Innkeepers

8 One of the last of the old summer hotels on Cape Ann, the Emerson's broad porches and Greek Revival architecture give it a classic majesty. Preserving the charm of yesteryear while keeping up with the times, the inn features a heated saltwater pool, a whirlpool and sauna, and a theater for movies. Popular seafood and shore specialties are always included on the menu. The Inn is right on the ocean and many rooms have an excellent ocean view. (*Traditional, Village, Inn. Member since 1973*)

THE RED LION INN

91 Rooms, $67/$155 EP
17 Suites, $165/$235 EP
Visa, MC, Amex, Diners, Discov
Private & Shared Baths
Open Year-round
Children Accepted
No Pets
Exercise room, Pool, Golf, Tennis, Massage Therapist; Tanglewood, Jacobs Pillow, Berkshire Theatre Festival, Norman Rockwell Museum, Chesterwood
Breakfast, Lunch, Dinner; MAP available for groups
Wine & Liquor available
Non-smoking dining rms
Conference Facilities (6-90)
Wheelchair Access (1 rm., dining rm)

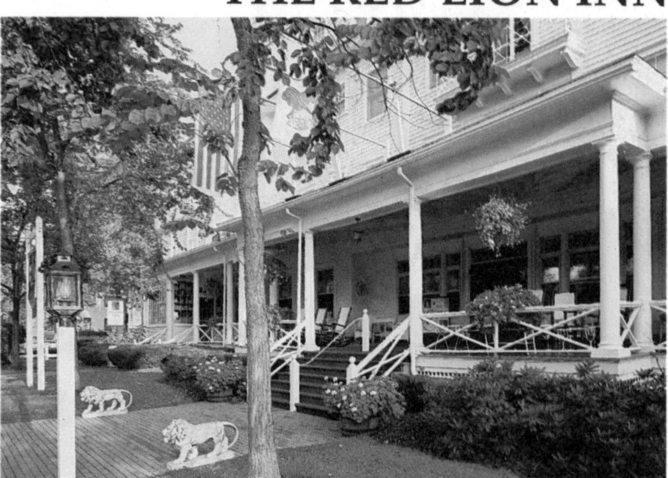

I-90, Exit 2 at Lee, to Rte. 102 (W) to Stockbridge.

TEL. 413-298-5545
FAX 413-298-5130
Main St.
Stockbridge, MA 01262
Jack & Jane Fitzpatrick, Owners
C. Brooks Bradbury, Innkeeper

2 This renowned, antique filled inn in the Berkshire Hills is still the lively, delightful focus of village activity it has been since 1773. As one of few American Inns continuously operated as such since the eighteenth century, the Red Lion welcomes travelers with cheerful cordiality born of longstanding tradition. Individually decorated rooms and suites. Traditional New England cuisine is served in the formal Main Dining Room, cozy Tavern or flower filled Courtyard in summer. Charming gift shop and Country Curtains store located in the Inn. (*Traditional, Village, Inn. Member since 1967*)

THORNCROFT INN

12 Rooms, $129/$349 B&B
1 Suite, $269/$309 B&B
Visa, MC, Amex, Discov, DC
All Private Baths
Open Year-round except Jan. 5–Feb. 1
Children over 12; No Pets
Beaches, Boating, Golf, Tennis, Bicycling, Fishing
Breakfast
No Smoking
Confrernce Facilities (10)
N/A

16 Thorncroft Inn is situated in two restored buildings on 3 1/2 acres of quiet, treed grounds on the Island of Martha's Vineyard. It is secluded, exclusively couples oriented and first class, with Mobil★★★★ and AAA♦♦♦♦ ratings. Most rooms have working, wood burning fireplaces and canopied beds. Some have 2 person whirlpool bathtubs or private 300 gallon hot tubs. Thorncroft Inn is an ideal honeymoon, anniversary or special couples getaway.
(Elegant, Colonial, Village, Breakfast Inn. Member since 1994)

Woods Hole/Martha's Vineyard Ferry (Car & Passenger, year 'round) from Cape Cod. Take R. at first stop sign; take next R. onto Main St. Inn 1 mile on L.

TEL. 508-693-3333
FAX: 508-693-5419
278 Main ST.
Vineyard Haven
Martha's Vineyard, MA 02568
Lynn & Karl Buder,
Owners/Innkeepers

THE VILLAGE INN

32 Rooms, $50/$195 EP
1 Suite, $220/$325 EP
Visa, MC, Amex, Discov, CB
All Private Baths
4 Jacuzzis
Open Year-round
Appropriate for Children over 6; No Pets
Downhill & XC Skiing, Golf, Riding, Tennis, Swimming, Fishing
Breakfast, English tea with homemade scones, Dinner of fine American regional cuisine exc. Mon. & Tues.
Smoking Permitted only in common rooms
Conference Facilities (50)
Wheelchair Access (6 rms.)

1 In the historic district of the Berkshire village of Lenox, this Colonial Inn, built in 1771, is near shops, galleries, library, churches, beautiful parks and wooded trails, Tanglewood and summer theatre and dance festivals, winter downhill and cross-country skiing, fall foliage and spring flower excursions, and year-round museums such as the Norman Rockwell, Clark, Grandma Moses, and Hancock Shaker Village. Every room is individually furnished with country antiques, some 4-posters and fireplaces, all with private baths and telephones, air conditioning in summer months.
(Traditional, Colonial, Village, Inn. Member since 1977)

Mass. Tpke. (I-90), Exit 2, Rte. 20(W) to Rte. 183(S). Turn L. for 1 mi. to R. on Church St. & inn. From Rte. 7 to Rte. 7A & Church St. in Lenox.

TEL. 413-637-0020
800-253-0917
FAX 413-637-9756
16 Church St. P.O. Box 1810
Lenox, MA 01240
Clifford Rudisill and
Ray Wilson, Innkeepers

THE WEATHERVANE INN

10 Rooms including 1 suite, $175/$200 MAP; $95/130 B&B

Visa, MC, Amex

All Private Baths

Open Year-round

Appropriate for Children Over 7; No Pets

Pool, Nature walks, Antiques, Museums, Tennis, Golf, Skiing, Tanglewood, Summer Theater; Downhill & Cross Country skiing, etc.

Breakfast & Dinner; B&B rates available weekdays

Wine & Liquor available

No smoking

Conference Facilities (20)

N/A

From NYC, Taconic Pkwy. to Rte. 23(E) 13 mi. to inn on R. From Mass. Tpke., Exit 2 & Rte. 102 to Rte. 7(S) to Rte. 23(W) to inn on L.

TEL. 413-528-9580
FAX 413-528-1713
P.O. Box 388, Rte. 23
South Egremont, MA 01258
Murphy Family,
Innkeepers

4 Renowned and caring Murphy family has been providing hospitality to their guests for the past 14 years in an elegant farm and coach house on ten acres in a quaint Berkshire village in southwestern Massachusetts. The charming fireside room with three common rooms and honor bar beckons guests seeking recreation and recuperation before experiencing the inns superb cuisine. A full breakfast is offered daily and when dinner is served a host of delectable appetizers and entrees entice you. An all seasons inn. (AAA 3 diamonds) (*Traditional, Federal, Village, Inn. Member since 1984*)

WHALEWALK INN

7 Rooms, $80/$115 B&B
5 Suites, $135/$175

VISA, MC

All Private Baths

Open April-November

Children over 12 Welcome; No Pets

Cape Cod National Seashore, Boating, Fishing, Biking, Golf, Whale Watching, Antiquing, Theater

Breakfast

No Smoking

Conference Facility (10)

N/A

Rte. 6 to Orleans Rotary. Rock Harbor exit off rotary. Left onto Rock Harbor Road. Right onto Bridge Road. Driving time from Boston 2 hours.

TEL 508-255-0617
FAX 508-240-0017
220 Bridge Road
Eastham MA 02642
Carolyn and Richard Smith,
Innkeepers

13 The owners of this inn promise you an unspoiled environment on outer Cape Cod, one of the country's most beautiful areas. This 1830's home has been authentically restored and decorated with handsome antiques. The site consists of three acres, located on a back road, only minutes by car or bike to beaches, bike trials, or Orleans Village. All 12 guest rooms have private baths and are beautifully decorated. Five of them are suites with kitchens. A full breakfast is served. Hor d'oeuvres provided each evening. (*Traditional, Federal, Village, Breakfast Inn. Member since 1993*)

YANKEE CLIPPER INN

26 rooms, $99/$215 B&B
13 Rooms w/ocean view
1 cottage, $1800/$2100 per wk
Visa, MC, Amex, Discov
All Private Baths
Closed Jan. 1–Mar. 1, Week before Christmas & Christmas Day
Appropriate for Children over 3; No Pets
Swimming pool, Tennis, Golf, Whale-watching, Deep Sea Fishing, Hiking, Biking
Breakfast & Dinner, BYOB
No Smoking
Conference facilities (50)
N/A

Fresh ocean breezes and sweeping panoramic views have greeted guests here for over 49 years. The Inn and the 1840 Bulfinch House, both with antique furnishings, and the more contemporary Quarterdeck all offer country inn blandishments. There are historic sites in Boston, Salem, Concord and Lexington, and life can be lazy or exciting with Rockport's famous art colony close by. The Inn has a lovely heated outdoor saltwater pool on a landscaped terrace overlooking the gardens and ocean. Our dining room features New England gourmet cuisine and is open to the public.
(Traditional, Waterside, Inn. Member since 1973)

Rte. 128 (N) to Cape Ann thru Gloucester. L. on Rte. 127 for 4 mi. to Rockport's 5 Corners & sharp L. & Pigeon Cove sign. Continue 1 mi. to inn.

TEL. 508-546-3407
800-545-3699
FAX 508-546-9730
96 Granite St., P.O. Box 2399
Rockport, MA 01966
Bob & Barbara Ellis, Innkps.

Rates are quoted for 2 people for 1 night and do not necessarily include service charges and state taxes. An asterisk after the rates indicates a per-person rate for AP and MAP plans. For more detailed information, ask the inns for their brochures.

AP — American Plan (3 meals included in room rate)

MAP — Modified American Plan (breakfast & dinner included in room rate)

EP — European Plan (meals not included in room rate)

B&B — Bed & Breakfast (breakfast included in room rate)

R — Represents recreational facilities and diversions either on the premises of an inn or nearby

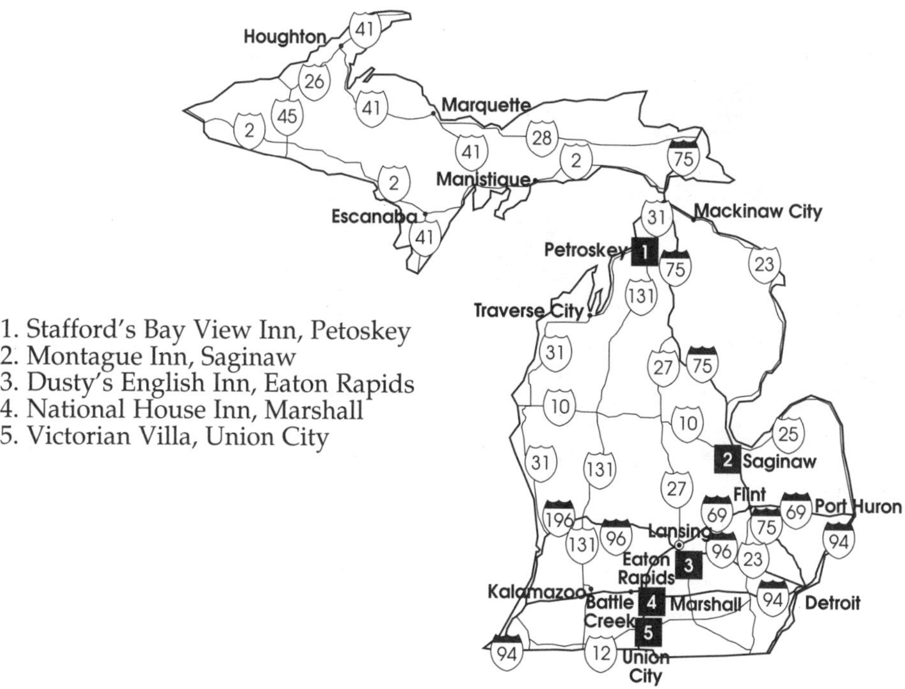

1. Stafford's Bay View Inn, Petoskey
2. Montague Inn, Saginaw
3. Dusty's English Inn, Eaton Rapids
4. National House Inn, Marshall
5. Victorian Villa, Union City

DUSTY'S ENGLISH INN

7 Rooms, $75/$175 B&B
1 Suite, $125/$195 B&B
2 Cottage, $110/$175 B&B
Visa, MC, Discov

All Private Baths

Open Year-round

2 Persons per room limit
Children not encouraged;
No Pet facilities

Golf, Fishing, Canoeing, Hiking, Biking, XC-Skiing, Antiquing

Breakfast, Lunch, Dinner; Authentic English pub; Wine, Beer, Ales, Liquor

Smoke-free Inn

Conference Facilities (50)

Wheelchair Access (4 rms., dining rm & conf. fac.)

From I-96 in Lansing, take M-99 (S) 8 mi. From I-94, take M-99 (N) 22 mi. Ninety miles west of Detroit. 20 miles south of State Capitol (Lansing) and Michigan State Univ. (E. Lansing).

TEL 517-663-2500
FAX 517-663-2643
728 S. Michigan Rd.
Lansing/Eaton Rapids, MI 48827
Dusty Rhodes, Innkeeper

3 A 1927 built Tudor-style riverside mansion on 15 acres. Rolling countryside with 2 miles of nature (xc-skiing in winter) trails along the Grand River and through woods. A 3 room suite and master bedroom are in the cottage complete with pool and fireplace sitting room. Six bedrooms in the inn find fireplaces, dining rooms, and walnut-paneled pub for cocktails, or pints of English ale.
(*Traditional, Country, Inn. Member since 1991*)

MONTAGUE INN

17 Rooms, $65/$150 B&B
1 Suite, $150
Visa, MC
16 Private Baths
1 Shared Bath
Open Year-round
Children Accepted; No Pets
Cultural; Marshall Frederick Sculpture Gallery, Saginaw Art Museum, Japanese Tea House. Shopping: Antique Warehouse, Birch Run Outlet, Frankennuth ½ hr South. Winter & Summer sports
Breakfast; Lunch & Dinner Tues.–Sat. Wine & Liquor available
No Smoking in guest rooms
Conference Facilities (1) (max. 25 people)
Wheelchair Access (2 rms., dining rm. & conf. fac.)

2 This Georgian Mansion, restored to its original splendor, is surrounded by spacious lawns with flower and herb gardens. Summer evenings may be spent under the trees watching the sun set over the lake. Enjoy winter evenings curled up in front of a roaring fire in our library. Fine cuisine is offered in our intimate dining room overlooking the beautiful grounds. The Montague Inn provides a peaceful and elegant oasis in the heart of the city.
(*Elegant, Georgian/Colonial, In-Town, Inn. Member since 1989*)

From I-75 exit west on Holland Ave. (W) for approx. 3.5 mi. Go L. on Washington Ave., 2 blocks to inn.

TEL. 517-752-3939
FAX 517-752-3159
1581 S. Washington Ave.
Saginaw, MI 48601

Willy Schipper, Innkeeper

THE NATIONAL HOUSE INN

16 Rooms, $69/$120 B&B
2 Suites, $120/$125 B&B
Visa, MC, Amex
All Private Baths
Closed Dec. 25
Children Welcome
No Pets
Gift shop, Garden, Park, Tennis, Antiquing, XC Skiing, National Historic Landmark District Tours
Breakfast & Catered Dinners; Wine Available
Area Smoking
Conference facilities (36)
Wheelchair Access (dining rm. & conf. fac.)

4 Marshall, a National Historic Landmark District and home of Win Schuler's restaurant, has many citations for its 850 structures of 19th-century architecture, including the National Register of Historic Places, on which this inn is also listed. Michigan's oldest operating inn, the first brick building in the county has been restored as a warm, hospitable inn, beautifully furnished, and lovely gardens. Afternoon Tea, Lectures, Candlelight Home Tours, Mystery Weekends, Historic Garden Tours.
(*Rustic, Village, Breakfast Inn. Member since 1978*)

I-94 to Exit 110; Rte. 27 (S) 2 mi. to Michigan Ave. Turn R. Marshall is halfway between Detroit & Chicago.

TEL. 616-781-7374
FAX: 616-781-4510
102 So. Parkview
Marshall, MI 49068

Barbara Bradley, Innkeeper

STAFFORD'S BAY VIEW INN

23 Rooms, $79/138 B&B
10 Suites, $145/$195 B&B

Visa, MC, Amex

All Private Baths

Open May-Oct. full time.
Lodging only Jan.-March
& Christmas week

Children Welcome
No Pets; Kennel nearby

Complimentary Croquet, Bikes. Hiking, XC Skiing, Beach, Golf, Tennis, Boating, Scenic Drives

Breakfast, Lunch, Dinner, & Sun. Brunch in summer, Sat. Dinner in winter

No Smoking Starting May 1995

Conference Facilities (60)

Wheelchair Access, most rooms

From Detroit, I-75 (N) to Gaylord exit, Rte. 32 (W) to Rte. 131 (N) Petoskey. From Chicago, I-94 to Rte. I96 (N) to Rte. 131 (N) to Petoskey.

TEL. 616-347-2771

613 Woodland Ave.
P.O. Box 3
Petoskey, MI 49770

The Stafford Smith Family, Innkeepers

Judged one of the "Ten Best Inns" in the nation, this grande dame of classic Victorian architecture on Little Traverse Bay in the Historic Landmark Victorian cottage community of Bay View, sets the standard in fine dining and gracious service. Guests swim, sail the Great Lakes, rock on the front porch, cross-country ski out the front door, or enjoy the finest Alpine skiing in the Midwest. (*Traditional, Lake-side, Inn. Member since 1972*)

THE VICTORIAN VILLA INN

6 Rooms, $75/$95 B&B
4 Suites, $95/$125 B&B
MAP rates available
Visa, MC, Discov, Diners
All Private Baths
Open year-round
Children Accepted
No Pets
Antiquing, Hiking, Canoeing, Golf, Tandem Bicycles, Croquet, Fishing, Lawn Games, Special Weekends, Summertime Villa Dinner Theatre Productions
Breakfast, Afternoon Tea, Lunch (in Summer) Dinner, Picnic baskets, Victorian theme Dinners, Wine & Liquor available
No Smoking
Conference Facilities (24)
Wheelchair Access (1 rm., dining rm. Conf. Fac.)

From I-69, exit M-60 (Exit 25); 7 mi. (W) to Union City & left on Broadway St. (the Main St. of town). Continue to inn on No. Broadway.

TEL. 517-741-7383; 800-34-VILLA; FAX 517-741-4002

601 No. Broadway St.
Union City, MI 49094
Jason Enos, Ron Gibson, Cynthia Coats, Innkeepers

A quiet and unhurried reflection of the 19th Century, the elegant and romantic Victorian Villa Inn offers distinctively furnished guest chambers, delicious hearty breakfasts, afternoon English Teas, and seasonal lunches. The Victorian Villa Inn also offers 19th Century gourmet 7-course Victorian dining, which has achieved national recognition in *Victoria Magazine*, *Midwest Living*, and *Wine Spectator*. Guests may also choose a special selection from over 200 wines from the Villa's own wine cellar, awarded *Wine Spectator*'s "Best of Award of Excellence." (*Elegant, Victorian, Village, Inn. Member since 1990*)

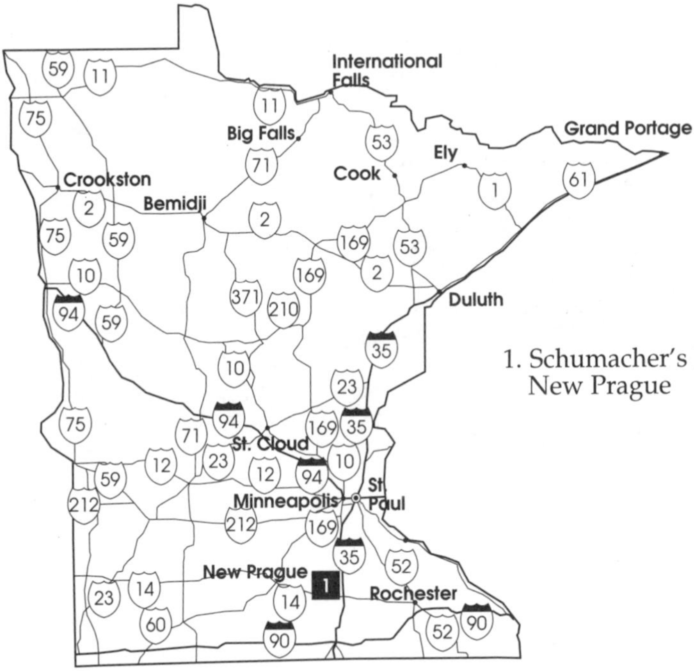

1. Schumacher's New Prague Hotel, New Prague

SCHUMACHER'S NEW PRAGUE HOTEL

11 Rooms, $105/$160 EP

Visa, MC, Amex, Discov

All Private Baths
11 Whirlpool Tubs

Year-round except Dec. 24–25

No Pets

18-hole Golf course, XC Skiing, Biking, Fishing, Casino

Breakfast, Lunch, Dinner
Wine, Beer & Liquor available

Smoking Permitted; No Pipes or Cigars

Conference Facilities (11)

Wheelchair Access (dining rm.)

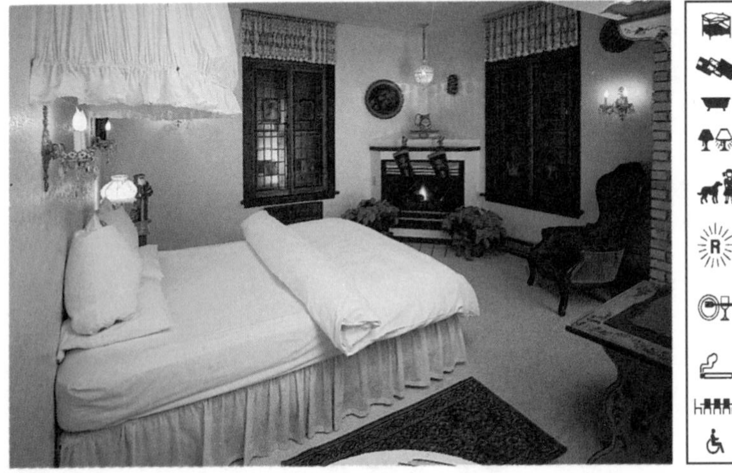

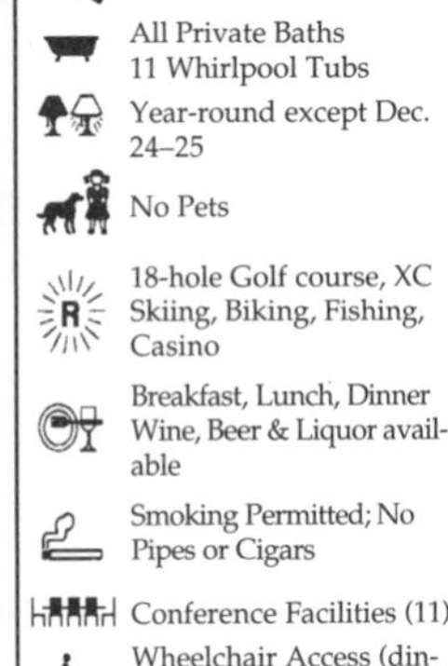

Named one of the "Ten Best Inns," 1992, one of the "Top Twelve Inns, 1991," and "National Pork Restaurant of the Year," 1992 and consistently named one of the favorite restaurants in Greater Minnesota, this charming Central European Inn is internationally known for its superb Czech and German cuisine by Chef/Proprietor John Schumacher. Bavarian folk painted furniture, eiderdown comforters, whirlpool tubs, gas fireplaces, Bavarian bar, and European gift shop add to the uniqueness of this inn. (*Elegant, Village, Inn. (Member since 1979*)

From Mpls., 35W (S) to Exit 76 Elko, New Market (County Rd. 2), W, turn R for 10 mi. At 13, turn L, S, follow 13 2 mi., merges w/19 W, follow 2 Hwys into New Prague. Hotel is on left hand side past center of New Prague.

TEL. 612-758-2133
FAX (612) 758-2400
212 W. Main St.
New Prague, MN 56071
Kathleen & John Schumacher, Innkeepers

COUNTRY INN CUISINE

Webster's Dictionary defines cuisine as *1. the kitchen 2. the style or way of cooking.* Certainly then, cuisine becomes a most essential consideration for the Inns described in this guidebook.

The approaches to cuisine among the Inns in the Independent Innkeepers' Association are as different as the Inns themselves. For some, breakfast is the primary meal presented to guests, and so no holds are barred in its design and preparation. Guests are literally awakened by the aroma of delicacies which our daily lives are too hurried to even consider. Some of these Breakfast Inns even publish their own Breakfast Cookbooks, though somehow one wonders if the items could ever smell and taste the same.

For a number of Country Inns, dining becomes the raison detre; the inn being established as a showcase for the chef/owner's self expression. The *"style or way of cooking"* part of the definition takes on particular meaning in these cases. At Chef-owned Inns, the diner can be assured that each meal will be an individually created masterpiece (or nearly so) prepared especially for him. Since the quality and design of the comestibles from such a kitchen carry with them the reputation and perhaps even livelihood of their creator, guests are treated to outstanding, sometimes innovative examples of what man can create for the palate. The cuisine will often be the first thing mentioned in the guest's bragging about this Inn.

Many, many people in America are "meat and potatoes" kinds of folks. They prefer comfortable, delicious everyday fare. The pot roast, recently enjoyed by this author, which was cooked on a wood burning kitchen stove at a farmhouse Inn in New Hampshire should not be missed by such a connoisseur. And the honest to goodness home cooking and farm fresh vegetables served from an abundant Lazy-Susan table on a mountain top in North Carolina is reason enough to go there.

Perhaps the more typical Country Inn cuisine for Independent Innkeepers' Association members is created by a talented chef working hand in hand with the innkeeper to complete the total hospitality experience for the guests of the Inn. Often he is well trained and widely experienced. Sometimes he has worked up through the ranks in the kitchen "learning from the school of hard knocks." Some Country Inn chefs formerly worked at larger hotels but simply do not enjoy impersonally produced cuisine. Whatever the route, Country Inn chefs usually feel they have finally found their niche.

It is the feeling of most Innkeepers that hospitality includes providing sustenance to meet their guests' needs. Whether this means hot cider in the parlor, the ever-ready coffee/hot chocolate pot, home-baked cookies, gourmet breakfast, a picnic lunch, or candlelit diner in an intimate dining room, Webster's *1. kitchen* and *2. style or way of cooking a*re not lightly considered by successful innkeepers.

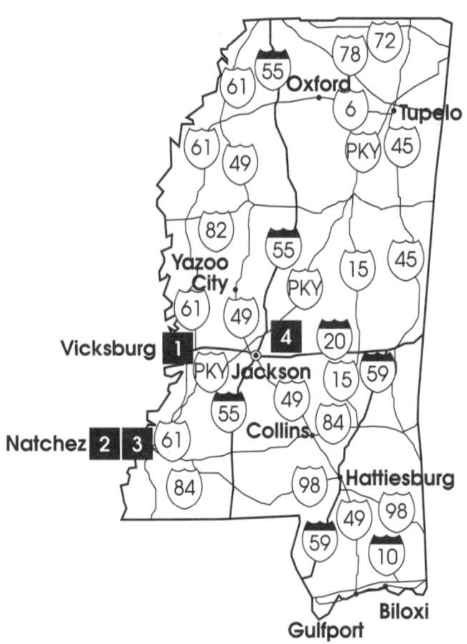

1. The Duff Green Mansion, Vicksburg
2. Monmouth Plantation, Natchez
3. The Burn, Natchez
4. Fairview, Jackson

THE BURN

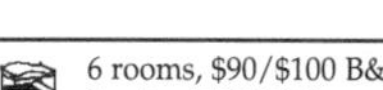 6 rooms, $90/$100 B&B
1 suite, $125 B&B

 Visa, MC, Amex, Diners

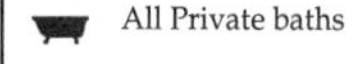 All Private baths

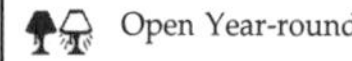 Open Year-round

 School-age Children
No Pets

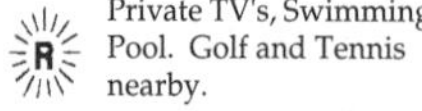 Private TV's, Swimming Pool. Golf and Tennis nearby.

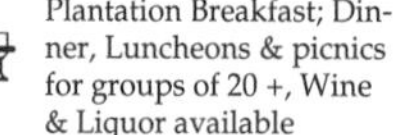 Plantation Breakfast; Dinner, Luncheons & picnics for groups of 20 +, Wine & Liquor available

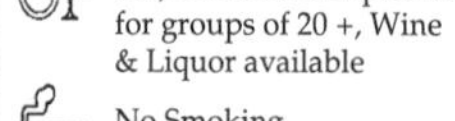 No Smoking

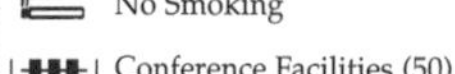 Conference Facilities (50)

Dining Room

3 The Burn: c. 1834 three story mansion especially noted for its semispiral stairway and unique gardens. Overnight guests are pampered with a seated plantation breakfast, tour of the home, and use of the swimming pool. Nightly turn down with sweets and wine. On site catering available for weddings, luncheons or special occasions. Member of Independent Innkeepers' Association.

(Traditional, Greek Revival, In-town, Inn. Member since 1990)

From I-55 at McComb, MS, exit to Hwy. 98 (Natchez). Meadville to Hwy. 98/84 to end & Hwy. 61 at Washington. Turn L. (W) to Natchez. R. onto No. Union to inn on L.

Tel. 601-442-1344
800-654-8859
FAX 601-445-0606
712 No. Union St.
Natchez, MS 39120
Larry & Debbie Christiansen, Owners
David & Ann White, Innkeepers

THE DUFF GREEN MANSION

5 Rooms, $65/$110 B&B
2 Suites, $105/$160 B&B
8% Sales Tax

Visa, MC, Amex
Private Baths
Open Year-round
Children Welcome
Small Pets Accepted, Swimming pool on grounds; Golf, Tennis, Fishing, Hunting nearby; many Historic Sites within walking distance
Plantation Breakfast, Lunch, Dinner, Refreshments, Wine & Liquor Available
Smoking in designated areas
Conference Facilities (75)
Wheelchair Access (4 rms., dining rm.)

From I-20 Exit 4B to Clay St. Turn R. on Adams. Turn right on First East St. & continue on.

TEL. 601-636-6968; 638-6662; 800-992-0037; FAX 601-634-1061
1114 First East St.
Vicksburg, MS 39180
Harry & Alicia Sharp, Innkeepers

One of the finest examples of Palladian architecture in the state (National Register of Historic Places), this 1856 mansion was pressed into service as a hospital for Confederate, and later Union, soldiers during the famous siege of Vicksburg. The 12,000-sq.-foot mansion in the historic Old Town was restored in 1985 and is luxuriously furnished in period antiques and reproductions.
(Traditional, In-town, Inn. Member since 1991)

FAIRVIEW

3 Rooms, $95 B&B
4 Suites, $165 B&B

Visa, MC, Amex, Personal Checks

All Private Baths
Open Year-round
Inappropriate for Children No Pets

Walking/jogging, exercise equipment on property. Nearby: golf, tennis, baseball stadium, Agricultural Museum, Art Museum, Old Capitol Museum, Manship House, New Stage Theatre, Shopping

Breakfast, Dinner (by arrangement); BYOB
No Smoking
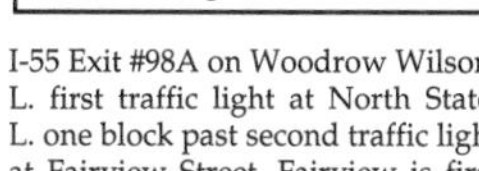
Conference Facilities (100)
Wheelchair Access (3 rms., dining rm. & conf. fac)

I-55 Exit #98A on Woodrow Wilson, L. first traffic light at North State, L. one block past second traffic light at Fairview Street. Fairview is first property on L.

TEL. 601-948-3429
FAX 601-948-1203
734 Fairview St.
Jackson, MS 39202
Carol & William Simmons, Innkeepers

In the heart of Mississippi's capital city stands Fairview, a National Register Colonial Revival mansion whose owners welcome guests in the hospitable tradition of the Old South. Guests may relax in the comfort of individually decorated bedrooms or suites or enjoy the eclectic interior design, various objets d'art, the oak-panelled library with its Civil War book collection, or stroll the extensive grounds and garden. Cover Feature and "Inn of the Month," Country Inns Magazine, October 1994.
(Traditional, In-town Breakfast Inn. Member since 1994)

MONMOUTH PLANTATION

12 Rooms, $105/$135
13 Suites, $145/$185
AAA Four Diamond
Visa, MC, Amex, Dicovr, Diners, Optima
All Private Baths
Open Year-round
No Pets; Children over 14
Croquet course, Fishing and Walking Trails
Breakfast and Dinner, Lunch for private parties only
No Smoking; Smoking is allowed outside the rooms
Conference Facility (100)
Wheelchair Access (4 rms., dining rm. & conf. fac.)

Monmouth Plantation, a National Historic Landmark circa 1818, a glorious return to the antebellum South. Rated "One of the ten most romantic places in the USA" by *Glamour Magazine* and *USA*. Today it tranquilly waits to enfold you in luxury and service. Walk our 26 beautifully landscaped acres. Twenty-five rooms and suites in the mansion and the 5 other historic buildings hold priceless art and antiques while providing every modern comfort. Mornings begin with a delightful complimentary Southern breakfast. Nights sparkle under candlelight and crystal during 5-course dinners. (*Elegant, Country, Inn. Member since 1993*)

East on State Street, 1 mile from downtown Natchez on the corner of John Quitmen Parkway and Melrose Avenue.

TEL. 601-442-5852
800-828-4531
FAX 601-446-7762
36 Melrose Avenue
Natchez, MS 39120
Ron Riches, Owner

WHAT DID YOU DO BEFORE INNKEEPING?

"How did you happen to get into this innkeeping business?" That is the question most often asked of innkeepers. And guests find the answers are as varied as the personalities of the innkeepers themselves.

One of the most common heroic replies is something about, "I got fed up with the impersonal corporate world (and/or the big city)." A few innkeepers just simply became disenchanted with their chosen vocations and "wanted a change." One gentleman, interested in historic restoration, discovered that the building he was so altruistically "returning to its original purpose, an 1835 stagecoach stop" was almost completed and *someone* was going to have to create a business for it. Suddenly he became an innkeeper.

And then there is the family that lived in a gracious and spacious southern plantation. By coincidence, one day when the father of the family was sitting at his desk looking at a $400.00 utilities bill, a prosperous acquaintance from a nearby city rang him to inquire if, just for a lark, he and his wife could bring another couple up to stay at his plantation while attending a nearby Saturday football game. The bill-paying plantation owner looked at the utilities bill and said, "Yes, of course you can. The charge will be $400, and we will serve you dinner." On that day his Inn was born, and he and his guests have been most pleased with that fortuitous decision ever since.

Each of the innkeepers in this book has a different background, a different story. Isn't that part of what makes inn-traveling such an adventure?

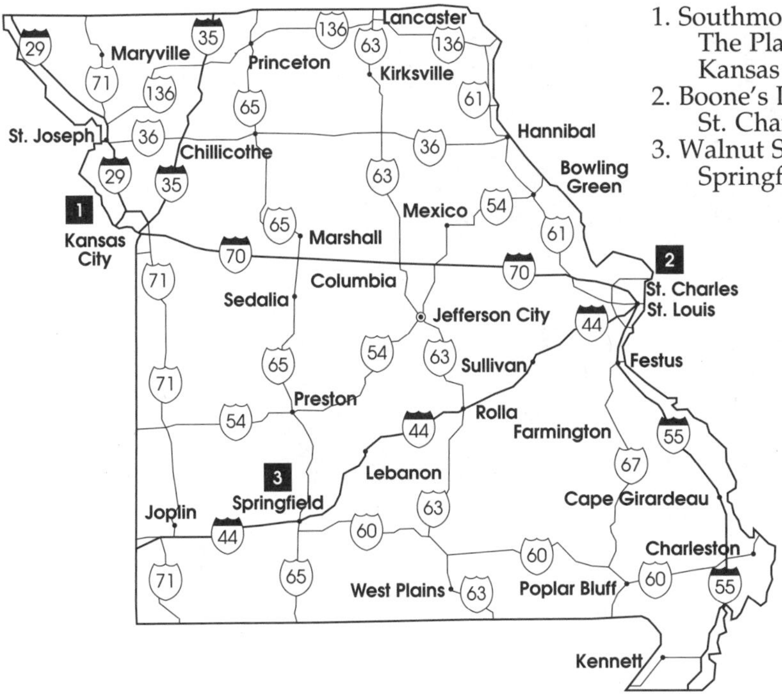

1. Southmoreland On The Plaza, Kansas City
2. Boone's Lick Trail Inn, St. Charles
3. Walnut Street Inn, Springfield

BOONE'S LICK TRAIL INN

4 Rooms, $75/$105 B&B
1 Suite, $95/$125 B&B
Visa, MC, Discov, Diners, Personal Checks
All Private Baths
Open Year-round
Children Accepted; No Pets; Kennels nearby
Historic District, Winery Antiquing, Dining, Riverboat Excursions, Goldernrod Showboat, Riverboat Gaming Casino, Katy Trail: State Park; Biking/Hiking
Full Breakfast, Lunches for Hikers/Bikers on Request
No Smoking
Conference Facilities (10-16)
Wheelchair Access Limited (2 Rooms)

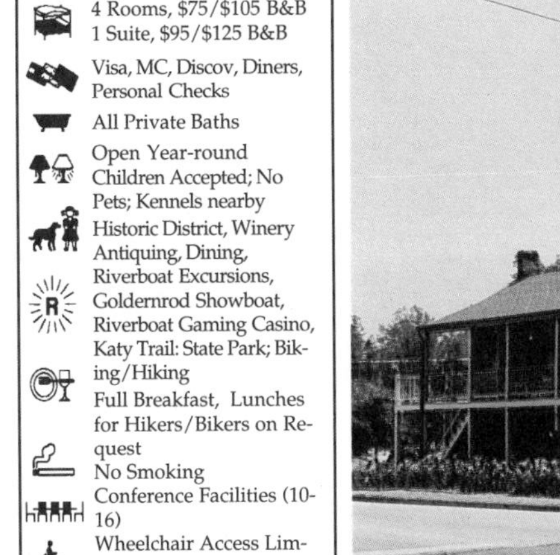

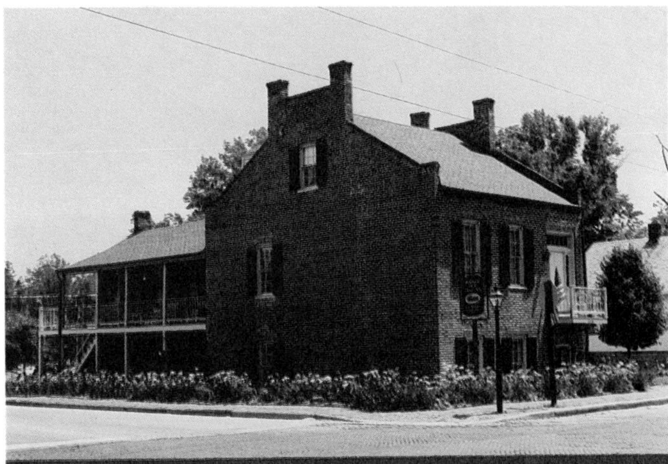

I-70 to exit 229 St. Charles Fifth St., (N) 3 blocks to Boonslick Rd. R. 4 blocks to Main St. Inn on SE corner of Main & Boonslick

TEL. (314) 947-7000
(800-366-2427 9-5 CST)

1000 South Main St.
St. Charles, MO 63301

V'Anne and Paul Mydler, Innkeepers

It was THE highway west, predating the Santa Fe & Oregon Trails. At first, they called it the "Boone's Lic" Trail. In the 1840's, a Federal style building rose in the village of St. Charles at the corner of Main Street and the Boonslick Road. Today, the inn, on the waterfront of "the Wide Missouri" River is surrounded and scented by rose and herb gardens, dressed in regional antiques and Folk Art, houses an antique, working, duck decoy collection, and serves delicacies like fresh lemon biscuits. Guests stroll the cobblestoned street of Missouri's largest Historic District. (Six miles to airport; 25 minutes to St. Louis.)
(Traditional, Federal, In-town, Breakfast Inn. Member since 1992)

SOUTHMORELAND ON THE PLAZA

12 Rooms $100/$145 B&B

Visa, MC, Amex

All Private Baths

Closed Christmas Eve & Christmas Day

Children over 13; No Pets

Nelson-Atkins Museum of Art, Country Club Plaza, Dining & Shopping, Theater, Dinner Playhouse, Tennis, Swimming, Royals Baseball, Chiefs Football, Crown Center, Historic Westport & River Market

Breakfast, Wine & Hors d'oeuvres nightly

Smoking areas designated

Conference Facilities; A-V Equip. Available (14)

Wheelchair Accessible First Floor

1 Award-winning Southmoreland's 1913 Colonial Revival styling brings New England to the heart of Kansas City's Historic, Arts, Entertainment and Shopping district—The Country Club Plaza. Business and leisure guests enjoy individually decorated rooms offering decks, fireplaces or double-Jacuzzi baths. Business travelers find respite at Southmoreland with its rare mix of business support services; in-room phones, FAX, message center, modem connections, 24-hour access and switchboard, and photocopier. Mobil Four-Star.
(*Traditional, Colonial, In-town, Breakfast Inn. Member since 1992*)

From I-70, I-35, I-29 in downtown Kansas City, Missouri, take the Main Street exit S. several miles to E 46th St., turn E (L), go 1 1/2 blocks to the Inn on the left.

TEL. (816) 531-7979
FAX (816) 531-2407
116 E. 46th St.
Kansas City, MO 64112
Susan Moehl &
Penni Johnson, Innkeepers

WALNUT STREET INN

14 Rooms, $80/$150 B&B

Visa, MC, Amex, Discov, Diners

All Private Baths

Open Year-round

No Pets; limited provisions for children

Nearby Lakes & Rivers, Golf, Tennis, Bass Pro, Caves, Bluffs, and Hiking Trails at the Nature Center. 45 min. from Branson, MO and Silver Dollar City

Breakfast; Wine & Beer Available

No Smoking except outside porches & balconies

Wheelchair Access (1 rm., dining rm.)

3 One of the "Top Twelve Inns in the Country" and recommended by *Glamour Magazine*, the 14-room luxury urban inn is in Springfield's Historic District and thirty minutes from Branson. Enjoy fireplaces, jacuzzis, private porches, and feather comforters for leisure travelers. In-room phones and fax for business travelers. Relax on the front porch swing, read a book by the fire, walk to the great Hall for the Performing Arts, museums, theaters and restaurants, or enjoy the Ozarks fine natural attractions.
(*Traditional, Victorian, In-Town, Breakfast Inn. Member since 1993*)

From I-44 take 65 S to Chestnut Expressway. West on Chestnut Expressway to Sherman Parkway; turn S 4 blocks to Walnut St.

TEL. 417-864-6346
FAX 417-864-6184
900 E. Walnut St.
Springfield, MO 65806

Nancy Brown & Karol Brown,
Innkeepers

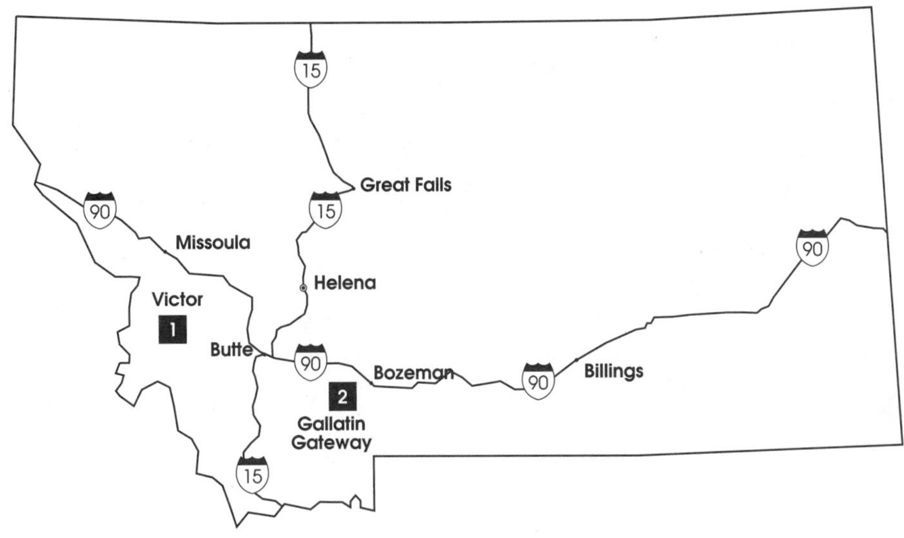

1. The Inn at Bear Creek, Victor
2. Gallatin Gateway Inn, Gallatin Gateway

THE INN AT BEAR CREEK

8 Rooms, $125 B&B; $295 AP

Visa, MC, Amex, Discov

All Private Baths

Open Year-round

Children over 13
Pets considered

Horseback Riding, Hiking, Mountain Biking, Fly Fishing, Excursion Tours, Rafting, Canoeing

Breakfast, Lunch, Dinner; Wine & Liquor Available

Smoking outside only

Conference facilities (16)

N/A

32 mi. S. of Missoula to the town of Victor on Hwy. 93. Go 2 mi. S. to Bear Creek Rd. Turn R. & follow signs.

TEL. 406-642-3750
800-270-5550
FAX 406-642-6847
1184 Bear Creek Trail
Victor, MT 59875
Terry & Audrey Coleman, Innkeepers

The Inn at Bear Creek is nestled on 74 scenic acres adjacent to the Selway Bitteroot Wilderness complex in southwest Montana. The inn features 8 rooms with private bath, each decorated with a mixture of old and new. Our mountain location enables us to offer our guests literally every type of mountain related recreation available.
(*Rustic, Country, Ranch. Member since 1994*)

MONTANA

GALLATIN GATEWAY INN

32 Rooms $65/$80 B&B
3 Suites, $90/$110 B&B
Visa, MC, Amex, Discov, JCB
33 Private Baths
Open Year-round
Children Welcome; Pets by Arrangement
65 mi. from Yellowstone Park, 30 mi. to Big Sky; Bring Your Bow! Ski Areas; Minutes from Hiking, Flyfishing, Rafting, Biking, Horseback Riding
Breakfast, Lunch, Dinner; Wine & Liquor Available
Smoking restrictions
Conference Facilities (25–150)
Wheelchair Access (1 rm., dining rm. & conf. fac.)

2 Fully restored to its original 1920's splendor, the Gallatin Gateway Inn is among the finest inns in the Rocky Mountain West. Designed to be a grand railroad hotel, its palatial structure features arched windows, Spanish-style corbels and carved beams. Rooms and suites are decorated in the warm, clean tones of the west and offer amenities required by today's busy traveler. The Inn's spacious restaurant, a local favorite, is well known for it's American Cuisine.
(*Elegant, Southwestern, Country, Inn. Member since 1994*)

13 mi. S of I-90 on Hwy. 191; Take the Balgrade Exit 17.

TEL. 406 -763-4672
FAX 406-763-4672 (Ext 313)
Highway 191 South
P.O. Box 376
Gallatin Gateway, MT 59730
Colin Davis, Innkeeper

THE STAFF AT A COUNTRY INN PERSONAL INTEREST AND SERVICE

It doesn't take many visits along the Country Inn circuit to realize that a key ingredient for any hospitality recipe is the staff who "keep it all together". Since the size of most Inns limits the number of employees needed, the sometimes cumbersome employer/employee structure is usually not necessary. Staff members take personal interest in what they do, thereby losing that "employee" aura.

Many innkeepers very quickly and proudly introduce staff members to guests since they are often considered members of the Inn family. Sometimes they actually are members of the innkeeper's family. Besides the expected mother/father/offspring team found at many Inns, guests are sometimes surprised to have the innkeeper introduce the dishwasher or desk clerk as his mother. One very successful innkeeper employs his mother-in-law as a housekeeper; in another inn a retired gentleman is employed by his niece as a waiter.

Because Inns are usually very highly respected businesses in a community, they are often considered prestigious places to work. I recall overhearing one staff member tell her friend, "My friends *have* to work at other establishments in town. I *get* to work at the Inn." It is very difficult to hide this attitude from guests.

Every staff member from the lawn boy to the desk person to the housekeeper has an important role in providing consummate hospitality for every guest. The personal interest and service of staff members at an Inn is a big measure of what brings guests to enjoy their visits. Fortunately, in our Inns it is easy for staff to feel the importance of their contribution. Certainly, guests perceive this Inn-family teamwork, and that makes all the difference . . . for everyone.

NEW HAMPSHIRE

1. Philbrook Farm Inn, Shelburne
2. Christmas Farm Inn, Jackson
3. Darby Field Inn, Conway
4. Stafford's in the Field, Chocorua
5. Corner House Inn, Center Sandwich
6. Moose Mountain Lodge, Etna
7. Dexter's Inn and Tennis Club, Sunapee
8. Hickory Stick Farm, Belmont
9. Colby Hill Inn, Henniker
10. Inn at Crotched Mountain, Francestown
11. The Hancock Inn, Hancock
12. Chesterfield Inn, West Chesterfield

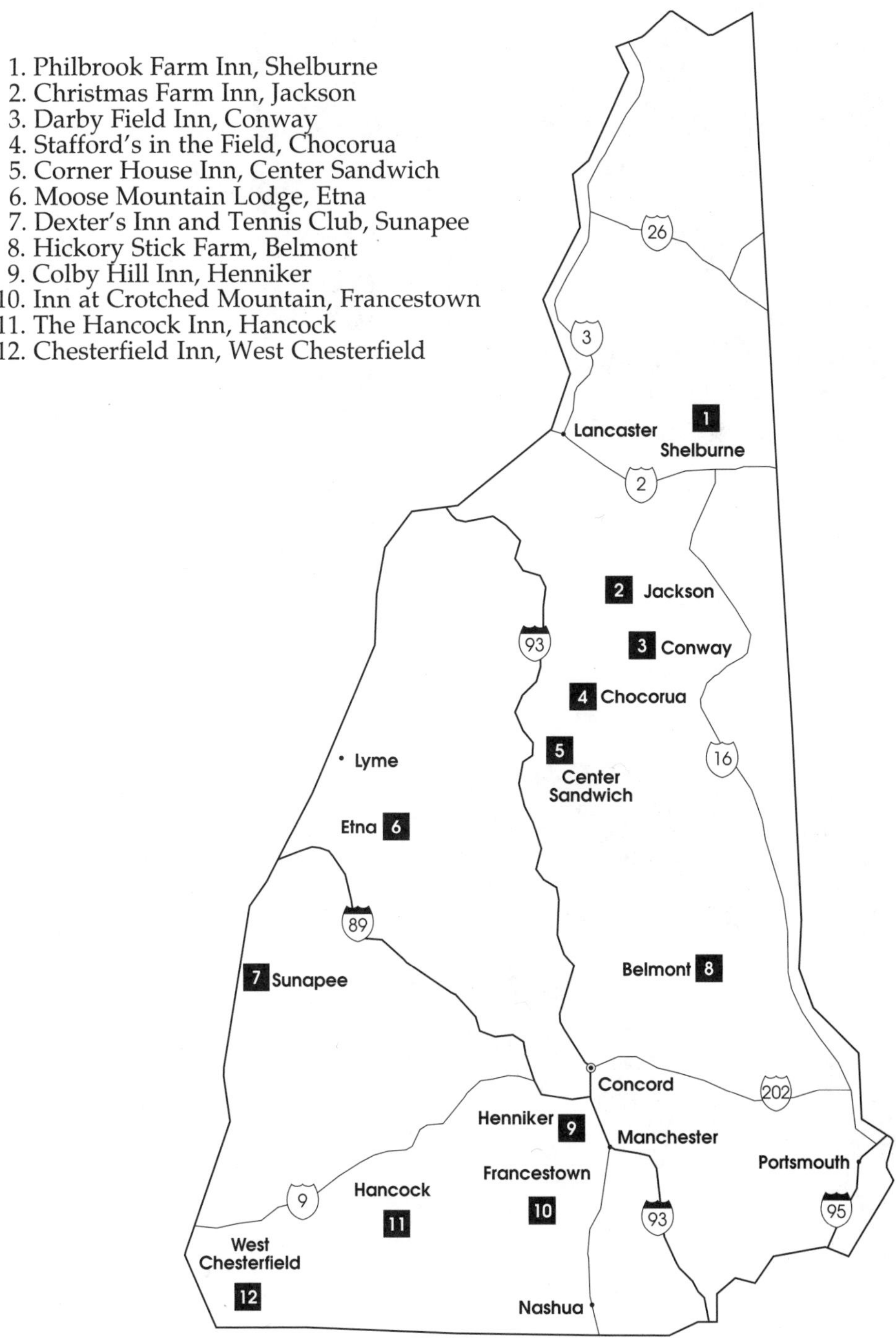

CHESTERFIELD INN

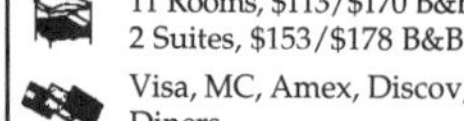

- 11 Rooms, $113/$170 B&B
  2 Suites, $153/$178 B&B
- Visa, MC, Amex, Discov, Diners
- All Private Baths
- Open Year-round except Christmas Eve & Day
- Children & Pets Welcome
- Arts, Crafts, Music in Keene & Brattleboro. Swimming & Boating on Spofford Lake
- Breakfast & Dinner Daily
  Wine & Liquor available
- Smoking restrictions: Dining room & 11 guest rooms are non smoking
- Conference Facilities (25)
- Wheelchair Access (2 rms. Dining & conf. fac.)

12 Serving since 1787 as a tavern, a farm, and a museum, the inn's guest rooms today are spacious; some with fireplaces, or outdoor balconies, all with private baths, air conditioning, TV & telephone. Outside, the meadow overlooks Vermont's Green Mountains. Guests enjoy the cuisine of chef Carl Warner and enter the dining room through the kitchen to observe his magic in action. Chesterfield Inn is a wonderful place to relax in comfortable elegance.
(*Elegant, Colonial, Country, Inn. Member since 1990*)

From I-91, take Exit 3 to Rte. 9 (E). Continue on Rte. 9 for 3 mi. to inn on L.

TEL. 800-365-5515
FAX: 603-256-6131
Route 9
West Chesterfield, NH 03443

Judy & Phil Hueber, Innkeepers

CHRISTMAS FARM INN

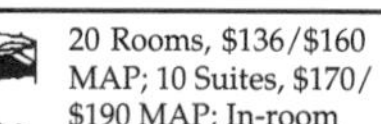

- 20 Rooms, $136/$160 MAP; 10 Suites, $170/ $190 MAP; In-room phones exc. M. Inn
- Visa, MC, Amex
- All Private Baths, 5 Jacuzzis
- Open Year-round
- Children Most Welcome
  No Pets
- Swimming Pool, Putting Green, Game Room, Shuffleboard, XC & Down-hill Skiing, Golf, Tennis
- Breakfast & Dinner
  Wine & Liquor available
- Non-Smoking Dining & Living Rooms
- Conference Facilities (50)
- Wheelchair Access (dining rm. & conf. fac.)

2 In a setting of majestic mountains, crystal-clear rivers and leafy woods, the cluster of buildings that make up this rambling inn invite you to share the good life. Whether inside in cozily decorated rooms, outside at the garden swimming pool, or in the candlelit dining room feasting on delectable, fresh meals, guests enjoy the at-home feeling.
(*Traditional, Village, Inn. Member since 1988*)

From Rte. 16 to Rte. 16A across covered bridge .5 mi. to schoolhouse. R. on Rte. 16B for .5 mi. to inn on R.

TEL. 603-383-4313
800-HI-ELVES
FAX 603-383-6495
Box CC, Route 16B
Jackson, NH 03846

The Zeliff Family, Innkeepers

COLBY HILL INN

16 Rooms, $85/$165 B&B

Visa, MC, Amex, Diners, Discov, CB

All Private Baths

Open Year-round

Appropriate for children over 7; No Pets, enjoy ours

Swimming, Games, Ice Skating, Skiing, Fishing, Books, Tennis, Antiques, and Canterbury Shaker Village

Full Breakfast Daily (for inn guests), Dinner Daily except Mon.–Tues. for everyone. Wine & Liquor Available

No Smoking except outside

Conference Facility (32)

N/A

17 miles west of Concord off Route 202/9. South 1/2 miles on Rt. 114 to blinking light and Pharmacy. Turn right. Inn is 1/2 mile on the right.

TEL. 603-428-3281
800-531-0330
FAX 603-428-9218

The Oaks, PO Box 778
Henniker NH 03242

Ellie, John, and Laurel Day, Innkeepers

9 Congenial inn-dogs Bertha and Delilah await with a handshake and the cookie jar beckons at this rambling 1795 inn, a complex of farmhouse, carriage house, and barns on five village acres. 16 antique-filled guestrooms, some with working fireplaces, all with private baths and phones. Now all fully air conditioned. And the food is memorable—from the bountiful breakfasts to the acclaimed candlelit dinners served in the gardenside dining room. Classic New England scenery abounds around this village on the river.
(*Traditional, Village, Inn. Member since 1993*)

CORNER HOUSE INN

3 rooms, $80 B&B

Visa, MC, Amex

All Private Baths

Open Year-round exc.Thanksgiving, Dec. 25

Children over 4
Well-behaved Pets allowed

Crafts & Antique Shops, Museum, Art Gallery, Squam Lake, Tennis, Hiking, Skiing

Breakfast, Lunch, Dinner
Wine & Liquor available

Smoking discouraged including dining rm.

Conference Facilities (70)

Wheelchair Access (dining rm. & conf. fac.)

I-93, Exit 23 & Rt. 104 (E) to Meredith. R. at light on Rt. 25 (E) to Ctr. Harbor. L. at 2nd light to Bean Rd. for 7 mi. to blinker. R. onto Main St. to inn.

TEL. 603-284-6219
FAX 603-284-6220

Main St., P.O. Box 204
Ctr. Sandwich, NH 03227

Jane & Don Brown, Innkeepers

5 The picturesque village of Center Sandwich and the surrounding lakes and mountain area, near "Golden Pond" (Squam Lake), offer delightful diversions in any season. A warm welcome awaits at the intimate 150-year-old Corner House, sparkling with country antiques and beautiful crafts made by many local artisans. The Inn boasts one of the area's most widely acclaimed restaurants.
(*Traditional, Village, Inn. Member since 1987*)

THE DARBY FIELD INN

 15 Rooms, $65/$90 MAP
1 Suite, $90/$100 MAP
(4)

 Visa, MC, Amex, Diners

 14 Private, 2 Shared Bath

Open Year-round exc. April

 Children over 2 Accepted
No Pets

 Swimming pool, XC ski trails, Canoeing, Golf, Tennis, Hiking, Rock climbing

 Breakfast & Dinner
Wine & Liquor available

 Smoking Restricted

 Wheelchair Access (dining rm.)

3 Beguiling guests with a spectacular view of distant mountains from its dining room, many guest rooms, and terrace swimming pool, this 1830 inn on the edge of the White Mountain National Forest is a favorite with outdoor enthusiasts. Well-groomed ski and hiking trails past rivers and waterfalls, a cozy pub, a massive stone fireplace, and hearty, delicious food are part of the picture.
(*Traditional, Mountain, Inn. Member since 1981*)

Rte. 16 (N) toward Conway. Turn L. .5 mi. before Conway at inn sign. 1 mi. to 2nd inn sign. Turn R. & continue 1 mi. to inn.

TEL. 800-426-4147
603-447-2181
FAX 603-447-5726
P.O. Box D, Bald Hill
Conway, NH 03818
Marc & Maria Donaldson, Innkeepers

DEXTER'S INN & TENNIS CLUB

 18 Rooms, $130/$170 MAP
1 Cottage, $187.50 MAP

 Visa, MC, Discover

 All Private Baths

 Closed Nov. 1 to May 1

 Children Accepted
Pets Accepted

 3 Tennis Courts, Pool, Lawn Games, Lake activities, Hiking, Golf

 Breakfast, Dinner
Wine & Liquor available

 Non-smoking Dining area

 Conference Facilities (25)

 N/A

7 Tennis buffs love Dexter's, but so do all the guests who come for the breathtaking views, idyllic gardens, green lawns, bright guest rooms and excellent, bountiful food. The Simpson-Durfor family runs the inn like a well-appointed private estate, which provides a perfect setting for weddings and family reunions. In addition to the outstanding tennis program and 3 excellent golf courses nearby, they offer friendly service and advice on the myriad diversions available in the area.
(Federal, Country, Inn/Resort. Member since 1978)

I-89 (N), Exit 12 & Rte. 11 (W) for 5.5 mi. to L. on Winn Hill Rd. for 1.5 mi. From I-91 (N), Exit 8 & Rte. 11/103 (E) for 18 mi. to Newport & Rte. 103 for .1 mi. to L. on Young Hill Rd. for 1.2 mi.

TEL. 800-232-5571
603-763-5571
Box 703IIA, Stagecoach Rd.
Sunapee, NH 03782
Michael Durfor & Holly Simpson-Durfor, Innkeepers

HICKORY STICK FARM

 2 Rooms, $70 B&B

 Visa, MC, Amex, Discov.

 All Private Baths

 Closed Mon.; Restaurant winter hours restricted

Appropriate for Children over 7; No Pets

 Hiking, Nature trails, Birdwatching, Swimming, Boating, Skiing, Shaker Village

 Breakfast (guests only) & Dinner by reservation Wine & Liquor available

 Smoking Restricted

Conference Facilities (25)

 N/A

I-93, Exit 20 & Rte. 3 toward Laconia, approx. 5 mi. over Lake Winnisquam bridge .3 mi. to R. on Union Rd. for 1.5 mi. & L. on Bean Hill Rd. for .5 mi. to inn.

TEL. 603-524-3333
60 Bean Hill Road
Belmont, NH 03220
Scott & Linda Roeder, Innkeepers

8 Since 1950 the Roeder family has been serving thoughtful meals in the delightful Early American atmosphere of their restaurant. The converted Colonial farm buildings offer great views over the back fields to the mountains from the dining room and screened gazebo. A varied menu is offered, with roast duckling the specialty. Two charming B&B rooms provide quiet relaxation to travelers.
(*Traditional, Colonial, Country, Inn. Member since 1983*)

INN AT CROTCHED MOUNTAIN

 13 Rooms, $120/$140 MAP

 No Credit Cards

 8 Private Baths

 Closed end of ski season to mid-May; late Oct. to Thanksgiving

 Children Accepted Pets Accepted

 Swimming pool, Tennis courts, XC and walking trails, Downhill Skiing, Ice Skating, Antique shops, Summer Theaters

Breakfast, Dinner Wine & Liquor available

 Cigars or Pipes restricted No smoking in Dining Room

Conference Facilities (26)

Wheelchair Access (4 Rms., dining rm. conf. fac.)

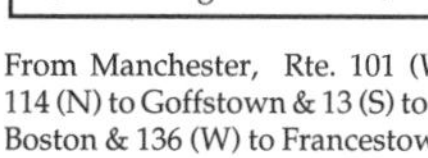

From Manchester, Rte. 101 (W) to 114 (N) to Goffstown & 13 (S) to New Boston & 136 (W) to Francestown. R. at 47 (N) 2.5 mi. to L. on Mountain Rd. for 1 mi. to inn.

TEL. 603-588-6840
Mountain Rd.
Francestown, NH 03043
Rose & John Perry, Innkeepers

10 This 170-year-old colonial house is located on the northern side of Crotched Mountain. An awe-inspiring setting and a spectacular view of Piscataquog Valley makes all the difference at this out-of-the-way Colonial inn. Walking and ski trails thread the woods; vegetable and flower gardens supply food and adornment for tables and rooms. Rose Perry's savory home cooking has the added zest of an occasional Indonesian dish. John and Rose, who have been operating the inn since 1973, look forward to welcoming you.
(*Traditional, Country, Inn. Member since 1981*)

THE HANCOCK INN

- 11 rooms, $88/$150 B&B
- Visa, MC, Amex, Discovr Diners
- All Private Baths
- Open Year-round
- Appropriate for Children over 12; No Pets
- Historic Touring, Walking, Mountain Climbing, Skiing, Skating, Bicycling, Swimming, Antiquing, Summer Theater
- Breakfast, Dinner, Wine & Liquor available
- No Smoking
- Conference Facilities (35)
- Ramp for Access

This is the oldest original inn in New Hampshire. The Inn and the homes on this beautiful tree lined Main Street are in the National Historic Register. Stroll the well-worn cow paths. Pass the village store, country school house, gazebo, and white steepled church to Norway Pond. Celebrate the evening in our award-winning dining rooms, decorated with sponge painted walls, soft lighting and period fabrics. Dine on succulent roasts and Indian pudding. Retire in four poster comfort, snuggle under a hand made quilt and let the Paul Revere church bell lull you to sleep.
(*Traditional, Village, Inn. Member since 1971*)

From Keene, Rte. 9 (N) to Rte. 123 (E) to Hancock. From Peterborough, Rte. 202 (N) to L. on Rte. 123 to Hancock.

TEL. 603-525-3318
Outside N.H. **800-525-1789**
FAX 603-525-9301
Main Street
Hancock, NH 03449

Linda & Joe Johnston,
Innkeepers

MOOSE MOUNTAIN LODGE

- 12 rooms, $120 B&B, $160 MAP
- Visa, MC
- 5 Shared Baths
- Open May 31–Oct 31, Dec 26–Mar 15
- Appropriate for Children over 5; No Pets
- Hiking & Skiing Trails, Swimming Pond, Large Porch, Appalachian Trail, Connecticut River, Dartmouth College
- Breakfast, Lunch & Dinner in winter; Breakfast & Dinner summer & fall
- No Smoking
- N/A

Perched high on the side of Moose Mountain, with hiking and ski trails threading through 350 acres of woods and meadows, this big, old, comfortable lodge offers ever-changing views of the Connecticut River Valley. Meals are healthy, plentiful and delicious; the welcome is warm and friendly. Far from the sounds of civilization, peace and quiet reign. (*Rustic, Mountain, Lodge. Member since 1984*)

I-89, Exit 18 (N) to Rte. 120 for 0.5 mi. to R. at Etna Rd. for 3.6 mi. to R. on Rudsboro Rd. for 2 mi. to L. on Old Dana Rd. for 0.4 mi. up mtn. to lodge.

TEL. 603-643-3529
Hanover, NH
Moose Mountain Rd.
P.O.Box 272
Etna, NH 03750

Peter & Kay Shumway,
Innkeepers

PHILBROOK FARM INN

21 Rooms, $109/$135 MAP
2 Cottages $525/week

No Credit Cards

Private & Shared Baths

Closed April 1 to May 1; Nov. 1 to Dec. 26

Children Welcome
Pets Accepted in Cottages

Swimming pool, Game room, Major Ski areas, Nat'l. forest Hiking, Golf
Full Breakfast, Trail Lunches to order, Dinner; B&B rates avail. BYOB

Conference Facilities (45)
Wheelchair Access (Dining rm.)

U.S. Rte. 2 (W—20 mi.) from Bethel, ME. or (E—6 mi.) from Gorham, NH. At inn sign turn on Meadow Rd. for 1 mi. to R. at North Rd. for .5 mi. to inn.

TEL. 603-466-3831
881 North Rd.
Shelburne, NH 03581

The Philbrook & Leger Families, Innkeepers

1 The latchstring has been out at this venerable (National Register of Historic Places) inn since 1861 and 5 generations of the Philbrook family have been dispensing New England hospitality and wholesome, hearty, home-cooked New England meals ever since. As they say, "you will find simplicity rather than luxury, genuineness rather than pretension" at this peaceful retreat.
(*Traditional, Mountain, Inn. Member since 1978*)

STAFFORDS-IN-THE-FIELD

12 Rooms, $120/$210 B&B DBL Occ.; $150/$210 MAP DBL Occ.—3 Cotts, $90/ $160 B&B DBL Occ.; $170/ $200 MAP DBL Occ.
Visa, MC
8 Private, 3 Shared Baths
Open Year-round
Inquire Regarding Children; No Pets, Kennel Nearby
Walking Trails, Tennis, Croquet, XC Skiing, Golf, Swimming, Climbing, Antiques, Wedding Receptions in Restored Barn
Breakfast & Dinner, Picnic Lunches; Wine & Liquor Available
Smoking Restricted
Conference Facility (250)
Wheelchair access (cotts, dining rm. & conf. fac.)

From Chocorua Village & Rte. 16, take Rte. 113 (W) 1 mi. to inn sign. From Rte. 93, Exit 23 to Rtes. 104 & 25 (E) to Rte. 16 (N) to village & Rte. 113 as above.

TEL. 603-323-7766
FAX 603-323-7531
Box 270
Chocorua, NH 03817
Fred & Ramona, Innkeepers

4 This New England farmhouse circa 1778, set amidst rolling fields & hidden from view by the surrounding forest, celebrates its centennial this year as a country Inn. Known the world over for its gourmet country dining. The herbs from Ramona's kitchen garden flavor the scrumptious dishes served in the lantern-lit dining room. Walk in the woods, sleep under down filled quilts, enjoy the peace and quiet of the country.
(*Traditional, Federal, Country, Inn. Member since 1972*)

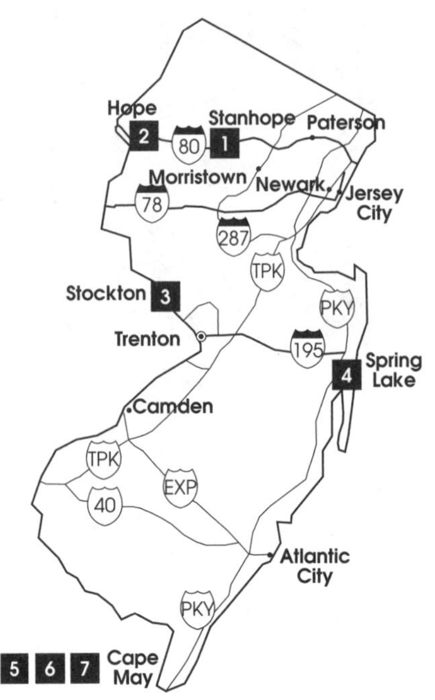

1. Whistling Swan Inn, Stanhope
2. Inn at Millrace Pond, Hope
3. Stockton Inn, Stockton
4. Sea Crest By The Sea, Spring Lake
5. Mainstay Inn & Cottage, Cape May
6. Manor House, Cape May
7. The Queen Victoria, Cape May

THE INN AT MILLRACE POND

17 Rooms, $85/$160 B&B
Corp. Rate Sun.– Thurs.
Visa, MC, Amex, Diners
All Private Baths
Open Year-round
Dining Room Closed for Dinner Christmas Day
Children Accepted (limited); No Pets
Tennis, Antiquing, Hiking, Fishing, Canoeing, Skiing, Golf, Bicycling, Winery tours, Waterloo Village.
Breakfast; Dinner daily
Sunday Lunch or Dinner served Noon- 8:00 p.m.
Wine & Liquor available
Smoking in designated rooms and areas
Conference Facilities (30)
Wheelchair Access (restaurant)

2 Originally a grist mill complex, Circa 1769, the original innkeepers restored these historic buildings in 1986, creating a lovely inn along Beaver Brook. Authentically decorated rooms in the Grist Mill, Millrace House, and stone Wheelwright's Cottage blend the quiet elegance of Colonial America with modern amenities. The Mill's rich industrial heritage is evident while enjoying the restaurant's acclaimed seasonal menu. Colonial traditions of hospitality, value and gracious service highlight a visit to historic Hope. AAA ◆◆◆ Mobile ★★★
(*Rustic, Village, Inn. Member since 1988*)

From I-80, Exit 12, take Rte. 521 (S) 1 mi. to 4-way stop., L. on Rte. 519 (N), .2 mi. to inn. From the south, Rte. 78 to Rte. 22 to Rte. 519 (N), travel 18 mi., take R. at blinker/4-way .2 mi. to inn.

TEL. 908-459-4884
1-800-7-INNHOPE
FAX: 908-459-5276
Rte. 519, P.O. Box 359
Hope, NJ 07844
Cordie & Charles Puttkammer, Innkeepers

MAINSTAY INN

 16 rooms, $105/$190 B&B
7 suites, $115/$220 B&B

 No Credit Cards; Personal Checks

All Private Baths

 Open Year-round

 Appropriate for children over six; No Pets

 Swimming, Biking, Hiking, Tennis, Golf, Birdwatching, Historic Attractions

 Breakfast, Afternoon Tea

 No Smoking

 Conference facilities (12)

 Wheelchair Access (1 unit)

Take Garden State Pkwy. (S). In Cape May, Pkwy. becomes Lafayette St. Take L. at first light onto Madison Ave. Go 3 blocks, R. at Columbia Ave. Inn on R.

TEL. 609-884-8690
635 Columbia Ave.
Cape May, NJ 08204

Tom & Sue Carroll,
Innkeepers

Once an exclusive gambling club, the Mainstay is now an elegant Victorian inn furnished in splendid antiques. Breakfast and afternoon tea are served each day either in the formal dining room or on the wide veranda. Located in Cape May's famous historic district, the inn is within walking distance of beaches, interesting shops and a vast selection of fine restaurants.
(*Traditional, Village, Breakfast Inn. Member since 1976*)

MANOR HOUSE

 8 Rooms, $68/$145 B&B
1 Suite, $105/$165 B&B

 Visa, MC, Discov

 7 Private, 2 Shared Bath

 Open Feb. 1–Jan.1

 Appropriate for Children over 12; Unable to Accommodate Pets

 Ocean swimming, Beach walking,Porch sitting, Birding, Golf, Historic Homes Tours, Napping

 Breakfast, Afternoon Tea

 Smoking Restricted

 Conference Facilities (12)

 N/A

From zero-mi. mark on Garden State Pkwy. to Rte. 109 South becoming Lafayette St., turn L. on Franklin for 2 blks. to R. on Hughes for 1 1/2 blks. to inn on L.

TEL. 609-884-4710
612 Hughes St.
Cape May, NJ 08204-2318

Nancy & Tom McDonald,
Innkeepers

On a tree-lined residential street in the heart of the historic district, Manor House offers guests an exceptionally clean and unpretentiously comfortable homestyle inn. Fluffy robes in the rooms and a generous cookie fairy are but a few of the fun touches found here. Relaxing on the porch, reading in the garden, or roaming the beaches and streets of Cape May occur with little effort. Traditional sticky buns and made-from-scratch breakfasts and the innkeeper's good-humoredness give the inn its reputation for fine food and its character.
(*Traditional, Village, Breakfast Inn. Member since 1991*)

NEW JERSEY

THE QUEEN VICTORIA®

17 Rooms, $75/$200 B&B
6 Suites, $115/240 B&B

Visa, MC, Amex

All Private Baths, 13 with Whirlpool Tubs

Open Year-round

Children Accepted
No Pets

Ocean swimming, Historic tours, Birding, Shopping, Dining, Biking (free inn bikes), Tennis, Golf, Fishing

Full Breakfast, Afternoon Tea, B.Y.O.B.

No Smoking Inside

Conference Facilities for 10-20

Wheelchair Access (1 suite)

7 The Wells family welcome you to three restored Victorian homes in the center of the Historic District with warm hospitality and special services. Relax on porches overlooking Victorian gardens. Fortify yourself with a hearty breakfast and afternoon tea for bicycle riding, antique shopping, historic touring or nature walks. Dine at several of New Jersey's best restaurants. Victorian ambiance yet modern amenities—air conditioning and whirlpool tubs. December, devoted to Christmas.
(*Traditional, Victorian, Village, Breakfast Inn. Member since 1992*)

Garden State Parkway to southern end: continue straight over bridge, past marinas and onto Lafayette St. At second light turn left onto Ocean Street. Go 3 blocks. Turn right on Columbia and right into loading areas.

TEL. 609-884-8702
102 Ocean St.
Cape May, NJ 08204
Joan & Dane Wells,
Innkeepers

SEA CREST BY THE SEA

12 Rooms, $110/$179 B&B
1 Suite, $195/$239 B&B

Visa, MC, Amex

All Private Baths

Open Year-round

No Children or Pets

Ocean Beach, Tennis, Golf, Playhouse, Race Track, Antiquing, Biking, Fishing, Sailing

Breakfast, Afternoon Tea

Smoking Outdoors Only

Conference Facility (11)

N/A

4 Your romantic fantasy escape. A Spring Lake Bed & Breakfast Inn just for the two of you. Lovingly restored 1885 Queen Anne Victorian for ladies and gentlemen on seaside holiday. Ocean views, open fireplaces, luxurious linens, feather beds, antique filled rooms, sumptuous breakfast and afternoon tea. A *Gourmet Magazine* "top choice." *Victoria* magazine calls it "a perfect ocean refuge." John & Carol Kirby welcome you with old fashioned hospitality to an atmosphere that will soothe your weary body and soul.
(*Elegant, Victorian, Village, Breakfast Inn. Member since 1993*)

From NY & N Garden Pkwy to 34. From Phil. & S I-195 to 34. On 34 go south to first traffic circle and 3/4 around to 524 east to ocean. Go 1 blk. and turn right on Tuttle Avenue.

TEL. 908-449-9031
19 Tuttle Ave
Spring Lake, NJ 07762

John & Carol Kirby,
Innkeepers

THE STOCKTON INN

 3 rooms, $60/$125 B&B
8 suites, $110/$165 B&B

 Visa, MC, Amex, Discov

 All Private Baths

 Closed Dec. 25
Children limited
No Pets

Canoeing, Rafting, Tubing, Ballooning, Fishing, Hiking, Riding, Antiquing, Museums, Galleries, Theater, Historic Sites & Parks, Shopping Outlet Centers

 Lunch, Dinner, Sun. brunch, Banquets to 200
Wine, Liquor & Beer available

 Conference Facilities (60)
Wheelchair Access (dining rm.)

N.J. Rte. 202 to N.J. Rte. 29 (River Rd.) 3 mi. (N) to Stockton. Inn is in center of town on Main St. (Across the river from New Hope, PA).

TEL. 609-397-1250
Main St., P.O.Box C
Stockton, NJ 08559

Andrew McDermott,
Innkeeper

The centerpiece of a small Delaware River town dates from 1710, serving travelers & neighbors since 1796. A colorful history and equally colorful guests include Rodgers & Hart, who were inspired to write the song "There's A Small Hotel (with a wishing well)." Romantic suites & bedrooms, many with fireplaces, in the Main Inn, Wagon, Carriage and Federal Houses. The restaurant boasts " 3 Star" Contemporary American & Continental Cuisine, fireplaces, murals of colonial Hunterdon & Bucks Counties, live entertainment & dancing. Seasonal Garden Dining.
(Traditional, Village, Inn. Member since 1983)

WHISTLING SWAN INN

 10 Rooms, $75/$110 B&B

 Visa, MC, Amex, Discov

 All Private Baths

 Open Year-round

 Children over 12 are Welcome; No Pets Please

 Near Waterloo Village, Wineries, Antiquing, Winter Sports, State forests, Shopping, Fairs, Shows, Flea Markets

 Full Buffet Breakfast, Wine, Lemonade, Coffee, Tea, Cider

 No Smoking

 Conference (10-12)

 N/A

Bus & Train via N.J. Transit to Netcong/Stanhope. Exit 27 off I-80 via route 183/206 one mile to Hess gasoline station. Turn on Main St. across from Hess.

TEL 201-347-6369
FAX 201-347-3391
110 Main St.
Stanhope, NJ 07874
Joe Mulay and Paula Williams , Innkeepers

Nestled in northwestern New Jersey's Skylands Tourism region only 45 miles west of New York City, this 1905 Victorian home has been converted to a B&B and renovated in two major segments of time. Each room has a private bath, queen size bed and period furnishings. The house is air conditioned. Much of what is in the house is from Paula's grandmother's home in Oklahoma. Enjoy the porch swing, hammock and picnic table or sherry, movies, fireplaces and Tubs-for-Two bathroom. We work with any dietary requirements.
(Traditional, Village, Breakfast Inn. Member since 1992)

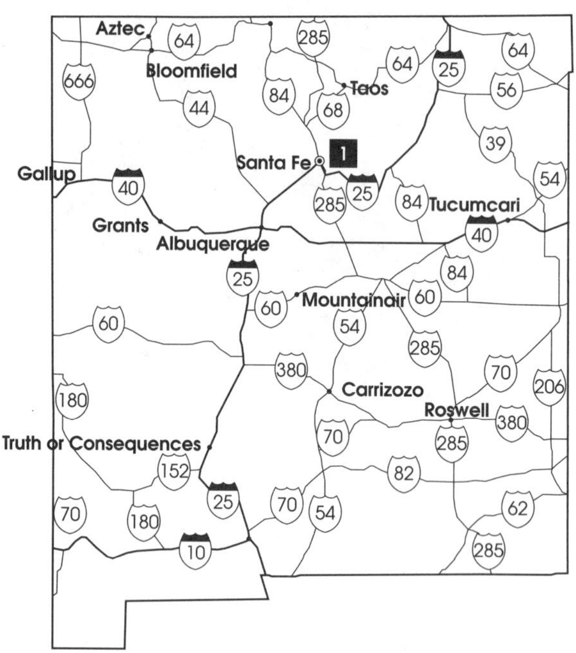

1. Grant Corner Inn, Santa Fe

GRANT CORNER INN

12 Rooms, $70/$140 B&B
Hacienda, $100/$115 B&B

Visa, MC

10 Private Baths, 1 Shared Baths

Open Year-round

Appropriate for Children over 6; No Pets

Skiing, Hiking, Fishing, Golf, Tennis, Swimming (fee)

Complimentary Breakfast; Picnic Lunches, Catered Dinners, Restaurant Serving Brunch to Public Sat. & Sun. Complimentary Wine

Smoke-free inn

Conference Facilities (20)

Wheelchair Access (1 rm.)

This delightful inn has an ideal location just two blocks from the historic plaza of downtown Santa Fe, among intriguing shops, galleries, and restaurants. Lush gardens, beautifully appointed guest rooms, fabulous gourmet breakfasts, and the gracious hospitality of the Walters family make this an experience not to be missed. Ample parking on the premises.

(*Traditional, In-Town, Breakfast Inn. Member since 1988*)

From Albuquerque, I-25 (N) Exit St. Francis L. (N) 3 mi.to R. at Alameda (W) .6 mi. L. (N) on Guadalupe .1 mi., R. (W) on Johnson .1 mi., parking on L.

TEL. 505-983-6678
122 Grant Ave.
Santa Fe, NM 87501

Louise Stewart & Pat Walter,
Innkeepers

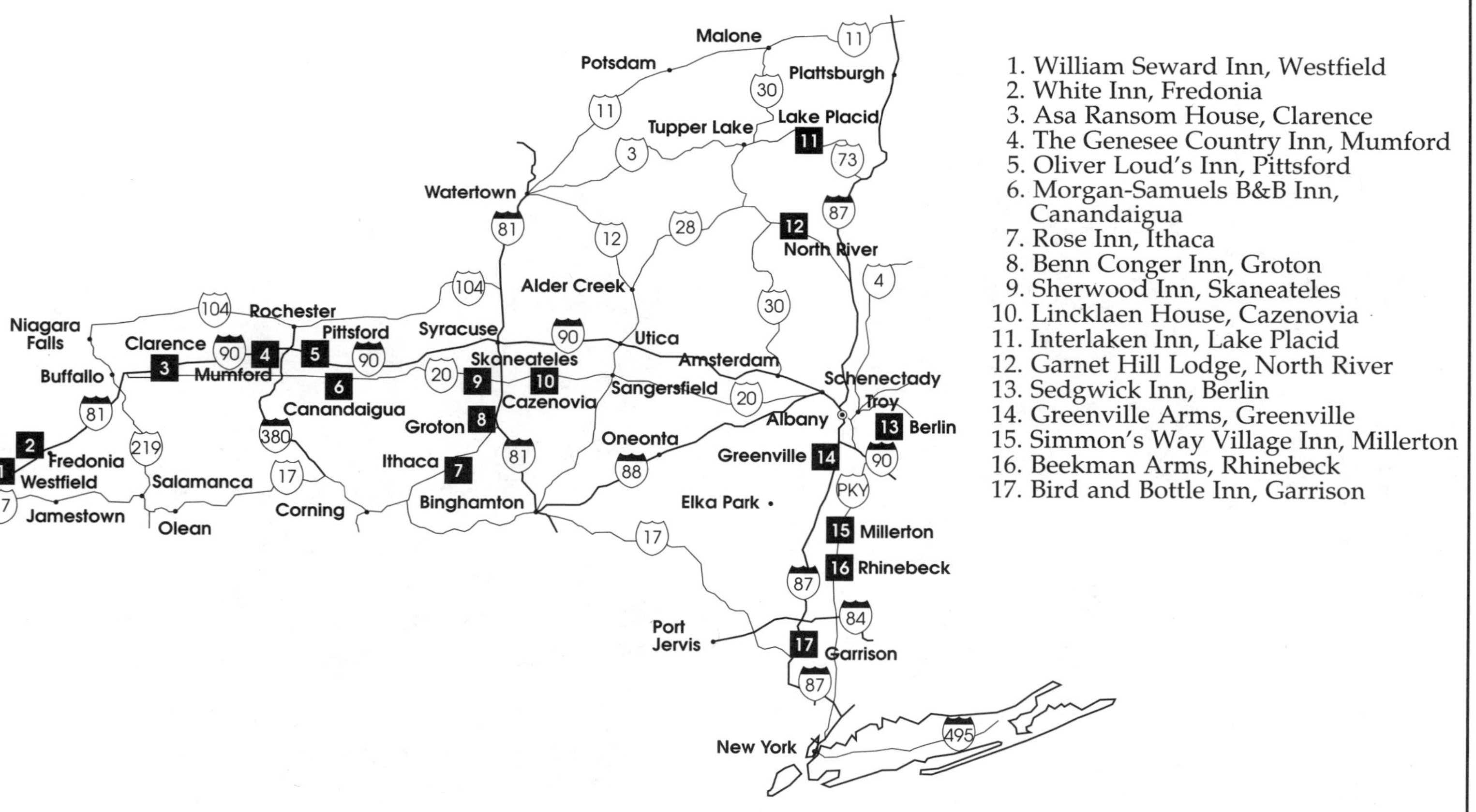
1. William Seward Inn, Westfield
2. White Inn, Fredonia
3. Asa Ransom House, Clarence
4. The Genesee Country Inn, Mumford
5. Oliver Loud's Inn, Pittsford
6. Morgan-Samuels B&B Inn, Canandaigua
7. Rose Inn, Ithaca
8. Benn Conger Inn, Groton
9. Sherwood Inn, Skaneateles
10. Lincklaen House, Cazenovia
11. Interlaken Inn, Lake Placid
12. Garnet Hill Lodge, North River
13. Sedgwick Inn, Berlin
14. Greenville Arms, Greenville
15. Simmon's Way Village Inn, Millerton
16. Beekman Arms, Rhinebeck
17. Bird and Bottle Inn, Garrison
Malone
Potsdam
Plattsburgh
Tupper Lake
Lake Placid
Watertown
North River
Alder Creek
Niagara Falls
Rochester
Pittsford
Syracuse
Utica
Clarence
Amsterdam
Skaneateles
Buffalo
Mumford
Sangersfield
Schenectady
Canandaigua
Cazenovia
Troy
Groton
Albany
Berlin
Fredonia
Oneonta
Westfield
Ithaca
Greenville
Salamanca
Jamestown
Corning
Binghamton
Elka Park
Olean
Millerton
Rhinebeck
Port Jervis
Garrison
New York
PKY

ASA RANSOM HOUSE

6 Rooms, $85/$125 B&B
3 Suites, $145 B&B

Visa, MC, Discov

All Private Baths

Closed Fri.; month of Jan.

Well-supervised Children welcome; No Pets

Niagara Falls, many Antique Shops within walking distance

Breakfast for House-guests; Dinner Sun. thru Thurs. (Sat.-Houseguests only); Wine & Liquor available

No Smoking

Conference Facilities (40)

Wheelchair Access

3 On the site of the first gristmill built in Erie County (1803), this historic village inn offers country gourmet dining and fine New York State wines. Guests are romanced in the winter by the glowing fireplaces in the guest rooms, and enchanted in the summer by spacious grounds full of herbs and flowers. Some rooms have porches or balconies and a full country breakfast is included for all guests. Clarence is known throughout the East for its antiques and treasures. Only 25 miles from Niagara Falls.
(*Traditional, Village, Inn. Member since 1976*)

Traveling (E): I-90, Exit 49, L. on Rte. 78 for 1 mi. to R. on Rte. 5 for 5.3 mi. Traveling (W): I-90, Exit 48A & R. on Rte. 77 for 1 mi. to R. on Rte. 5 for 10 mi. to inn.

TEL. 716-759-2315
FAX 716-759-2791
10529 Main St. (Rte. 5)
Clarence, NY 14031-1684
Robert Lenz & Judy Lenz, Innkeepers

BEEKMAN ARMS

59 Rooms, $80/$110 EP
2 Suites, $125/$125 EP

Visa, MC, Amex, Diners

All Private Baths

Open Year-round

Children restricted to certain accommodations only; 4 persons to room, Children under 3 free
No Pets exc. motel unit

Hyde Park, Rhinebeck WW1 Aerdrome, Culinary Instit. of Amer., Golf, Swimming, Fishing, XC Skiing Nearby

Breakfast, Lunch, Dinner
Wine & Liquor available

4 rooms Non-smoking
Non-smoking Dining area

Conference Facilities (20)

Wheelchair Access (2 rms, dining rm. & conf. fac.)

16 The focus of activity in bustling, historic Rhinebeck, this inn has seen history being made since 1766 when its original section was built. Today its offers authentically furnished guest rooms, some with working fireplaces, a Colonial Tap Room and a beautiful greenhouse dining area where casual but elegant country fare is served.
(*Traditional, Village, Inn. Member since 1967*)

NY Thruwy. (I-90) Rhinecliff Bridge Exit to Rte. 9 (S) 2 mi. to Rhinebeck Village. From Taconic Pkwy. take Rte. 199 (W) to L. on Rte. 308 to Rhinebeck Village.

TEL. 914-876-7077
FAX 914-876-7077
4 Mill St., Route 9
Rhinebeck, NY 12572

Chuck LaForge, Innkeeper

BENN CONGER INN

 2 Rooms, $110/$130 B&B
3 Suites, $120/$220 B&B

 Visa, MC, Amex, Diners

 All Private Baths

 Open Year-round

 Children Welcome
No Pets—Kennel nearby

 Hiking, Biking, XC Skiing, Golf, Tennis, all Lake Sports, Antiques, Wineries

 Breakfast, Dinner
Wine & Liquor available

 Smoking limited

 Conference Facilities (40)

N/A

From I-81, Exit 12 (Homer) (S) on Rte. 281 for 2 mi. R. (W) on Rte. 222 for 9 mi. to Groton. Cross Rte. 38, making no turns. Inn is up hill on R.

TEL. 607-898-5817
206 W. Cortland St.
Groton, NY 13073

Alison & Peter Van der Meulen, Innkeepers

8 A revival mansion built for industrialist Benn Conger, the Inn is best known as a hideaway for mobster Dutch Schultz. Eighteen pastoral acres, gracious public rooms, including a library and conservatory, oversized suites, antiques, imported linens, amenities, Mediterranean-inspired cuisine and over 100 fine wines will please the most discriminating traveler. ("Wine Spectator" Award 1987-94).

(Elegant, Village, Inn. Member since 1991)

THE BIRD & BOTTLE INN

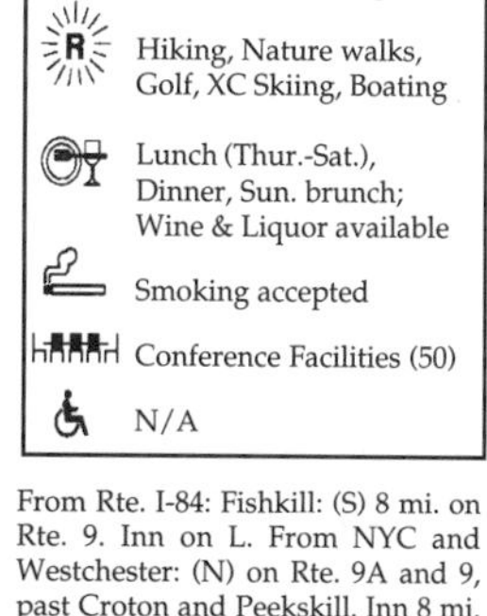

2 Rooms, $210/$220 MAP
2 Suites, $240 MAP

Visa, MC, Amex, Diners

All Private Baths

Open year-round

Not appropriate for Children; Pets not accepted

Hiking, Nature walks, Golf, XC Skiing, Boating

Lunch (Thur.-Sat.), Dinner, Sun. brunch; Wine & Liquor available

Smoking accepted

Conference Facilities (50)

N/A

From Rte. I-84: Fishkill: (S) 8 mi. on Rte. 9. Inn on L. From NYC and Westchester: (N) on Rte. 9A and 9, past Croton and Peekskill. Inn 8 mi. beyond Peekskill on Rte. 9 in Garrison area.

TEL. 914-424-3000
Old Albany Post Rd. (Rte. 9)
Garrison, NY 10524

Ira Boyar, Innkeeper

17 A famed landmark on the old Albany-New York Post Road since 1761, this inn continues to welcome travelers with traditional Hudson River Valley hospitality. An authentic old country inn, it is internationally renowned for its gourmet cuisine served in 3 dining rooms with working fireplaces and comfortable, cozy rooms with woodburning fireplaces, 4-poster or canopied beds, private baths, and Colonial furnishings. *Hudson Valley Magazine* voted . . . "Best Restaurant Putnam County, NY 1993."

(Colonial, Country, Inn. Member since 1972)

GARNET HILL LODGE

22 Rooms, $120/$170 MAP

Visa, MC

All private baths

Closed Nov. 20–30

Supervised Children Welcome; No Pets

Swimming, Tennis, Hiking, Boating, Fishing, XC Skiing, Museums, Downhill Skiing

Breakfast, Lunch, Dinner Wine & Liquor Available

Non-smoking Dining Area

Conference Facilities (60)

Wheelchair Access (1 rm)

12 Garnet Hill is nestled in the Adirondack Mountains and overlooks beautiful Thirteenth Lake. This rustic resort-inn was built in 1936 in the area of a historic garnet mine. Guests are welcomed into a dining/living room with great log pillars and a large garnet stone fireplace. The inn features distinctive guest rooms and a menu highlighted by homebaked breads and desserts, special vegetarian dishes, and heart-healthy entrees.
(Rustic, Mountain, Resort. Member since 1980)

From Albany on I-87 Exit 23 (Warrensburg). (N) on Rte. 9 to Rte. 28. (W) on Rte. 28, 22 mi. to North River. L. on 13th Lake Rd. 4.5 mi. to inn.

TEL. 518-251-2444
FAX 518-251-3089
13th Lake Rd.
North River, NY 12856

George & Mary Heim,
Innkeepers

THE GENESEE COUNTRY INN

9 Rooms, $80/$130 B&B
2 nite min (some wkends)

Visa, MC, Diners

All Private Baths

Closed Dec. 24 & 25

No Pets; Inn has pets in residence

Trout fishing, Walking, Biking, Genesee Country Museum, Letchworth St. Pk., Rochester, Discount shopping, Gift Shop

Breakfast houseguests; Luncheon for conferences; Tea, Cheese & Crackers; BYOB

No Smoking

Conference Facilities (14)

Wheelchair Access (1 rm)

4 GIVE YOURSELF A HIDEAWAY BREAK... Savor the magic quiet of our award-winning historic storybook stonemill in the century village of Mumford. See blue heron as you flyfish secluded "A-rated" troutstreams, visit nearby village-museum, our "18th century Williamsburg of Western NY," or Letchworth Park known as "The Grand Canyon of the East," then just relax and enjoy our hospitality. Tea, breakfast, some fireplaces, canopy beds, giftshop. Near fine restaurants. AAA, MOBIL, *Country Inns and Backroads.*
(Traditional, Colonial, Village, Breakfast Inn. Member since 1988)

From NY Thrwy. (I-90) take Exit 47 and Rte. 19 S. to LeRoy. Go (E) on Rte. 5 to Caledonia, (N) on Rte. 36 to Mumford. L. on George St. 1 1/2 blocks—Inn on R.

TEL. 716-538-2500
FAX 716-538-4565
948 George St.,
Mumford, NY 14511-0340
Glenda Barcklow, Proprietor,
Kim Rasmussen,
Innkeeper

GREENVILLE ARMS

12 Rooms, $95/$145 B&B
1 Suite, $145 B&B

Visa, MC, Discov

All Private Baths

Closed Dec. 1–28

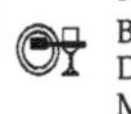
Not appropriate for children under 12; No Pets

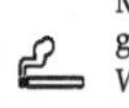
Swimming pool, Tennis, Golf, Bicycling, Hiking, Hudson Valley & Catskill Sightseeing

Breakfast for houseguests
Dinner by reservation May 1–Oct. 31 & Thanksgiving

Wine & Beer available

No Smoking

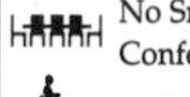
Conference Facilities (30)

N/A

From NYC: 2 hrs. (N) on I-87 to Exit 21 & Rte. 23(W) for 9 mi. Then (N) on Rte. 32 for 9 mi. to Greenville. Inn is on L., before traffic light.

TEL. 518-966-5219
P.O. Box 659, South St.
Greenville, NY 12083-0659

Tish Dalton & Eliot Dalton, Innkeepers

Built in 1889 in the foothills of the Northern Catskills, this lovely Queen Anne Victorian inn has welcomed guests for over 40 years. Two buildings are set on 6 acres of lawns, shade trees and gardens. Antiques, original artwork and Victorian details add to an atmosphere of warmth and relaxed comfort. After a full country breakfast, guests enjoy hiking, biking, sightseeing or relaxing by the inn's pool. In the evening, guests are treated to delicious seasonal American cuisine, completing a memorable experience. (*Traditional, Village, Inn. Member since 1991*)

INTERLAKEN INN

11 Rooms, $60/$110 B&B
$110/$170 MAP
1 Suite, $180 MAP

Amex, MC, Visa

All Private Baths

Open Year-round; B&B only Apr. & Nov.

Children accepted over 5
No Pets

Golf, Skiing, Boating, Skating, Canoeing, Hiking, Biking, X-Country Skiing, Olympic Venues

Full Breakfast, Dinner, Afternoon Tea, Sherry in each room, Wine & Liquor Available

Smoking limited to common rooms

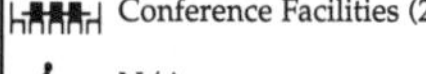
Conference Facilities (20)

N/A

I-87 to 73 to Lake Placid, 1st stoplight left (Main St.) to Mirror Lake Dr. to Interlaken

TEL. 518-523-3180
800-428-4369
15 Interlaken Ave.
Lake Placid, NY 12946

Roy and Carol Johnson, Innkeepers

In the heart of the Adirondack Mountains, site of the 1932 and 1980 winter Olympics, this 1906 Victorian Inn offers a wonderfully romantic setting with uniquely decorated, antique furnished rooms. Enjoy a peaceful setting and four seasons of outdoor activities. The Inn offers fine dining using the season's freshest bounty to provide guests with a unique dining experience. (*Traditional, Village, Inn. Member since 1992*)

LINCKLAEN HOUSE

18 rooms, $94/$109 B&B
3 suites, $120/$140 B&B

Visa, MC,

All Private Baths

Open Year-round

Children accepted
Pets accepted

Swimming, Golf, Tennis, Downhill & XC Skiing

Lunch, Dinner; Sun. Brunch; Dining room closed Mondays
Wine & Liquor available

Smoking accepted

Conference facilities (50)
Banquet facilities (200)

N/A

10 Built in 1835 as a luxurious stopover for 19th century travelers, the Lincklaen House has long been a local landmark and has hosted such luminaries as President Grover Cleveland and John D. Rockefeller. The old-world atmosphere is now combined with modern comfort and gracious service, offering guests a return to an era of elegant hospitality. (*Traditional, Village, Inn. Member since 1968*)

From NY Thruwy. (I-90): Exit 34, take Rte. 13 (S) to Cazenovia. R. on Rte. 20, 1 block. From I-81: Exit 15 (La Fayette), E. on Rte. 20. 18 mi. to Cazenovia.

TEL. 315-655-3461
FAX 315-655-5443
79 Albany St., Box 36
Cazenovia, NY 13035

Howard M. Kaler,
Innkeeper

MORGAN-SAMUELS B&B INN

5 Rooms, $109/$195 B&B
1 Suite, $195/$225 B&B
Business Rate/$69–$99
All rms. have fireplaces
Visa, MC, Discov
All Private Baths
Open Year-round exc. Dec. 24–25
Children under 3 or over 10; Pets outdoors only
Tennis, Golf, Nearby Lake, Wineries, Outdoor Symphonies & Concerts, Sonnerberg Gardens, Horse drawn Sleigh Rides, 2100-ft. elevation downhill skiing (11 m.)
Candlelit Gourmet Brkfast w/ Mozart, Dinner prix fixe by Reservation Fri.–Sat. or special request of 8+; BYOB
No Smoking
Conference Facilities (15)
Wheelchair Access (dining rm.)

6 As you travel the 2,000-ft. tree-lined drive to the secluded 1810 English style mansion you sense the difference between ordinary and legendary. The Inn sits like a plantation on a rise surrounded by 46 acres. Four patios, a lily pond with waterfall, five acres of lawn and gardens are canopied by 250 noble trees. Three rooms with French doors and balconies, ten active fireplaces, and a tea room with stone wall with 6-ft. glass window and pot-bellied stove. Library, common room, large screened and furnished porch, 2 jacuzzis, museum quality antiques, oil paintings. Mobil ★★★ AAA ◆◆◆
(*Elegant, Victorian, Village, Breakfast Inn. Member since 1992*)

I-90 from E Exit 43 R. on 21 to 488; L. 1st R. to stop sign continue 3/4 mile to Inn on R.

TEL. (716) 394-9232
FAX (716) 394-8044
2920 Smith Rd.
Canandaigua, N.Y. 14424

Julie & John Sullivan,
Innkeepers

OLIVER LOUD'S INN

8 Rooms, $135/$155 B&B

Visa, MC, Amex, CB, Diners Club

All Private Baths

Open Year-round

Children 13 & over welcome; No Pets; kennel nearby

Erie Canal towpath for hiking, Jogging, XC Skiing, Biking, Boating, Golf, Tennis, Museums, Sight-seeing

Cont. Breakfast hamper, Richardson's Canal House rest.; Wine & Liquor available

Smoking/non-smoking rms.

Conference Facilities (20)

Wheelchair Access (1 rm.)

NY Thruwy. (I-90) Exit 45, to I-490 (W) for 3 mi. to Bushnell's Basin exit (#27), turn R. & continue to Marsh Rd. signal & bear R. to inn.

TEL. 716-248-5200
FAX 716-248-9970
1474 Marsh Rd.
Pittsford, NY 14534

Vivienne Tellier, Innkeeper

5 Feeding ducks, building snowmen, visiting nearby shops, or rocking on the porch over-looking the Erie Canal, are some ways to relax at this circa 1810 stagecoach inn. Authentically furnished with antiques and period artwork, guests are pampered with V.I.P. welcome trays, as well as a breakfast hamper delivered to your room. King sized and canopy beds available. (*Elegant, Village, Inn. Member since 1989*)

ROSE INN

10 Rooms, $100/$160 B&B
5 Suites, $175/$250 B&B

Visa, MC

All Private Baths

Open Year-round

Children over 10 or prior arrangements; No Pets, kennel next door

Cayuga Lake Sports, X-Country Skiing, near Downhill Skiing, Golf, Fishing, Wineries, Cornell University, Antiques

Breakfast, Dinner prix fixe by reservation Tues.–Sat.; Wine & Liquor available

No smoking

Conference Facilities (60)

Wheelchair Access (conf. fac.)

10 m. N of Ithaca on 34 N. From Ithaca 13 exit, 34 N, 6 m. to "T" (red flashing light). R. for .5 m. to fork, stay L., Inn is 3.5 m. on R.

TEL. 607-533-7905
FAX 607-533-7908
Rte. 34 North, P.O. Box 6576
Ithaca, NY 14851-6576

Charles & Sherry Rosemann, Innkeepers

7 A spectacular Inn in a lovely country setting. Located halfway between NYC and Niagara Falls, in the heart of the Finger Lakes. This 1850 Italianate mansion is a gem of woodcraft, with a stunning circular staircase of Honduran Mahogany. Large, high ceilinged rooms are luxuriously furnished with antiques from around the world accented by lush colors and fabrics. Extraordinary cuisine is romantically served in elegant private dining rooms. Sherry and Charles welcome you to New York's only Mobil **** and AAA ◆◆◆◆ inn.
(*Elegant, Country, Inn. Member since 1986*)

NEW YORK
THE SEDGWICK INN

4 Rooms, $85/$95 B&B
1 Ste, $100/$120 B&B
Annex $65/$75
Visa, MC, Amex, Diners, Discov
All Private Baths
Open Year-round
Children accepted in annex; Pets accepted in annex
Library, Gift & Gourmet shops, Downhill & XC Skiing, Swimming, Theatre, Tanglewood Music Festival, Art Museums
Breakfast, Light lunches, Gourmet Dinners
Wine & Liquor available
No Smoking in Inn bedrooms
Conference Facilities (25)
Wheelchair Access (annex, dining rm.)

13 This historic inn, once a stagecoach stop, sits on 12 acres in the beautiful Taconic Valley on the New York side of the Berkshires, within easy access to Albany, Western Massachussets and Southern Vermont. Comfortable, yet elegant, it has been described as "the quintessential country inn." Rooms are furnished in antiques. Fireplaces, fine art and interesting artifacts grace both the handsome living room and the well-stocked library where the original indentures, date 1791, are displayed. The restaurant is renowned for its fine food and the carriage house features unusual gifts.

(Traditional, Country, Inn. Member since 1985)

From Albany: Rte. 787 N to Troy. Exit Rte. 7 E to Rte. 278. R. on 278 to Rte. 2, L. on Rte. 2 for approx. 15 m. to Rte. 22. R. on 22 S, 6 m. to inn. From N.Y.C.: Taconic Pkwy N, Exit Rte. 295 E to Rte. 22. L. on Rte. 22 N for 22 m.

TEL. 518-658-2334
800-845-4886
FAX 518-658-3988
Rte. 22, Box 250
Berlin, NY 12022
Edie Evans, Innkeeper

THE SHERWOOD INN

16 Rooms, $65/$100 B&B
5 Suites, $85/$145 B&B
3 Bedroom Hospitality Suite W/Fully Equipped Kitchen
Visa, MC, Amex, Diners, CB
All Private Baths
Open Year-round
Peak rates effective Fri. & Sat. nights year-round
Children Accepted
No Pets
Swimming, Boating, Golf, Downhill and XC Skiing, Fishing, Bicycling, Hiking, Antiquing
Continental Breakfast, Lunch, Dinner; Dining room closed 12/24 & 25;
Wine & Liquor available
Non-smoking dining area
Conference/Banquet Facilities for 25/250
N/A

9 From the handsome lobby with its fireplace and gift shop to the pleasant guest rooms, many of which overlook beautiful Skaneateles Lake, gracious service and comfort are the keynotes here. American cuisine with a Continental touch has been featured in *Bon Appetit*, and is served in the dining rooms and the friendly, casual tavern. Cocktail Cruises aboard our restored vintage Chris Craft. Featured in USAIR Magazine as one of the ten top historic country inns. The lovely village of Skaneateles offers many activities.

(Traditional, Village, Inn. Member since 1979)

From N. Y. Thruwy: Exit Weedsport, Rte. 34 (S) to Auburn. (E) on Rte. 20, 7 mi. to Skaneateles. From (S): Rte. 81 (N) to Cortland, Rte. 41 (N) to Skaneateles. L. on Rte. 20 for 1 mi.

TEL. 315-685-3405
1-800-3-SHERWOOD
FAX 315-685-8981
26 West Genesee St.
Skaneateles, NY 13152
William Eberhardt and Claire O'Boyle Downey, Innkeepers

SIMMONS' WAY VILLAGE INN & RESTAURANT

 9 Rooms, $145/$175
1 Suite, $320

 Visa, MC, Amex, Diners

All Private Baths

 Open Year-round

 Children Accepted
No Pets

 Skiing, Golf, Tennis, Swimming, Concerts, Summer Stock, Auto Racing, Antiquing, Historical sites

 Breakfast (guests only), Brunch, Dinner; MAP available

 Wine & Liquor available
Smoking in restricted areas

Conference Facilities (25)

 N/A

From N.Y.C. (90 mi.): Taconic Pkwy. to Rte. 44(E) or I-684 to Rte. 22 (N) to Rte. 44 (E) (Main St.). From Boston (160 mi.): Mass. Tpke., Exit 2, Rte. 102 (W) to Rte. 7 (S) to Rte. 44 (W). From Hartford: Rte. 44 (W) to Millerton.

TEL. 518-789-6235
FAX 518-789-6236
33 Main St.
Millerton, NY 12546
The Carter Family, Owners & Innkeepers

15 Graceful retreat in grand Victorian elegance and civility. Located near CT border in Berkshire foothills. Antiques, fireplaces, porches and historic, candlelit silver service highlight memorable accommodations and internationally acclaimed cuisine and wine selections. Selected by American Express/Hertz as "Quintessential Country Inn 1991" for a national ad campaign. Simmons' Way has been awarded a rare distinction of 4-star rating at local, national and international levels.
(*Victorian, Village, Inn. Member since 1990*)

THE WHITE INN

 12 Rooms, $59/$89 B&B
11 Suites, $89/$159 B&B

 Visa, MC, Amex, DC, Discov.

 All Private Baths

 Open Year-round

 Children welcome
No Pets

Antiquing, Wineries, Chautauqua Institution, SUNY college activities, Golf, Bicycling, XC/alpine skiing

 Breakfast included; Lunch, Dinner, Wine & Liquor available

 Some Non-smoking rms.
Non-smoking Dining area

Conference Facilities (65)

 Wheelchair access (dining rm. & conf. fac.)

NY Thruwy. Exit 59. At traffic light L. on Rte. 60 (S) to traffic light, R. on Rte. 20 (W), Main St. Inn on R.

TEL. 716-672-2103
FAX 716-672-2107

52 East Main St.
Fredonia, NY 14063

Robert Contiguglia & Kathleen Dennison, Innkeepers

2 Built on the 1868 homesite of the county's first physician, The White Inn features beautifully restored and decorated guest rooms and suites. Antiques and period reproductions adorn the guest rooms and public spaces. Superb cuisine has gained an enthusiastic following among guests and townsfolk. The Inn offers fine dining and banquets as well as casual and late-night fare.
(*Traditional, In-Town, Inn. Member since 1989*)

WILLIAM SEWARD INN

14 Rooms, $85/$155 B&B
Visa, MC, Discov.
All Private Baths
Open Year-round
Children over 10 are welcome; No Pets, Boarding available nearby
Chautauqua Institution, Lily Dale, Wineries, Antique & Speciality Shops, Skiing, Swimming, Boating, Tennis, Golf nearby.
Full Breakfast; Prix Fix Dinner available Thursday-Sunday by advance Reservation only; BYOB
No Smoking inside
Conference Facilities (15)
Wheelchair Access (2 Rms.)

Although Chautauqua Institution is a major attraction, many travelers come specifically to stay at this 1821 antique-filled inn for rest and relaxation. The formal but comfortable ambiance created with period antiques (mid-1800s-early 1900s) in the 1821-1880 portion of Inn as well as the period reproduction setting in the new carriage house lend well to total relaxation for guests.
(Traditional, Greek Revision, Country, Inn. Member since 1992)

4 mi. S. on Rte. 394 from I-90, Exit 60. 2.5 hrs. NE of Cleveland, OH; 2.5 hrs. N of Pittsburgh, PA; 1.5 hrs. SW of Buffalo, NY; 3 hrs. SW of Toronto, Canada

TEL. 716-326-4151
FAX 716-326-4163
RR2, Box 14, S. Portage Rd.
Westfield, NY 14787
Jim and Debbie Dahlberg, Innkeepers

INN ARCHITECTURE

The architecture of the Inns in this book is a good part of what makes them so interesting. The variations in vintage, style and design lend to the charm and ambiance that makes each of them different and exciting.

Some Country Inns are housed in beautifully restored historic structures ranging from Colonial through Ante-bellum to Victorian. They encompass ornate woodwork, cut and stained glass, intricate detailing, even Doric columns and fanciful porches. Some are farmhouses and some are row houses. One Inn is made up of reclaimed century old log cabins. Another has guest rooms in the silo. Inn guests can encounter a contemporary structure that juts into the trees or a Scandinavian Inn that looks as if it has been transported from Europe. A couple of Inns are in old stone mills, one with the mill stream running through the building.

If you are a lover of architecture and design, your fascination can be captured forever by going from one Inn to another enjoying the history and beauty of the buildings and appreciating the talent and ingenuity that went in to each of one of them. For many of the vintage structures, not only can one enjoy those features which were designed and created so long ago, but visitors also have the opportunity to appreciate the way in which our heritage is being preserved and protected by the careful restoration and adaptive use of these structures.

Certainly the grandeur and size of some historic edifices make them perfect for adaptation as overnight accommodations, Country Inns. And with each adaptation, architecture connoisseurs get to enjoy this win-win effort. Is it any wonder that a number of our Independent Innkeepers' Association innkeepers were once architects?

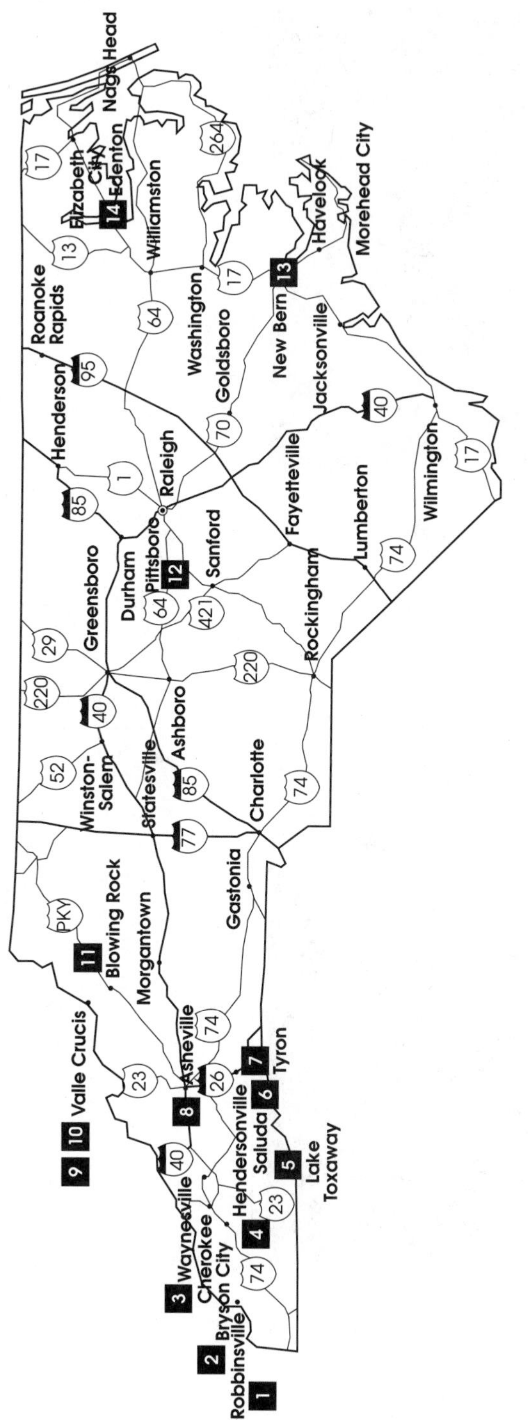

1. Snowbird Mountain Lodge, Robbinsville
2. Hemlock Inn, Bryson City
3. Swag Country Inn, Waynesville
4. Waverly Inn, Hendersonville
5. The Greystone Inn, Lake Toxaway
6. Orchard Inn, Saluda
7. Pine Crest Inn, Tryon
8. Richmond Hill Inn, Asheville
9. Inn at Taylor House, Valle Crucis
10. Mast Farm Inn, Valle Crucis
11. Gideon Ridge Inn, Blowing Rock
12. Fearrington House, Pittsboro
13. Harmony House Inn, New Bern
14. Lords Proprietor's Inn, Edenton

NORTH CAROLINA

THE FEARRINGTON HOUSE

15 Rooms, $150/$250 B&B
9 Suites, $200/$250 B&B
Visa, MC, Amex
All Private Baths
Open Year-round
No children under 12; No Pets
Swimming, Biking, Walking, Bird watching, Golf, Tennis, Sailing, Fishing, Antique Shopping
Breakfast, Lunch, Dinner Outstanding Wine list; BYOB
Smoking limited
Conference facilities (40)
Wheelchair Access (1 rm.)

12 In a cluster of low, attractive buildings surrounded by gardens and rolling countryside, this elegant inn offers luxurious quarters in a country setting. A member of Relais et Chateaux, the restaurant's sophisticated regional cuisine, prepared in the classical techniques, has received national acclaim, including AAA's ◆◆◆◆◆ award and Mobil's 4-star.
(*Elegant, Village, Inn. Member since 1987*)

Chapel Hill, U.S. 15-501 (S) 8 mi. to Fearrington Village.

TEL. 919-542-2121
FAX 919-542-4202
2000 Fearrington Village Center
Pittsboro, NC 27312

Jenny & R.B. Fitch, Owners; Richard Delany, General Manager

GIDEON RIDGE INN

9 Rooms, $100/$150 B&B
Visa, MC, Discovr., Amex
All Private Baths
Open Year-round
Appropriate for Children over 12; No Pets
Hiking, Horseback Riding, Golf, Tennis, Village & Crafts shops, Blue Ridge Pkwy. Grandfather Mtn.
Full Breakfast, Dinners & Lunches for groups by prior request; BYOB
Smoking limited
Conference Facilities (12-16)
N/A

11 Gideon Ridge Inn is nine delightful guest rooms with mountain breezes. French doors and stone terraces. Ceiling fans and wicker chairs. Antiques and good books. Fine breakfasts to linger over. Earl Grey Tea and shortbread cookies to savor. And a piano with a breathtaking view of the mountains. Really.
(*Traditional, Mountain, Breakfast Inn. Member since 1990*)

U.S. 321, 1.5 mi. (S) of village of Blowing Rock, turn (W) on Rock Rd., L. on Gideon Ridge Rd. at fork. Go to top of the ridge.

TEL. 704-295-4586
6148 Gideon Ridge Rd.
P.O. Box 1929
Blowing Rock, NC 28605
Cindy & Cobb Milner,
Jane & Cobb Milner,
Innkeepers

THE GREYSTONE INN

32 Rooms, $260/$380 MAP
1 suite $410/$475 MAP

Visa, MC, Amex
All Private Baths

Open Apr. 1–Jan. 1; Beginning Apr. 1, 1995, open year-round; weekends only Jan. thru Mar.

Children Welcome; No Pets

Golf, Tennis, Swimming Pool, Croquet, Sailing, Water Skiing, Fishing, Hiking, Waterfalls, Champagne Cruise; Spa Facilities

High-Country Breakfast, mid afternoon tea; Gourmet Dinner, Wine & Liquor Available
Non-smoking in public areas
Conference Facilities (30)
Wheelchair Access (1 rm) (Dining Room)

From Asheville: I-40 to I-26 E., Rt. 280S (Exit #9) to Brevard. US 64 W for 17 m. to Lake Toxaway Country Club/Greystone Inn sign. Turn R. for approx. 3.5 mi. to inn.

TEL. 704-966-4700
800-824-5766 (in NC)
Greystone Lane
Lake Toxaway, NC 28747
Tim/Boo Boo Lovelace, Inkps.

With all the diversions of spectacularly beautiful Lake Toxaway at its doorstep, this intimate, historic (National Register) resort-inn combines the lure of its wild mountain setting with the comfort of modern luxuries and an exceptional cuisine. Romantic and tranquil. Complimentary tennis, sailboat, bassboat, ski boat, canoe and daily champagne cruise at all times and complimentary golf certain months. ◆◆◆◆
(Elegant, Waterside, Resort. Member since 1991)

HARMONY HOUSE INN

9 Rooms, $85 B&B
1 suite, $140 B&B

Visa, MC, Amex, Discovr

All Private Baths

Open Year-round

Well-behaved Children accepted
No Pets

Historic district, Tryon Palace, 2 rivers, Croatan Forest, Golf, Tennis, Boating, Museums, Antique Shops

Full Breakfast; Wine & Liquor Available

No Smoking

Conference facilities (10-15)
N/A

I-95, Exit 70 (E) to 4th New Bern exit to E. Front St., then L. on Pollock St. Hwy. 17 runs 1 blk. (N) of Pollock St.

TEL. 919-636-3810
800-636-3113
FAX: 919-636-3810
215 Pollock St.
New Bern, NC 28560

Ed & Sooki Kirkpatrick, Innkeepers

As the Ellis family grew, so did their ca. 1850 home, with additions ca. 1860 (the Union troops were billeted in this home) and ca. 1880. In 1900, the home was sawed in half by the Ellis brothers, moved apart and rejoined with a second front door, hallway and staircase plus a wonderful front porch. Located in the historic district, this unusually spacious Greek Revival inn is decorated with antiques, locally made reproductions, Complimentary wine hour.
(Greek Revival, Village, Breakfast Inn. Member since 1990)

NORTH CAROLINA

HEMLOCK INN

23 rooms, $118/$134 MAP
3 cotts., $140/$162 MAP

No Credit Cards

All Private Baths

Open mid-April-Oct.

Children welcome
No Pets

Hiking, Ping-pong, Shuffle-board, Skittles, Smoky Mtn. Natl. Park, Tubing, Cherokee Indian Res.

Breakfast at 8:30 A.M., Dinner at 6 P.M., Mon. to Sat. & 12:30 P.M. Sun.

Non-smoking dining room

Wheelchair access (8 rms.)

High, cool, quiet, and restful, this inn is beautifully situated on top of a small mountain on the edge of the Great Smoky Mountains National Park. There's a friendly informality in the family atmosphere and authentic country furniture. Honest-to-goodness home cooking and farm-fresh vegetables are served bountifully from Lazy Susan tables. (*Rustic, Mountain, Inn. Member since 1973*)

Hwy. 74, Hyatt Creek Rd.- Ela exit & bear R. to L. turn on Hwy. 19 for approx. 1 mi. to R. turn at inn sign. Take country road 1 mi. to L. turn at next inn sign.

TEL. 704-488-2885
Galbreath Creek Rd.
P.O. Drawer EE,
Bryson City, NC 28713
Morris & Elaine White; Ella Jo & John Shell, Innkeepers

THE INN AT THE TAYLOR HOUSE

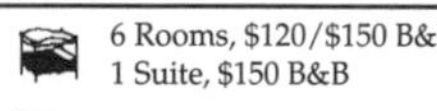

6 Rooms, $120/$150 B&B
1 Suite, $150 B&B

Visa, MC

All Private Baths

Open Apr. 1–Dec. 1

Children by prior arrangement; No Pets

Hiking, Fishing, Horseback riding, Canoeing, Championship Golf, Skiing, Grandfather Mtn., Blue Ridge Parkway, Shops & Restaurants

Breakfast; Arrangements for private parties, weddings & family reunions

Smoking on porch only

Wheelchair Access (1 rm.) (dining room)

A bit of Europe in the peaceful, rural heart of the Blue Ridge Mountains, this charming farmhouse is decorated with fine antiques, oriental rugs, artwork, and European goose-down comforters on all the beds. Bright fabrics, wicker furniture and flowering plants invite guests to rock on the wide wraparound porch, while the friendly hospitality and memorable breakfasts add to their pleasure. (*Elegant, Country, Breakfast Inn. Member since 1990*)

Boone/Banner/Elk accessible from any direction. NC Hwy. 105(N) for 2.8 mi. to Valle Crucis. L. on Hwy. 194 for 8/10 mi. to inn.

TEL. 704-963-5581
FAX 704-963-5818
Highway 194, P.O.Box 713
Valle Crucis, NC 28691

Chip & Roland Schwab, Innkeepers

THE LORDS PROPRIETORS' INN

 20 Rooms, $155/$215 MAP; B&B (Sun. & Mon.)

 None. We will bill.

 All Private Baths

Open Year-round Exc. Dec. 24 & 25

 Children Welcome No Pets

 Swimming at owners' country estate, Fishing, Tennis nearby, Golf privileges, Two Waterfront Courses

 Breakfast, Dinner (Tues.–Sat.); Wine available with dinner

 Smoking in parlors and on porches

Conference Facilities (30)

 Wheelchair Access (1 rm., dining rm. & conf. fac.)

From N.C. 32 and U.S. 17 continue on Broad St. to the inn.

TEL 919-482-3641
FAX 919-482-2432
300 No. Broad St.
Edenton, NC 27932

Arch & Jane Edwards, Innkeepers

14 The Inn offers twenty spacious guest rooms in three restored homes on over an acre of grounds in Edenton's Historic District. Breakfast and dinner are served to guests in the Inn's dining room. Guest reactions: "We've enjoyed some fairly decent lodgings—Shepherds, the St. Francis, the George V. We have never felt as well cared for as at your Inn. The quality of the surroundings and management, the attention to detail, and the genuine friendliness you and your staff offer make the Lords Proprietors' Inn truly exceptional." "The food is unsurpassable."
(*Traditional, Village, Inn. Member since 1990*)

MAST FARM INN

9 Rooms, $100/$150 MAP
3 Cabin Cottages, $150/$175

Visa, MC

10 Private, 1 Shared Baths

Open Dec. 27–Mar. 5; Apr. 20–Nov. 6

Appropriate for Children over 12; No Pets

 Fishing, Hiking, Skiing, Golf, Canoeing

 Breakfast, houseguests only; Dinner, Tues.- Sat.; Sun. Lunch; BYOB

No Smoking

 Wheelchair Access (1 rm., dining rm.)

Boone/Banner Elk area accessible from any direction. Watch for Valle Crucis sign on NC 105. Mast Farm Inn is 2.6 mi. from NC105 on SR1112.

TEL. 704-963-5857
FAX 704-963-6404
P.O.Box 704
Valle Crucis, NC 28691

Sibyl & Francis Pressly, Innkeepers

10 Nestled in the beautiful mountain valley community of historic Valle Crucis near the Blue Ridge Parkway, the inn sits on an 18-acre operating farm. The inn features extensive flower gardens and the farm's freshest vegetables and salads help provide guests with a special dining experience. Life at this restored, antique-filled inn (National Register of Historic Places) is pleasant and peaceful. Lodgings are in the main house or in the renovated blacksmith shop, woodwork shop or loom house.
(*Traditional, Country, Inn. Member since 1988*)

NORTH CAROLINA

THE ORCHARD INN

9 Rooms, $105/$130 B&B
3 Cottages $150/$175 B&B

MC, Visa

All Private Baths

Open Year-round except 3-4 days at Christmas

Appropriate for children over 10; No Pets

Walking Paths, Birding, Antiquing, Biltmore Estate, Blue Ridge Parkwy, Golf

Breakfast; Lunch-private parties of 12 or more only; Dinner, BYOB

No Smoking

Conference Facilities (20)

N/A

6 Guests enjoy a truly memorable dining to the strains of Mozart and Vivaldi on the glassed in wrap-around porch with a breathtaking view of the Southern Blue Ridge Mountains. This turn-of-the-century-country house invites you to relax in its exceptional living room with a large fireplace, antiques, folk art, books, and puzzles. Or stay in one of the three cozy fireplaced cottage suites, complete with whirlpool baths and decks.
(*Traditional, Country, Inn. Member since 1985*)

I-26, NC Exit 28 & turn toward Saluda for 1 mi. to L. on Hwy. 176 for .5 mi. to inn on R.

TEL. 800-581-3800
704-749-5471
FAX 704-749-9805
P.O. Box 725
Saluda, NC 28773

Veronica & Newell Doty,
Innkeepers

PINE CREST INN

21 Rooms, $95/$165 B&B
9 suites, $140/$165 B&B

Visa, MC, Amex, Discov

All Private Baths

Open Feb. 1–Jan. 2

Children Welcome
No Pets

Golf, Tennis, Swimming, Hiking, Horseback riding, Biltmore House & Gardens, Blue Ridge Pkwy., Chimney Rock., Fence Equestrian & Nature Ctr. Whitewater Rafting, Waterfalls, Shops & Antiques, Putting green & Volleyball

Full Breakfast, Picnic Baskets Available, Dinner; Liquor & Wine available

Smoking Limited

Conference Facilities (up to 60)

Wheelchair Access 1 rm., dining rm. (conf. fac.)

7 The famed hunt country and foothills of the Blue Ridge Mountains are the setting for this classic Inn. Listed on the National Register, the Pine Crest Inn features luxurious guest rooms, fireplaces, verandas, crisp mountain air, exceptional dining, and gracious service. Fresh grilled seafood, Maryland crab cakes, rack of lamb, and roast duck are the Chef's specialties. An extensive library, intimate bar, and manicured grounds add to the atmosphere of casual elegance. Hiking trails, nature walks, and natural waterfalls are nearby. AAA Four Diamond Award.
(*Elegant, Mountain, Inn. Member since 1991*)

From I-26, Exit 36 to Tryon. Follow Rte. 108/176 to town of Tryon. Turn on New Market Rd. Follow signs to inn.

TEL. 800-633-3001
704-859-9135
FAX: 704-859-9135
200 Pine Crest Lane
Tryon, NC 28782

Jeremy & Jennifer Wainwright,
Innkeepers

RICHMOND HILL INN

 33 Rooms, $130/$235 B&B
3 Suites, $150/$325 B&B

 Visa, MC, Amex

 All Private Baths

 Open Year-round

 Children Welcome; Pets Not Permitted

 Croquet Lawn on site, Biltmore Estate tours, Blue Ridge Pkwy., Antiques & Crafts Shopping

 Breakfast, Dinner; Sun. Brunch; Wine & Liquor Available

 Non-Smoking Guest Rooms

Conference Facilities (64)

Wheelchair Access (1 rm., dining rm. & conf. fac.)

From I-240, take 19/23 Weaverville exit. Take exit 251 (UNC-A). L. at bottom of Ramp; L. onto Riverside Dr., R. on Pearson Bridge Rd., R. on Richmond Hill Dr.

TEL. 704-252-7313
800-545-9238
FAX 704-252-8726
87 Richmond Hill Dr.
Asheville, NC 28806
Susan Michel, Innkeeper

This 1889 Queen Anne mansion was one of the most elegant and innovative structures of its time. Now on the National Register, the Inn's rich oak paneling, handcarved fireplaces, and high ceilings provide an unusually luxurious setting in the Blue Ridge Mountains. Canopy and 4-poster beds, a highly acclaimed gourmet restaurant, and fresh mountain air are just a few of the attractions.
(*Elegant, Mountain, Inn. Member since 1991*)

SNOWBIRD MOUNTAIN LODGE

 22 Rooms, $119/$125 AP

 Visa, MC

 All Private Baths

 Open April 14–Nov. 12

 Children over 11 welcome; No Pets

 Hiking, Rafting, Horseback riding, Smoky Mountain Railroad, Cherokee Indian sites nearby, Billiards, Ping-pong, Shuffleboard on site

 Breakfast, Lunch, Dinner BYOB

 Smoking in restricted areas

Wheelchair Access (2 rooms and dining room)

Robbinsville, at Hardees, Rte. 129 N for 1. 5 mi. to L. on NC Rte. 1116 for 3.3 mi. to R. at stop sign (Rte. 1127) for 6.7 mi. to lodge. (Also, by following signs to Joyce Kilmer Memorial Forest you will find us.

TEL 704-479-3433
275 Santeetlah Rd.
Robbinsville, NC 28771
Bob & Connie Rhudy, Innkeepers

High up in Santeetlah Gap, not far from the giant hardwood trees of the Joyce Kilmer virgin forest, is this secluded, rustic and picturesque mountain lodge, built of chestnut logs and native stone. Huge fireplaces, comfortable beds in pleasant rooms, a spectacular view and plentiful, delicious meals make this an exceptional vacation retreat. The lodge is on the National Register of Historic Places.
(*Traditional, Mountain, Lodge. Member since 1973*)

NORTH CAROLINA

THE SWAG COUNTRY INN

 13 rooms, $190/$375 AP
2 cabins, $275/$375 AP

 Visa, MC, Discovr

 All Private Baths

 Mid-May–End of October

Children in cabins only; No Pets

 Hiking trails, Racquetball, Badminton, Croquet, Horseshoes, Pond with boat and dock

 All 3 Meals, hors d' oeuvres; Coffee beans & grinders in rooms; BYOB

 No inside Smoking

 Conference Facilities (20)

Wheelchair Access (1 rm.; dining rm. & conf. fac.)

This mountain hideaway is built of hand-hewn logs and is situated on 250 acres of secluded and unspoiled land. The Swag Country Inn is perched at 5,000 feet, with a private entrance into The Great Smoky Mountains National Park. Guests enjoy 50-mile breathtaking views. It offers countless amenities, such as a fine library, fireplaces, Jacuzzis, and exceptional cuisine.

(*Rustic, Mountain, Retreat. Member since 1991*)

NC I-40, Exit 20 to Hwy. 276 for 2.8 mi. to Swag sign. Just after sign, turn R. 4 mi. up blacktopped road to Swag gate. L. on gravel driveway 2.5 mi. to inn.

TEL. 704-926-0430; 926-3119; FAX 704-926-2036
212-570-2071 Off Season
FAX: 212-5709-9756

Hemphill Rd.,Rte. 2, Bx 280A
Waynesville, NC 28786
Deener Matthews, Innk.

THE WAVERLY INN

15 Rooms, $90/$120 B&B
1 Suite, $165 B&B

 Visa, MC, Amex, Discov.

 All Private Baths

 Open Year-round

 Children Welcome
No Pets

 Biltmore Estate, Flat Rock Playhouse, Antiquing, Golf, Blue Ridge Pkwy., Hiking, Horseback Riding, Fishing

 Full Breakfast; Refreshments; Evening Social Hour; Arrangements for Private Parties, BYOB

 Smoking Limited

Wheelchair Access (dining room)

In an area rich with history and natural scenery, this National Register inn is the oldest surviving inn in Hendersonville's historic district. Walking distance to fine restaurants, exceptional shopping and antiquing. Polished wood, turn-of-the-century fittings, 4-poster beds, wide porches and rocking chairs are only part of the picture that brings guests back to this comfortable, friendly place. Join us for our daily social hour between 5 and 6 P.M. or just raid the cookie jar for one of Darla's famous inn house delectables.

(*Traditional, In-Town, Breakfast Inn. Member since 1991*)

From I-26, NC Exit 18B, US-64 (W); Continue 2 mi. into Hendersonville. Bear R. onto Rte. 25(N) for 800 yards. Inn is on L. at corner of 8th Ave. & N. Main.

TEL. 800-537-8195; 704-693-9193; FAX 704-692-1010

783 N. Main St.
Hendersonville, NC 28792

John & Diane Sheiry, Darla Olmstead, Innkeepers

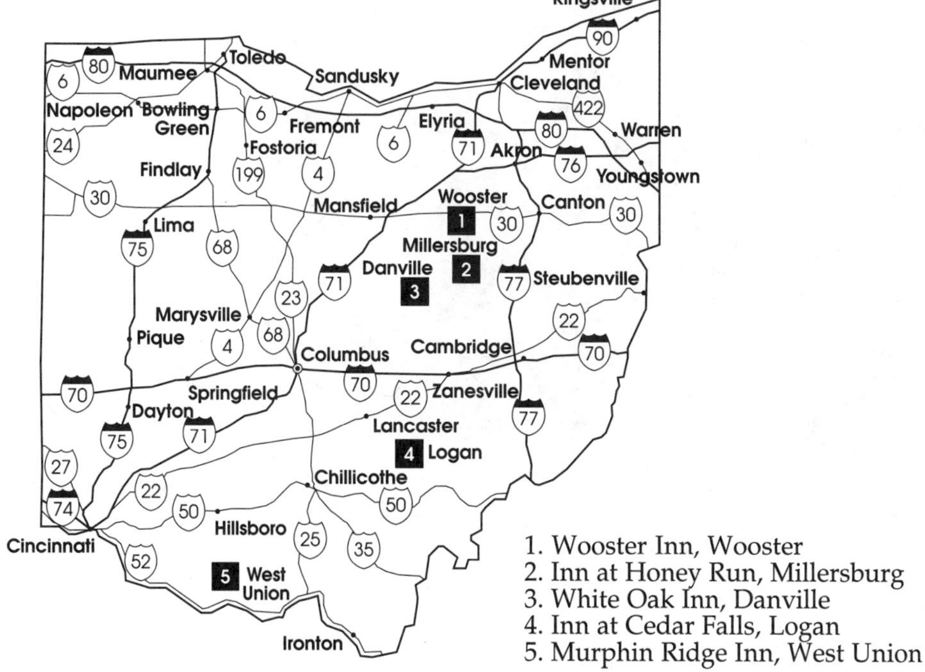

1. Wooster Inn, Wooster
2. Inn at Honey Run, Millersburg
3. White Oak Inn, Danville
4. Inn at Cedar Falls, Logan
5. Murphin Ridge Inn, West Union

THE INN AT CEDAR FALLS

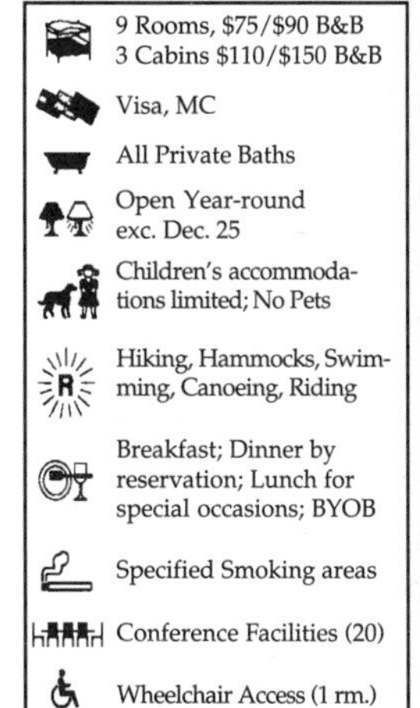

9 Rooms, $75/$90 B&B
3 Cabins $110/$150 B&B

Visa, MC

All Private Baths

Open Year-round exc. Dec. 25

Children's accommodations limited; No Pets

Hiking, Hammocks, Swimming, Canoeing, Riding

Breakfast; Dinner by reservation; Lunch for special occasions; BYOB

Specified Smoking areas

Conference Facilities (20)

Wheelchair Access (1 rm.)

From Columbus: Rte. 33 (S) to Logan exit, R. on Rte. 664, 9.5 mi. L. on Rte. 374. Inn is 1 mi. on L.

TEL. 614-385-7489
FAX: 614-385-0820
21190 State Route 374
Logan, OH 43138

Ellen Grinsfelder, Innkeeper

4 The restored and comfortably rustic 1840 Log House is an open kitchen-dining room, serving the most refined of gourmet dishes, prepared from home-grown produce. Guest rooms in the barn-shaped Inn building combine antique beds, private baths, and sweeping views of meadows, woods and wildlife. Fully-equipped 1800 log cabins, accommodating up to four, feature privacy. Facilities are appropriate for small business retreats, as well. The rugged and beautiful Hocking Hills State Park with glorious caves, waterfalls and forests flanks the Inn on three sides. *(Rustic, Country, Inn. Member since 1989)*

THE INN AT HONEY RUN

39 rooms, $75/$150 B&B
2 Two Bedroom cottages, $150/$275 (4 pers.) B&B
Visa, MC, Amex
All Private Baths
Open Jan. 16 (95)–Dec. 17; Dec. 26 (95)–Jan. 1 (96)
Children accepted in Inn only, not honey combs or cottages
No pets
Birdwatching, Nat. trails, Game room, Amish Ctry, Cheese Factories, Craft Shops, Golf, Tennis, Hiking Trails
Breakfast, Lunch (except Sun.), Dinner
BYOB for guest rooms only
Some Non-smoking rooms & areas, No smoking in dining room
Conference Facilities (72)
Wheelchair Access (1 rm., dining rm., conf. fac.)

2 Located on sixty acres of woods and pasture, this prize winning, contemporary inn offers a serene blend of nature and luxury. Stay in the INN and watch birds from your picture window. Enjoy breakfast in your earth-sheltered Honeycomb Room with its stone fireplace and sliding glass door overlooking a wild flower meadow. Relax in a two-bedroom Guest House with panoramic views of Holmes Country hills. Explore the sights, crafts and backroads of scenic Holmes County, home to the world's largest Amish population.
(*Contemporary, County, Inn. Member since 1984*)

From Millersburg: Rtes. 62/39 (E) for 2 blocks. L. on Rte. 241 (N) for 1.9 mi. R. (E) on County Rd. 203 for 1.5 mi.

TEL. 216-674-0011
800-468-6639
FAX. 216-674-2623
6920 County Road 203
Millersburg, OH 44654

Jim Root, Innkeeper

MURPHIN RIDGE INN

10 Rooms, $75/$90 B&B

No Credit Cards
All Private Baths

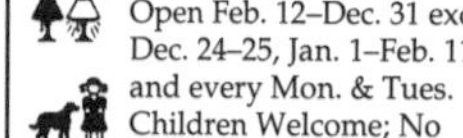

Open Feb. 12–Dec. 31 exc. Dec. 24–25, Jan. 1–Feb. 11 and every Mon. & Tues.
Children Welcome; No Pets
Amish Shops, Serpent Mound, Appalachia Preserve, Golf, Herbs, Scenic Drives nearby
Lunch & Dinner Wed. thru Sun.; BYOB for guest rooms only
No Smoking
Conference Facilities (25-30)
Wheelchair Access (6 rms.)

5 An historic, tranquil 717-acre woodland farm is the setting for this prize-winning Inn. The brick farmhouse (1810) blends 3 attractive dining rooms, original fireplaces, unique Adams County crafted gifts and Art Gallery. Guests enjoy delicious entrees; homemade soups, made daily; luscious desserts from the professional kitchen staff. The custom furnished contemporary guesthouse includes fireplace rooms, porches, gathering room. Swimming, tennis, nature trails, horseshoes, shuffleboard, basketball, croquet on premises.
(*Country, Inn. Member since 1992*)

Rte 32 E. Rte. 41 S. To Dunkinsville 6 mi, R. on Wheatridge 1 1/2 mi. R. on Murphin Ridge 1/2 mi.

TEL. (513) 544-2263
750 Murphin Ridge Rd.
West Union, OH 45693

Mary & Robert Crosset Jr., Innkeepers

WHITE OAK INN

 10 Rooms, $75/$140 B&B (3 Rms. with Fireplaces)

 Visa, MC, Discov

 All Private Baths

Closed Christmas

 Appropriate for Children over 12; No Pets

 Lawn games, Bicycling, Amish country touring, Antiquing, Golf, Fishing, Canoeing, Hiking

 Breakfast; Dinner by reservation; BYOB

 No Smoking

Conference facilities (25)

 N/A

From I-71: Rte 36 (E) or Rtes. 95 (E) and 13 (S) to Mt. Vernon. Then U.S. Rte 36 (E) 13 mi. to Rte 715. From I-77: Rte. 36 (W) 43 mi. to Rte 715. Take Rte. 715 (E) 3 mi. to inn.

TEL. 614-599-6107
29683 Walhonding (S.R. 715)
Danville, OH 43014

Ian & Yvonne Martin, Innkeepers

Turn-of-the-century farmhouse in a quiet, wooded country setting. Antiques and period decor, fireplace and square grand piano in the common room, front porch with swings and rockers, a screened house, and elegant meals, all make your stay a memorable one. Experience simple country pleasures. The Inn is close to Ohio's Amish area for quilts, oak furniture, antiques, and cheeses. We also offer guest participation in our onsite archaeological dig and other special event packages. (*Traditional, Country, Inn. Member since 1989*)

THE WOOSTER INN

 15 Rooms, $75/$85
2 Suites, $100/$120

 Visa, MC, Amex, Diners, Discov.

 All Private Baths

 Closed Dec. 25–26

 Well Supervised Children accepted; Pets Accepted

 Golf, Tennis, Amish settlements, Football Hall of Fame in Canton, Wooster College activities

 Breakfast, Lunch, Dinner, Wine & Beer available

 Non-Smoking Dining Room

Conference Facilities (50)

 Wheelchair Access (3 rms., dining rm.)

I-71 (S) to Burbank. L. on Rte. 83 (S), 18 mi. Wooster Exit, R. at Rte. 585 (S) for 200 ft. R. at Wayne Ave. Inn .7 mi. on L. I-71 (N) to US-30 E., 24 mi to Wooster Exit at Madison R. Follow to Bever to Wayne Ave. 2 mi. Turn R, 2 blks. to inn.

TEL. 216-264-2341
FAX 216-264-9951 (24 hr.)
801 E. Wayne Ave.
Wooster, OH 44691
Andrea Lazar, Innkeeper

The spacious campus of the College of Wooster is the setting for this pleasant inn, which overlooks the college golf course, where inn guests may play. Tastefully decorated rooms offer modern comfort and quiet, and cuisine in the attractive dining room is excellent and fresh. The Ohio Light Opera and college events provide cultural and recreational diversions.
(*Traditional, In-Town, Inn. Member since 1988*)

OREGON

1. The Johnson House, Florence
2. Steamboat Inn, Steamboat
3. Tu Tu' Tun Lodge, Gold Beach
4. Jacksonville Inn, Jacksonville
5. The Winchester Country Inn, Ashland 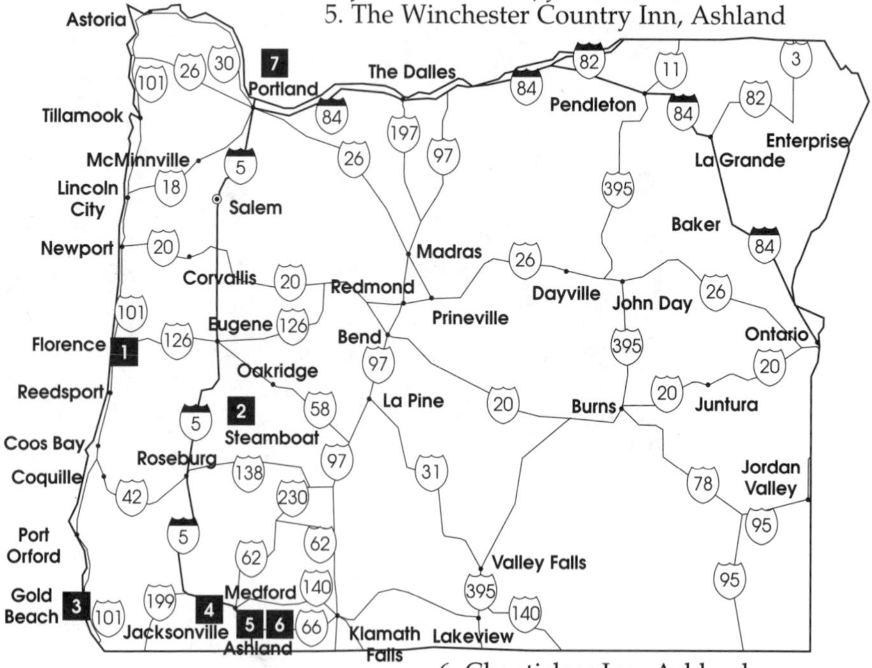
6. Chanticleer Inn, Ashland
7. Heron Haus, Portland

CHANTICLEER INN

6 Rooms, $90/$160 B&B
Visa, MC
All Private Baths
Open Year-round
Children Accepted
No Pets
Bike tours, hot air ballooning, horseback riding, scenic air flights, rock climbing, soaring, mountaineering, snowmobile tours, water skiing, helicopter rides, tennis and golf, nature trips, hang gliding, canoeing, scenic trips, sky diving, caving, carriage rides, sailplane rides, jet skiing, scuba diving, and much more.
Breakfast; Wine & Liquor available
Smoking outside only
N/A

6 Cozy and comfortable inn nestled between the Siskiyou and Cascade mountains in the charming village of Ashland, home of the award-winning Oregon Shakespeare Featival. Recreational opportunities abound as well as excellent restaurants and shopping. Luxuriously appointed guest rooms all with A/C, private baths. Sumptuous breakfasts, outstanding views, quite, tranquility, gorgeous gardens 1/3 acre, close in location. Off-season packages, corporate rates and innkeeping workshops available. (*Traditional, Village, Breakfast Inn. Member since 1994*)

From Hwy. 5 N.: Exit at Siskiyou Blvd. N. to Stratford Inn (about 2.5 mi.), turn left at Union St. Go two blocks to Fairview. Turn R. Go 1 block to Gresham. Turn R. Located at corner of Fairview & Gresham. From Hwy. 5 S.: Exit at 1st Ashland Exit #19, proceed to end of exit ramp. Turn R. Proceed to stop light. Turn L., go about 2.5 mi. into the center of town. Turn R. onto Gresham, just past the Manna Bakery. Go two blocks to 120 Gresham, inn is on the L.

TEL. 800-898-1950
FAX: 503-482-1919
120 Gresham St.
Ashland, OR 97520
Pebby Kuan, Innkeeper

HERON HAUS

5 rooms, $125/$250
$85.00 Single

Visa, MC

All Private Baths

Open Year-round

Children over 10
No Pets

1 1/2 hr to beach (Oregon Coast), 1 hr Mt Hood, Skiing, Hiking, 1 hr Touring Wine Country—Willomette Valley

Breakfast

No Smoking

N/A

Located in Northwest Portland, minutes from city center.

TEL. 503-247-1846
FAX 503-243-1075
2542 N.W. Westover Rd.
Portland, OR 97210
Julie Keppeler, Innkeeper

7 This elegant, three-story, turn of the century tudor sits high in the west hills, offering versatile accommodations for both the business traveler and romantic get-a-ways. Each room has sitting areas, work areas, phones with computer hook-ups, and TV's. All have queen or king size beds. The baths offer special extras—one has spa on windowed porch; another has shower with seven shower-heads. Off-street parking is provided. Two and a half blocks down the hill is the Nob Hill area with little boutiques, specialty shops and some of the best eating places in Portland. (*Elegant, In-Town, Breakfast Inn. Member since 1994*)

JACKSONVILLE INN

8 rooms, $80/$125 B&B
1 Suite, $175 B&B

Visa, MC, Discov, Amex, Diners

All Private Baths

Open Year-round

Children Accepted
No Pets

Museum, Antiques, Hiking, Wineries, Swimming, White Riv. Rafting, Shopping, Shakespeare Fest., Britt Music Festival

Restaurant, Bistro
Sun. Brunch, Lounge
Wine & Liquor available

Non-smoking Rooms

Conference Facilities (80)

N/A

I-5(N), Ex. 30, R. Crater Lk. Hwy (Hwy. 62) to Medford. R. on McAndrews, L. on Ross Lane, R. on W. Main (238), R. on Calif. St. I-5(S), Exit 27, L. on Barnett, R. on Riverside; L. on Main St. R. on Calif.

TEL. 503-899-1900; 800-321-9344; FAX 503-899-1373
175 E. California St.
Jacksonville, OR 97530
Jerry & Linda Evans, Innkps.

4 Housed in one of Jacksonville's early (1861) permanent structures, built during the gold rush, the inn has locally quarried sandstone walls flecked with bits of gold in the dining room and lounge. In addition to guest rooms furnished with restored antiques, the inn boasts one of Oregon's most award-winning restaurants, with superb dining and a connoisseur's wine cellar.
(*Traditional, Village, Inn. Member since 1991*)

THE JOHNSON HOUSE

6 rooms (including a small garden cottage), $75/$105 B&B

Visa, MC

3 Private Baths

Open Year-round

Appropriate for Children over 12; No Pets

Ocean Beaches, Dunes, Woods, Lakes, River, Whale-watching, Horseback Riding, Hiking, Fishing, Golf

Full Breakfast

Smoking on porches

N/A

This is like "grandmother's house," with treasured heirlooms, amusing photographs and curios, where you are welcomed with a cup of tea. The faithfully restored 1892 Victorian inn is in the center of Old Town, a waterfront community on Oregon's scenic central coast. Just a block away from docks and small commercial fishing fleet. Blue and ivory guest rooms feature lace curtains, down comforters, and many books. Breakfasts are lavish and imaginative.
(*Traditional, Village, Breakfast Inn. Member since 1991*)

1 block (N) of Siuslaw River; 2 blocks (E) of Coast Hwy. 101; corner First & Maple in Old Town.

TEL. 503-997-8000
216 Maple St.
PO Box 1892
Florence, OR 97439

Ronald & Jayne Fraese,
Innkeepers

STEAMBOAT INN

8 Cabins, $90 EP
7 Cotts./suites, $135/$215

Visa, MC

All Private Baths

Closed Jan.–Feb. & limited service Mar.–Apr.

Children Accepted
No Pets

Fishing for steelhead, 35 mi. of public water, Backpacking, Hiking

Breakfast & Lunch, Dinner by reservation
Wine Available

No Smoking

Conference facilities (70 day mtg. & 40 overnight)

Wheelchair Access (2 rms., dining rm. & conf. fac.)

Nestled among towering firs, choose from cozy streamside cabins, cottages in the woods or luxurious suites on the river. You may want a picnic for a days outing to Crater Lake, local waterfalls, swimming holes, hiking trails or the wineries of Douglas County. Be sure to be back for the evening dinner. This creative meal, featuring fresh local ingredients and Oregon wine, will add the perfect finish to an already perfect day!
(*Traditional, Waterside, Inn. Member since 1984*)

I-5 to Roseburg. Steamboat Inn is 38 mi. (E) on Rte. 138. Inn is 70 mi. (W) of Crater Lake and 40 mi. (W) of Diamond Lake, on Rte. 138.

TEL. 503-498-2411
FAX 498-2411 (1 ring +*2)
42705 North Umpqua Hwy.
Steamboat, OR 97447-9703

Sharon & Jim Van Loan,
Innkps.
Patricia Lee, Manager

TU TU' TUN LODGE

16 rooms, $85/$165 EP
4 Suites, Guesthouses, $165/$275 EP

Visa, MC

All Private Baths
Open Year-round

Children Welcome;
No Pets Welcome

Guided Fishing, White Water Boat Trips, Self-guided Hiking Trails, Beachcombing, 9-hole Golf Course, 4-hole Pitch & Putt, Horseshoes.

Breakfast, Lunch (Reg. Guests Only), Dinner, MAP available; Wine & Liquor Available

No Smoking

Conference Facilities (40)

Wheelchair Access (8 rms., dining rm. & conf. fac.)

Gold Beach, Hwy. 101 (E) 7 mi. along north side of Rogue River to Lodge.

TEL. 503-247-6664
FAX 504-247-0672
96550 North Bank Rogue
Gold Beach, OR 97444

Dirk & Laurie Van Zante, Innkeepers

Nestled on the banks of the Rogue River, Tu Tu' Tun Lodge combines the comforts of a first-class resort with the congeniality of a small hideaway. Guests enjoy hors d'oeuvre around the large stone fireplace, gourmet dining overlooking the river and madrone wood fires on the terrace at dusk. Come, partake in the serious challenge of the steelhead and salmon, experience the excitement of a white water excursion or simply enjoy some solitude.

(*Rustic, Waterside, Lodge. Member since 1989*)

THE WINCHESTER COUNTRY INN

12 Rooms, $89/$125 B&B
6 suites, $115/$170 B&B

Visa, MC, Discovr.

All Private Baths

Open Year-round

Children Accepted
No Pets

White water rafting, Hiking, XC & Downhill Skiing, Shakespeare Festival, Boating, Sailing, Music

Breakfast, Sunday brunch, Dinner; Wine & Liquor available

Smoke-free Inn

Conference facilities (35)

Wheelchair Access (1 rm., conf. fac.)

From I-5 (S), 1st Ashland exit. R. on Valley View, L. on Hwy. 99 for 3 mi. to Ashland. R. on 2nd St. From I-5 (N), 1st Ashland exit, for 4 mi. to Ashland. L. on 2nd St.

TEl. 503-488-1113
800-972-4991
FAX: 503-488-4604
35 So. Second St.
Ashland, OR 97520
Michael and Laurie Gibbs, Innkeepers

A true country inn in the heart of the city, this handsomely restored, century-old Victorian home (National Register) invites you to enjoy an atmosphere of sophisticated country living. Beautiful tiered gardens and gazebo welcome guests each morning for breakfast. Guest rooms offer antiques, balconies and patios. Gourmet dinners and champagne Sunday brunch are served.

(*Traditional, Victorian, In-Town, Inn. Member since 1991*)

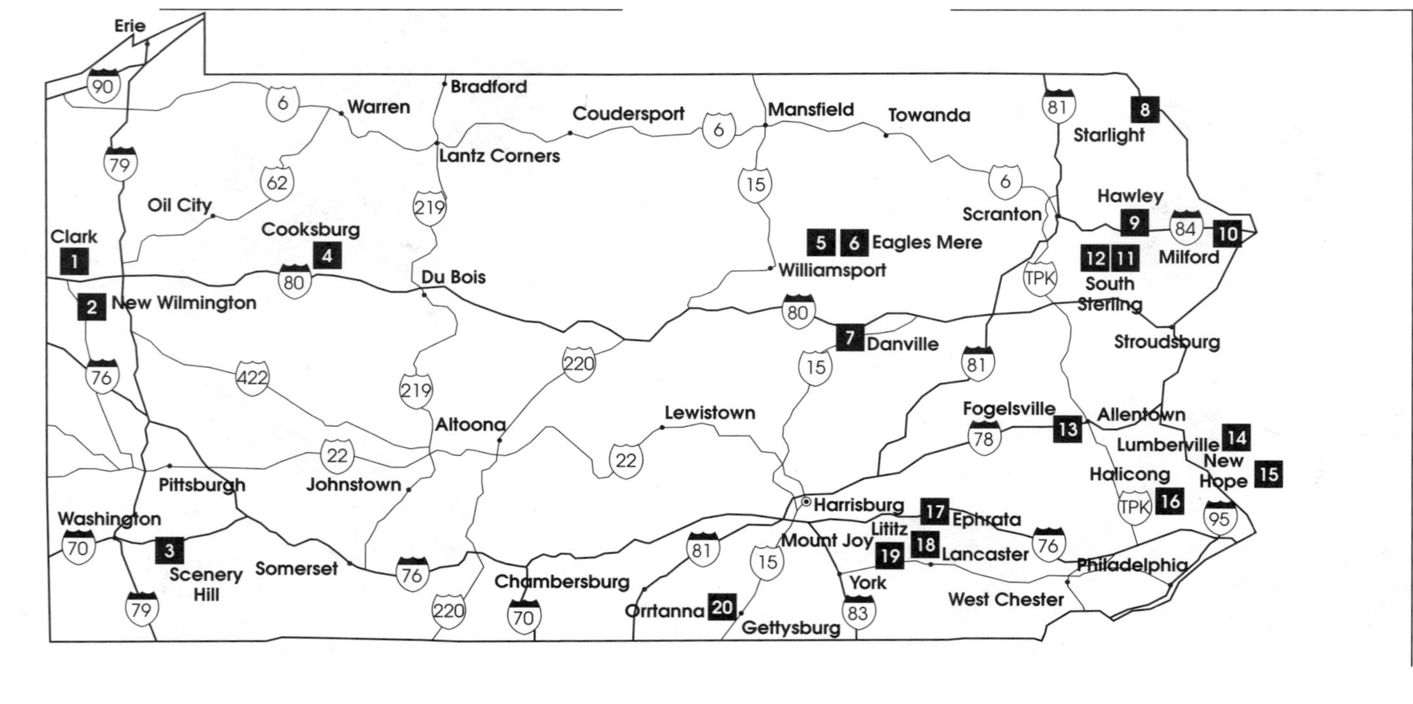

1. Tara, Clark
2. The Tavern, New Wilmington
3. Century Inn, Scenery Hill
4. Gateway Lodge, Cooksburg
5. Crestmont, Eagles Mere
6. Eagles Mere Inn, Eagles Mere
7. Pine Barn Inn, Danville
8. Inn at Starlight Lake, Starlight
9. The Settlers Inn, Hawley
10. Cliff Park, Milford
11. The French Manor, South Sterling
12. Sterling Inn, South Sterling
13. Glasbern, Fogelsville
14. 1740 House, Lumberville
15. Whitehall Inn, New Hope
16. Barley Sheaf Farm, Holicong
17. Smithton Inn, Ephrata
18. Swiss Woods B&B, Lititz
19. Cameron Estate Inn, Mount Joy
20. Hickory Bridge Farm, Orrtanna

BARLEY SHEAF FARM

8 Rooms, $150/$170 B&B
2 Suites, $145/$195 B&B

Visa, MC, Amex

All Private Baths

Closed only Christmas week

Children allowed if their behavior will permit other guests to enjoy the quiet atmosphere No Pets

Pool, Croquet, Flea Markets, Shopping, Historic touring, Antiquing, Sports

Full Country Breakfast; Wine & Cheese for afternoon treat ocasionally

Smoking restricted to the outside areas

Conference Facilities (25)

N/A

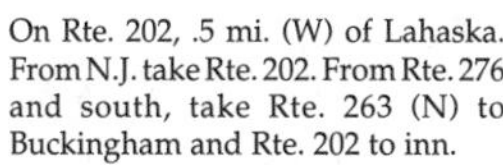

On Rte. 202, .5 mi. (W) of Lahaska. From N.J. take Rte. 202. From Rte. 276 and south, take Rte. 263 (N) to Buckingham and Rte. 202 to inn.

TEL. 215-794-5104
FAX 215-794-5332
Route 202, Box 10
Holicong, PA 18928

Veronika & Peter Süess, Innkeepers

16 Barley Sheaf is an early Bucks County farm comfortably situated on 30 acres at the end of a long tree-lined drive. Once owned by the playwright George S. Kaufmann, it was the gathering place in the 30's and 40's for some of Broadway's brightest illuminaries, ie. Dorothy Parker, Mose Hart, the Marx brothers, etc. A park-like setting provides beauty and seclusion ideally suited for a romantic getaway. Lovely guest rooms, gracious common rooms, exceptional hospitality and an outstanding breakfast are Barley Sheaf hallmarks.
(*Traditional, Village, Breakfast Inn. Member since 1982*)

CAMERON ESTATE INN

18 Rooms, $65/$110 B&B

Visa, MC, Amex, Diners, Discov

16 Private, 2 Shared Baths

Closed Christmas Eve & Day

Appropriate for Children over 12; No Pets

Library, TV, Lawn Games, Golf, Swimming & Tennis nearby

Breakfast, Dinner, Sun. Brunch; Wine & Liquor available

Smoking Accepted

Conference Facilities (60)

N/A

Rte. 283 to Rte. 772(S) to 1st light in Mt. Joy and R. on Main, 2nd light L. (S. Angle St.), R. on Donegal Springs Rd. at stop turn, L. on Colebrook, R. back onto Donegal Springs Rd., 1/4 mile on R.

TEL. 717-653-1773
FAX 717-653-9432
1895 Donegal Springs Rd.
Mount Joy, PA 17552
Stephanie Seitz, Larry Hershey, & Mindy Goodyear, Innkeepers

19 The Inn & Restaurant occupy the rural Lancaster County estate of Simon Cameron, Abraham Lincoln's first Secretary of War. Rooms at Cameron are furnished in grand style and are individually decorated; 7 have fireplaces. The restaurant offers a fine selection of American and classic foods as well as the appropriate wines. Groff's Farm Restaurant, the county's finest, is also nearby. Mobil Guide★★★
(*Elegant, Country, Inn. Member since 1982*)

CENTURY INN

	3 Rooms, $85/$100 EP 10 Suites, $95/$150 EP
	No Credit Cards
	All Private Baths
	Open Year-round (lodging & parties)
	Children Accepted No Pets
	Tennis, Croquet, Volleyball Court, Many Small Shops in Scenery Hill
	Breakfast, Houseguests only; Lunch, Dinner (Dining rm. open Mar. 19–Dec. 30) ; Wine & Liquor Available
	Smoking accepted
	Conference Facilities (175)
	N/A

3 It's not hard to believe this is the oldest operating inn (1794) on the National Pike (U. S. 40) when you see the hand-forged crane in the original kitchen and the vast array of rare antiques adorning this intriguing inn. Called one of the dining super stars in the Pittsburgh area, the inn, now celebrating its 200th year in operation, is a favorite destination for both country inn buffs and gourmands.
(Traditional, Village, Inn. Member since 1972)

From I-70, Bentleyville Exit. Rte. 917(S) to Rte. 40. 1 mi.(E) to the inn.

TEL. 412-945-6600
FAX: 412-945-5114
Scenery Hill, PA 15360
Megin Harrington, Innkeeper

CLIFF PARK INN & GOLF COURSE

	18 rooms, $103/$155 B&B
	Visa, MC, Amex, Diners, Discov
	All Private Baths
	Open Year-round
	Children Accepted with Parents; No Pets
	9-hole Golf Course, Hiking Trails, XC Skiing, Delaware River for Swimming, Fishing, Rafting, Canoeing
	Breakfast, Lunch & Dinner; MAP rates available; Wine & Liquor Available
	Smoking Permitted
	Conference Facilities (60 day, 36 overnight)
	Wheelchair access (5 rms., dining rm. & conf. fac.)

10 Historic Country Inn (1820) on secluded 600-acre estate, surrounded by long-established golf course (1913). Spacious rooms, some with fireplaces. This historic inn offers old-fashioned hospitality, heirlooms reflecting the life and times of the Buchanan family. Antiques and lace grace the guest rooms and the maple-shaded veranda overlooks the golf course. Their master chef specializes in American, French and Cajun cuisine. Golf, Honeymoon and Country wedding packages.
(Traditional, Country, Inn. Member since 1990)

I-80 to Ex. 34B; Rte. 15N becomes 206N, into Milford, PA. Thru traffic light, 2 blks. L. onto 7th & go 1.5 mi. to inn. From I-84, Ex. 10, Milford, (E) on Rte. 6 for 2 mi. R. on 7th St. for 1.5 mi. to inn.

TEL. 717-296-6491
800-225-6535
FAX 717-296-3982
RR4, Box 7200
Milford, PA 18337-9708
Harry W. Buchanan III, Innkp.

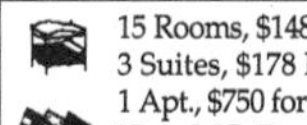

CRESTMONT INN

15 Rooms, $148 MAP
3 Suites, $178 MAP
1 Apt., $750 for 6 nights, EP
Visa, MC, Personal Checks
All Private Baths
Open May 1–Nov. 1; Late Fall & Winter Weekends
Children Welcome; No Pets
Swimming pool, Har-Tru Tennis, Golf, Lake Activities, Hiking trails, Ice Skating, XC Skiing, Tobogganing, Cultural activities, summer months
Country Breakfast & Dinner
Wine & Liquor available
Smoking in limited areas
Conference Facilities (30)
Wheelchair Access (9 rms., cocktail lounge, dining rm.)

From I-80, Exit 34 to 42 (N) for 33 mi. to Eagles Mere village. Continue thru town & follow Crestmont signs.

TEL. 717-525-3519
Res: 800-522-8767
Crestmont Dr.
Eagles Mere, PA 17731

Kathleen & Robert Oliver, Innkeepers

5 Situated atop the highest mountain in Sullivan County, Crestmont Inn is a perfect place to relax, unwind and enjoy the peaceful quietude of our natural woodland setting, and spacious grounds. Enjoy skiing or hiking through some of the most spectacular scenery in the state. Try sailing or canoeing on crystal clear Eagles Mere Lake. Classical music, gourmet dining by candle light, fresh mountain air, and warm hospitality beckon you to a special place that has kept people returning for almost a century.
(*Traditional, Federal, Country, Inn. Member since 1989*)

EAGLES MERE INN

13 Rooms, $129/$175 MAP
2 Suites, $165/$195 MAP
15% Serv Charge, 6% Tax
Visa, MC, Pers. Checks
All Private Baths
Open Year-round
Children Welcome
No Pets
Swimming, Boating, Beautiful Scenery & Hiking Trails, Golf, Tennis, XC Skiing, Ice Toboggan
Full Breakfast & 5 course Gourmet Dinner included; Wine and Liquor available
Smoking allowed in Pub only
Conference Facilities (30)
N/A

From East take Rte. 80 west to Exit #34 (Buckhead) to Rte. 42 (N) From West take Rte. 80 to Rte. 220 (N) then to Rte. 42 (N)

TEL. 717-525-3273
800-426-3273
Mary & Sullivan Avenues
Eagles Mere, PA 17731

Susan & Peter Glaubitz, Innkeepers

6 Called by Norman Simpson: "The last unspoiled resort," this Mountain top Inn offers Ultimate Stress relief! Peace & quiet 400 paces from a private, pristine, crystal clear, lake and thousands of acres of Forest. Incredible Waterfalls & Vistas! Innkeeper has run 3 & 4 star Hotels & Restaurants. Guests enjoy personal attention, warm Hospitality, Gourmet meals, outstanding Wines and peaceful relaxation. Excellent for couples seeking a quiet & relaxing getaway or for small Family reunions. Featured as a special vacation spot in numerous Travel Writer articles. Call for Brochure
(*Traditional, Mountain, Inn. Member since 1993*)

PENNSYLVANIA

THE FRENCH MANOR

- 6 Rooms, $120/$180 B&B
  3 suites, $160/$225 B&B
- Visa, MC, Amex, Discov
- All Private Baths
- Open Year-round
- Not suitable for Children
  No Pets
- Hiking, Croquet, Beautiful scenery, Swimming, Tennis, XC Skiing, Ice Skating nearby
- Breakfast, Lunch, Dinner; French restaurant; MAP rates available; Wine & Liquor available
- Non-smoking Dining
- Conference Facilities (18)
- Wheelchair Access (1 rm.)

11 The French Manor is an elegant country inn, secluded and private, like a secret lookout separate from the populace. You may choose from four spacious guest rooms in the Manor, three suites (one with jacuzzi and fireplace) or two comfortable rooms in the Carriage House. Enjoy a hearty breakfast with a view of the mountains from our dining room or in your room by request. Dinner is a celebration of authentic French cuisine in an atmosphere of elegance and refinement unmatched in the area.
(*Elegant, Country Inn. Member since 1991*)

From NYC: I-80(W), PA Exit 52 to Rte. 447(N) to Rte. 191(N) to S. Sterling. Turn L. on Huckleberry Rd. From Phila: NE extension of PA Tpke. to Pocono Exit 35. Follow Rtes. 940(E), 423(N) to 191(N) 2.5 mi. to Huckleberry Rd.

TEL. 717-676-3244
FAX: 717-676-9786
RES. 800-523-8200
Box 39, Huckleberry Rd.
South Sterling, PA 18460
Ron & Mary Kay Logan, Innkps.

GATEWAY LODGE

- 8 Rooms, $85/$95 EP, $105/$115 B&B, $155/$165 MAP; Cottages & B&B $138/$208 MAP; $188/$308 EP $100/$125
- Visa, MC, Amex, Discov
- 11 Private Baths
- Open Year-round exc. Wed. & Thur of Thanksgiving week & Dec. 24–25 (EP Cottages remain open)
- Children 8 & over
  No Pets
- Canoeing, Innertubing, Hiking, Biking, Antiquing, Birdwatching, Swimming, Golf, Tennis & Horseback Riding nearby, Ice Skating, Cross-country Skiing
- Breakfast; Lunch Limited (May–Oct.) Dinner
  Wine & Liquor Available
- Smoking on porch
- Meeting Facilities (50)
- Wheelchair Access (8 cottages, dining rm. & conf. fac.)

4 Amid some of the most magnificent forest scenery east of the Rocky Mountains, this rustic log cabin inn has been awarded one of the ten best country inns in the U.S. Guests gather around the large stone fireplace in the living room and savor wonderful home-cooked meals by kerosene light. Main inn guests may enjoy the indoor swimming pool, sauna, tea time, and turn-down service.
(*Rustic, Country, Inn. Member since 1983*)

From W I-80 to Exit 9 (Clarion). Turn L, go to 3rd Light. Go Straight thru Light (Rte. 68), travel 10 mi. to stop sign. At stop Sign turn R on Rte. 36 (S) go 4 mi, cross over bridge. Continue 1/4 mi. S. Lodge on L. From E I-80 to Exit 13 (Brookville), R on Rte. 36 (N). Travel 16 mi. Lodge on R.

TEL. 814-744-8017
800-843-6862 (PA/MD)
FAX 814-744-8017
Route 36, Box 125
Cooksburg, PA 16217
Joe & Linda Burney, Innkps.

GLASBERN

 10 Rooms, $105/$120 B&B
13 Suites, $120/$235 B&B

 Visa, MC

 All Private Baths, 16 Whirlpools

 Open Year-round

 Children Accepted
No Pets

 Swimming pool, Trails thru 100 acres, Bicycling, Hot air ballooning, Fishing

 Breakfast; Dinner Daily, Wine & Liquor Available

 Smoking Allowed

 Conference Facilities (16)

Wheelchair Access (4 rms, dining rm. & conf. fac.)

From I-78 take Rte. 100(N) for .2 mi. to L. at light (W) for .3 mi. to R. on Church St. (N) for .6 mi. to R. on Pack House Rd. for .8 mi. to the inn.

TEL. 610-285-4723
FAX 610-285-2862
2141 Pack House Rd.
Fogelsville, PA 18051-9743

Beth & Al Granger, Owners

13 Fireplaces and whirlpools embellish this farm established in the early-1800's, contemporized as an inn in 1985. Contemporary American cuisine is served under the Barn's timbered cathedral ceiling. Flower and vegetable gardens flourish where a farm family once labored for basic provisions. Pastoral landscape, complemented by streams, ponds and paths, provides illusions of the past mingled with present-day comforts—private phones, TV's and VCR's. AAA & Mobil 3 stars; ABBA 4 crowns. (*Traditional, Country, Inn. Member since 1988*)

HICKORY BRIDGE FARM

6 Rooms, $79/$89 B&B

Visa, MC

All Private Baths

Closed Christmas week

Children and Pets Accepted

Gettysburg touring, Fishing, Swimming, Hiking, Bicycling, Golf, Skiing

Breakfast (Houseguests), Dinner, Fri., Sat., Sun.

No Smoking

Conference facilities (125)

Wheelchair Access (conf. fac.)

Gettysburg, Rte. 116(W) to Fairfield and R. 3 mi.(N) to Orrtanna. Or Rte. 977 to Rte. 30(E) for 9 mi. Turn (S) at Cashtown for 3 mi. to inn.

TEL. 717-642-5261
96 Hickory Bridge Rd.
Orrtanna, PA 17353

Robert & Mary Lynn Martin, Dr. & Mrs. James Hammett, Innkeepers

20 A quaint country inn, offering 3-bedroom farmhouse accommodations and four private cottages and a delightful restaurant in a restored barn, filled with antiques, located 8 miles west of Gettysburg on a family operated farm. Fine, family-style dining Friday, Saturday and Sunday. Inn open seven days a week with bountiful morning meals. A quiet, rural setting with a country store museum, gift shop . . . a wonderful "country place!"
(*Traditional, Country, Breakfast Inn. Member since 1978*)

THE INN AT STARLIGHT LAKE

26 Rooms, $110/$154 MAP
Cottage Rooms $127/ $154 MAP
1 Suite, $170/$200 MAP
Visa, MC
20 Private Baths
Open Year-round
Children Accepted
No Pets
Swimming, Boating, Tennis, Ice Skating, XC Skiing, Lawn Sports, Fishing, Golf
Breakfast, Lunch, Dinner, Sunday Brunch
Wine & Liquor available
No Smoking in Dining Room
Conference facilities (20)
Wheelchair Access (dining rm.)

8 Since 1909, guests have been drawn to this classic country inn on a clear lake in the rolling hills of northeastern Pennsylvania. The atmosphere is warm, congenial, and informal. Twenty-two Mainhouse and cottage rooms, (one w. fireplace), suite w. Jacuzzi, and a family house and conference center complete this delightful little universe. There are activities for all seasons: swimming, boating, fishing, tennis, cycling, hiking; in winter, x-c skiing and ice-skating. Lakeside dining offers outstanding cuisine with emphasis on fresh ingredients, baked goods, and homemade pastas.
(Traditional, Waterside, Inn. Member since 1976)

From N.Y. Rte. 17, Exit 87 (Hancock). On Rte. 191 (S) 1 mi. to Rte. 370 (W), turn R. 3 mi. to sign on R. take R. 1 mi. to inn. From I-81, Exit 62, local roads; map sent on request.

TEL. 717-798-2519
800-248-2519
FAX 717-798-2672
Starlight, PA 18461
Judy & Jack McMahon, Innkeepers

THE PINE BARN INN

75 Rooms, $46/$68 EP
Visa, Amex, CB, Disc, MC, Diners
All Private Baths
Open Year-round
Children Accepted; Pets (ltd. accommodations)
Golf, Tennis, Swimming, Horseback riding, Racquetball nearby
Breakfast, Lunch, Dinner
Wine & Liquor available
Non-smoking dining area
Conference Facilities (50)
N/A

7 A part of the history and tradition of Danville for over 100 years, this inn began life first as a barn and then as a riding stable. Today, the restaurant and original rooms still occupy the original barn, with many additional rooms in more recently completed buildings. The restaurant has been renowned for decades for its fresh seafood and home-made pies and pastries.
(Rustic, Village, Inn. Member since 1976)

From I-80, Exit 33, Rte. 54 (E) 2 mi. to Danville. L. 1st traffic light, signs to Medical Ctr. Inn at entrance to Geisinger Med. Ctr.

TEL. 717-275-2071; 800-627-2276; FAX 717-275-3248
#1 Pine Barn Place
Danville, PA 17821
Martin & Barbara Walzer, Innkeepers

1740 HOUSE

23 Rooms, $75/$115 B&B
1 Suite, $100/$175 B&B

Personal Checks Accepted

All Private Baths

Open Year-round

No Children
No Pets

Pool at inn, Canoeing, Riding, Golf, Individual A/C

Breakfast, Daily to houseguests; Dinner, served on special occasions; BYOB

Non-smoking Dining Room

Conference facilities (22)

N/A

From NY & NJ use 202 (S) to Rte. 32. From I-95 use New Hope/Yardley exit (N) to New Hope. Lumberville is 7 mi. (N) of New Hope on Rte. 32.

TEL. 215-297-5661
River Rd. (Hwy. 32)
Lumberville, PA 18933

Robert John Vris, Innkeeper

14 An intimate view of the river from a lovely room with a private terrace or balcony is only one of the pleasures at this 18th-century, restored farmhouse on the the banks of the Delaware River. *Newsweek, McCall's, Glamour, & Harper's Bazaar* have all listed The 1740 House as one of their 10 favorite inns. The excellent restaurant is open to the public seasonally.
(*Traditional, Waterside, Breakfast Inn. Member since 1973*)

THE SETTLERS INN

16 Rooms, $75/$100 B&B
3 Suites, $110/$140 B&B

Visa, MC, Amex

All Private Baths

Open Year-round
Appropriate for Children
No Pets

Lake Wallenpaupack, Upper Delaware River, Promised Land State Park, Golf, Skiing, Horseback, Canoeing, Fishing, Glass Museum, Antique Shops

Breakfast, Lunch, Dinner
Wine & Liquor available

Smoking designated areas

Conference Facilities (100)

Wheelchair Access (dining rm.)

I-84 Exit 7, Route 390N. to Route 507 N. to Rt. 6 W., then 2 1/2 miles to Inn

TEL. 717-226-2993
800-833-8527
FAX 717-226-1874
Four Main Avenue
Hawley, PA 18428

Jeanne & Grant Genzlinger, Innkeepers

9 Reminiscent of a small European hotel, this Tudor Manor is in the small turn-of-the-century town of Hawley. Chestnut wood beams, a bluestone fireplace, leaded windows, outdoor patio & herb gardens add to the ambiance. The dining room is well known for a cuisine based on our region's food traditions highlighting products from local farms. Lake Wallenpaupack, the upper Delaware River, and Promised Land State Park are nearby providing many recreational activities. Antique shops and summer theatre in town. (*Traditional, Village, Inn. Member since 1992*)

SMITHTON INN

8 Rooms, $65/$135 B&B
1 Suite, $140/$170 B&B
Visa, MC, Amex
Private Baths, some Whirlpools
Open Year-round
Children and Pets by prior arrangement
Library, Gardens, Touring, Antiques, Epharta Cloister, Farmers Country Markets, Golf, Craft Center, Museums, Art Galleries
Breakfast
No Smoking
Wheelchair Access (1 rm.)

17 A romantic 1763 stone inn located in Lancaster County among the Pennsylvania Dutch. Rooms are large, bright and cheerful with working fireplaces, canopy beds, desks, leather upholstered furniture, Penn. Dutch quilts, candles, chamber music, refrigeration, feather beds (by prior arrangement), books, reading lamps, fresh flowers and night shirts. Common rooms are warm and inviting with fireplaces. The Inn is located in the Penn Dutch farmlands where visiting the farm homes of Amish, Mennonites & Brethern people is an easy matter.
(Colonial, Village, Breakfast Inn. Member since 1987)

From North, PA Take. Exit 21 & Rte. 222 (S). From South, Hwy. 30 to Rte. 222 (N). From North or South, Exit Rte. 222 at Rte. 322 (W) for 2.5 mi. to inn.

TEL. 717-733-6094
900 W. Main St.
Ephrata, PA 17522

Dorothy Graybill, Innkeeper

THE STERLING INN

38 Rooms, $130/$160 MAP EP
16 Suites, $170/220 MAP EP
Visa, MC, Amex, Discov
All Private Baths
Open Year-round
Children Accepted
No Pets
Indoor Pool, Lake, Tennis, Hiking, Horseback Riding, Golf, XC Skiing, Sleigh Rides, Antiquing
Breakfast, Lunch, Dinner. B&B rates on request
Wine & Liquor available
No Smoking in Dining area
Conference facilities (100)
Wheelchair Access (3 rm., dining rm. & conf. fac.)

12 The country inn you've always looked for, but never thought you'd find. A friendly, romantic atmosphere with beautiful gardens, crystal clear streams, a waterfall, Victorian suites with fireplaces, & horse-drawn sleigh rides. Attractive rooms, indoor pool & spa, & outstanding meals make this family operated, 130-year-old inn everything you thought a country inn should be. Honeymooners may enjoy the "Innkeeping with Romance" Package. Social groups and family reunions can be accommodated in the lodge or guest house.
(Traditional, Country, Inn. Member since 1974)

I-84, Exit 6, Rte. 507 (S), 3 mi. to Rte. 191 (S), 3 mi. to inn. I-80 (W) Exit 50, Rte. 191 (N) 25 mi. to inn. I-80 (E) Rte. 380 to Rte. 423 (N), to 191 (N), .5 mi. to inn.

TEL. 717-676-3311
RES: 800-523-8200
FAX: 717-676-9786
Rte. 191
South Sterling, PA 18460
Ron & Mary Kay Logan, Innkeepers

SWISS WOODS

7 Rooms, $75/$125 B&B
1 Suite, $105/115

Visa, MC, Discov

All Private Baths

Open Year-round except Dec. 24–26

No Pets, Children Welcome ($15 add. per person)

Canoe at lake, Hiking and Birdwatching

Breakfast

No Smoking

N/A

From PA Tpk Exit 21 to 222 S. to 322 W. Follow to Rt. 501. Take 501 S. 1 mi. to first crossroads. Turn R. on Brubaker Valley Rd. Go 1 mi. to the lake. Turn R. on Blantz Rd. The Inn is on your left.

TEL. 717-627-3358; 800-594-8018; FAX 717-627-3483

500 Blantz Rd.

Lititz, PA 17543

Werner & Debrah Mosimann, Innkeepers

Surrounded by meadows and gardens, Swiss Woods is a quiet retreat on 30 acres in Lancaster's Amish Country. All rooms here feature patios or balconies, some with views of the Speedwell Forge Lake, and decorated with light furnishings so popular in Europe. Fabulous breakfasts in a sunlight common room highlight your stay. Take a hike, watch the birds and relax! German spoken.
(*Traditional, Country, Breakfast Inn. Member since 1993*)

TARA — A COUNTRY INN

25 Rooms $250/$350 MAP
2 Suites $430/430 MAP
Visa, MC, Amex, Discov
All Private Baths
Open Year-round
Not appropriate for Children
Kennels nearby for Pets
Bocci, Croquet, Boating, Golf, Biking, Pool Table, Antiquing, XC Skiing, Swim Pools, Sauna, Steam
Breakfast, Lunch, Dinner, B&B rates available
Wine & Liquor available
Smoking in designated areas
Conference Facilities (60)
Wheelchair Access (din-ing rm. & conf. fac.)

From I-80, exit 1N, Rte. 18 (N) for 8 mi. Inn is located on (E) side overlooking Lake Shenango

TEL. 412-962-3535
800-782-2803

3665 Valley View, Box 475

Clark, PA 16113

Jim & Donna Winner, Innkeepers

If you loved the movie *Gone With the Wind*, you will love Tara. Built in 1854, this magnificent mansion reflects the golden days of the antebellum South, with rooms charmingly decorated to recall the grace and grandeur of yesteryear. Delightfully different cuisine, from gourmet to family-style, is served in the three totally different restaurants. Mobil 4-star and AAA 4-diamond.
(*Elegant, Country, Inn. Member since 1986*)

PENNSYLVANIA

THE TAVERN AND LODGE

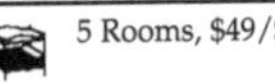
5 Rooms, $49/$60, B&B

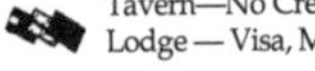
Tavern—No Credit Cards; Lodge — Visa, MC

All Private Baths

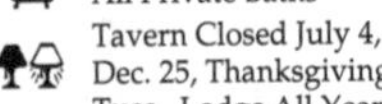
Tavern Closed July 4, Dec. 25, Thanksgiving & Tues., Lodge All Year

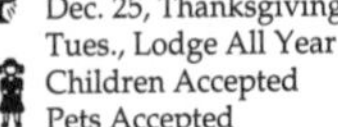
Children Accepted
Pets Accepted

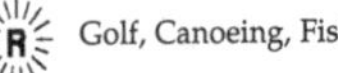
Golf, Canoeing, Fishing

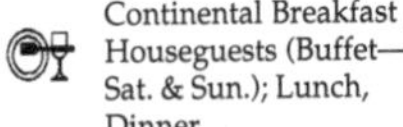
Continental Breakfast, Houseguests (Buffet—Sat. & Sun.); Lunch, Dinner

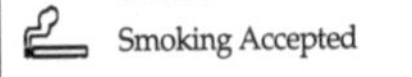
Smoking Accepted

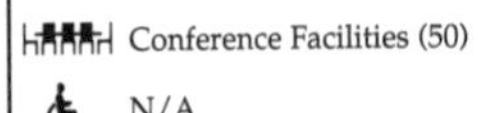
Conference Facilities (50)

N/A

Turn back the clock & escape the rush of today. Awaken the clip-clop of horse-drawn buggies, visit the nearby mills & covered bridges, explore the many unique shops featuring local handcrafted items, see a simpler way of life in the Amish country of western Pennsylvania. Enjoy our legendary sticky rolls as your server calls the menu of our bounteous homestyle cooking which has kept guests returning for over 60 years. After dinner retire to one of our comfortable guest rooms for a relaxing evening.
(Traditional, Village, Inn. Member since 1974)

I-80 E; Exit 1S onto Rte. 60 (S), to Rte. 18 (S). (E) on Rte. 208, 1 mi. to inn. I-80 W to Exit 2 (Mercer) south on Rte. 19 to West on 208, 8 miles to Inn.

TEL. 412-946-2020
Lodge: 412-946-2091
101 N. Market St.
New Wilmington, PA 16142

Mary Ellen Durrast,
Innkeeper

THE WHITEHALL INN

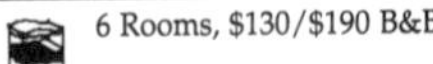
6 Rooms, $130/$190 B&B

Visa, MC, Amex, CB, Diners, Discov.

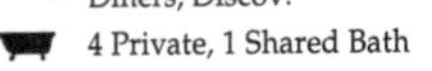
4 Private, 1 Shared Bath

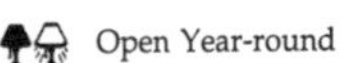
Open Year-round

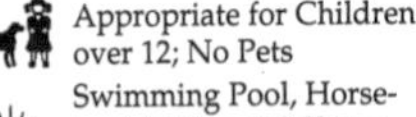
Appropriate for Children over 12; No Pets

Swimming Pool, Horseback Riding, XC Skiing, Public & Private Golfing, Tennis, Hiking, Delaware River Water Sports

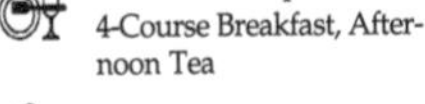
4-Course Breakfast, Afternoon Tea

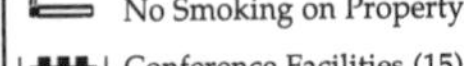
No Smoking on Property

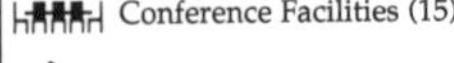
Conference Facilities (15)

N/A

Experience a "Top 10 B&B Inn"! With heirloom sterling and European china and crystal, indulge in a four-course candlelight breakfast and afternoon high tea called "sumptuous" by *Bon Appetit*. The culinary genius of Suella abounds! Most rooms with fireplaces. Enjoy the pool, rose garden, and horses—all situated on the grounds of our 1794 estate. Evening turn-down service with our own Whitehall chocolate truffles. "After years in their niche, the Wasses continue to stand above the rest." It's all very special! Ask about our Spring Tea Concerts.
(Traditional, Country, Breakfast Inn. Member since 1990)

Hwy. 202 (S) from New Hope to Lahaska. L. on to Street Rd. to 2nd intersection, bear R. on Pineville Rd. Continue 1.5 mi. to inn on R.

TEL. 215-598-7945
800-37-WHITE
RD2, Box 250
1370 Pineville Rd.
New Hope, PA 18938
Mike and Suella Wass,
Innkeepers

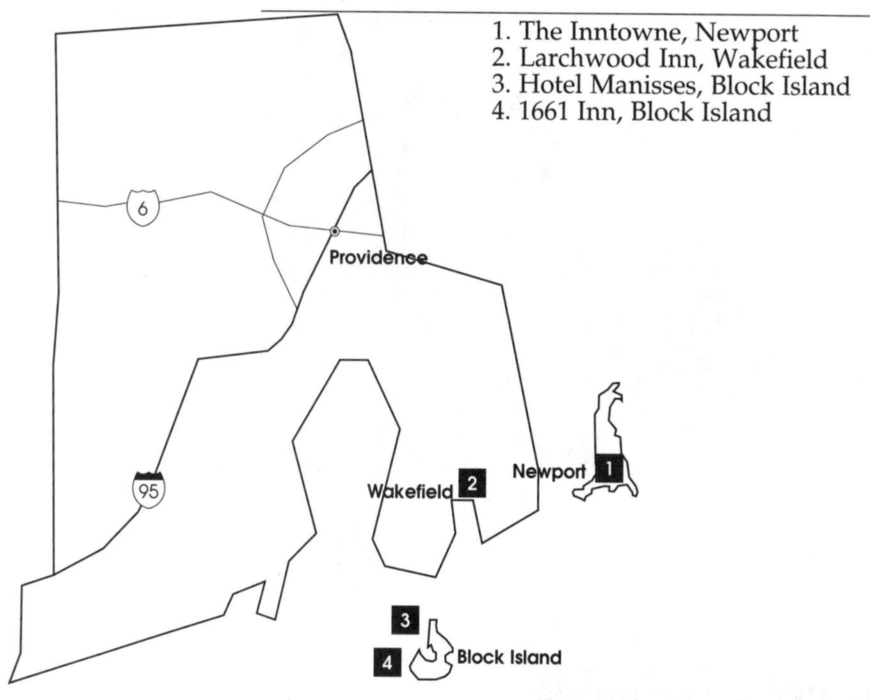

HOTEL MANISSES

 17 Rooms, $75/$350 B&B

 Visa, MC, Amex

 All Private Baths; 4 Jacuzzis

 Open year-round

Appropriate for Children over 10; No Pets

Swimming, Yachting, Hiking, Biking, Horse-back Riding

 Breakfast, Lunch, Dinner Wine & Liquor available

 Non Smoking rooms available

 Conference Facilities (80)

N/A

By ferry: Providence, Pt. Judith, Newport, RI & New London, CT. By air: Newport, Westerly, Providence, RI & New London, Waterford, CT. Contact inn for schedules.

TEL. 401-466-2421;
401-466-2063
FAX 401-466-3162
Spring St.
Block Island, RI 02807
Joan & Justin Abrams,
Rita & Steve Draper,
Innkeepers

Step into 19th Century yesteryear with a stay at this Romantic Victorian hotel featuring 17 meticulously appointed rooms with private baths and authentic Victorian furniture; some rooms with jacuzzis. The award-winning dining room serves dinner every evening. Sample delicious selections from our varied menu as featured in *Gourmet* magazine. Tableside flaming Coffees, After dinner drinks & Desserts served nightly in the upstairs parlour.
(*Elegant, Victorian, Village, Inn. Member since 1982*)

THE INNTOWNE

21 Rooms, $110/$200 B&B
5 Suites, $195/$250 B&B

Visa, MC, Amex

All Private Baths

Open Year-round

Appropriate for Children over 12; No Pets

Beaches, Tennis Boating, Mansion touring

Continental Breakfast, Afternoon Tea

Smoking Accepted

Conference Facilities (15)

N/A

This in-town Colonial inn with a garrison roof is right in the center of bustling Newport, just a block from the water. Rooms are bright and cheerful with elegant antiques, good reproductions, and paintings. A few steps from the door are beautiful sunsets, towering sailboat masts, quaint and fashionable shops, and many restaurants.
(*Traditional, In-Town, Inn. Member since 1982*)

Cross Newport bridge, R. at 1st exit sign. R. at bottom of ramp, straight to Thames St. Inn is on corner of Thames and Mary Sts. across from Brick Marketplace.

TEL. 401-846-9200; 800-457-7803; FAX 401-846-1534
6 Mary St.
Newport, RI 02840
Carmella Gardner, Innkeeper

LARCHWOOD INN

19 Rooms, $40/$100 EP

Visa, MC, Amex, Discov, CB, DC

12 Private Baths

Open Year-round

Children Accepted ($10)
Pets Allowed ($5)

Ocean Swimming, Fishing, Golf, Tennis, Historic Touring, Bicycling, Boating

Breakfast, Lunch, Dinner
Wine and Liquor available

Non-smoking dining area

Conference Facilities (125)

Wheelchair Access (dining rm. & conf. fac.)

Watching over the main street of this quaint New England town for 160 years, this grand old house, surrounded by lawns and shaded by stately trees, dispenses hospitality along with good food and spirits from early morning to late night. Historic Newport, picturesque Mystic Seaport, Foxwood Casino, and salty Block Island are a short ride away. Conveniences such as telephones, computers, and fax are available within the confines of this country inn with Scottish flavor. If you've never stayed at the Larchwood Inn, you're in for a real treat!
(*Traditional, In-Town, Colonial. Member since 1969*)

NYC and S.; I-95 (N) to Exit 3A(Rte. 138E) to Kingston, 108 to Wakefield; R. on Main St., follow to inn on R. From Boston and N.; I-95(S) to Exit 9(Rte. 4) which becomes Rte.1. Exit at 1st sign for Wakefield, follow Main St. to inn on R.

TEL. 401-783-5454; 1-800-275-5450; FAX 401-783-1800
521 Main St.
Wakefield, RI 02879
Francis & Diann Browning, Innkeepers.

THE 1661 INN

21 Rooms, $75/$350 B&B (3 w/fireplaces)

Visa, MC, Amex

16 Private Baths; 5 Jacuzzis

Open Year-round

Children of All Ages
No Pets

Swings, Biking, Hiking, Yachting, Swimming, Shelling (9 mos of the yr)

Breakfast, Lunch, Dinner (available at Hotel Manisses); Comp. Wine & Nibble hr.; Wine & Liquor Available

Smoking restrictions

Conference Facilities (80)

N/A

By Ferry: Providence, Pt. Judith, Newport, RI, and New London, CT. By air: Newport, Westerly, Providence, RI or charters. Contact inn for schedules.

TEL.401-466-2421
401-466-2063
FAX 401-466-2858
Spring Street
Block Island, RI 02807
Joan & Justin Abrams
Rita & Steve Draper, Innkeepers

Enjoy the spectacular views of the Atlantic ocean at The 1661 Inn. Most rooms feature ocean views, private decks, jacuzzis and some rooms have fireplaces. The ocean view dining deck with a canopy is a wonderful place to enjoy a relaxing buffet breakfast and special dinners.
(*Elegant, Colonial, Waterside, Inn. Member since 1976*)

The Independent Innkeepers' Association Gift Certificate

A Lovely Gift for Someone Special

The gift of an overnight stay or a weekend at a country inn can be one of the most thoughtful and appreciated gifts you can give your parents or children, dear friends, or valued employees for Christmas, a birthday, an anniversary, or any special occasion. Innkeepers and other employers are discovering this is an excellent way of rewarding their employees, while at the same time giving them some much needed rest and relaxation.

An Independent Innkeepers' Association gift certificate means that you can give the gift of a stay at any one of over 250 member inns from Kennebunkport, Maine to Southern California; from Quebec, Canada to Key West, Florida; from Martha's Vineyard, Massachusetts to Seaview, Washington. We have inns in the Blue Ridge Mountains, on ranches in the western desert, near state parks and forests and nature preserves, in restored villages in historic districts, on lakes and by the sea. Choose your pleasure.

An Independent Innkeepers' Association gift certificate is good for two years and may be purchased through the Independent Innkeepers' Association office by personal check or Mastercard or Visa. With each gift certificate we send along a brand new copy of the *Innkeepers' Register*. For further information call **800-344-5244**.

A five dollar ($5) postage and handling fee will be added to all gift certificate purchases.

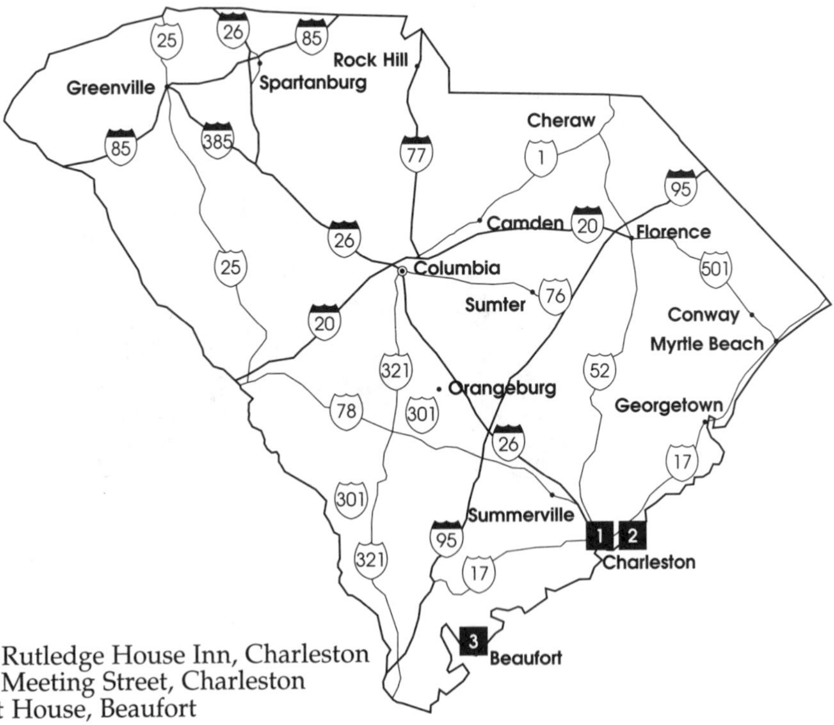

1. John Rutledge House Inn, Charleston
2. Two Meeting Street, Charleston
3. Rhett House, Beaufort

JOHN RUTLEDGE HOUSE INN

16 Rooms $135/$235 B&B
3 Suites, $235/$285 B&B

Visa, MC, Amex

All Private Baths

Open Year-round
Appropriate for Children
No Pets

Historic District, Homes & Garden Tours, Market area within walking distance

Continental Bfkfast. incl., Full Brkfast. available.

Walking distance to many restaurants for lunch and dinner. Afternoon tea w/ light refresh. Evening wine and sherry.

Smoking Restrictions

Conference Facilities (20)

Wheelchair Access (2 rms., conf. fac.)

Built in 1763 by John Rutledge, a signer of the United States Constitution, this elegant home is now a bed and breakfast inn. All guests receive wine and sherry in the ballroom, evening turndown with chocolate at bedside and continental breakfast and newspaper delivered to the room each morning. Free on-site parking. AAA Four Diamond & Mobil Four Star. Historic Hotels of America.

(*Elegant, In-Town, Breakfast Inn. Member since 1992*)

From the Charleston Visitor's Center turn R. onto John St. then L. onto King St. Go one mi. to the Broad St. intersection. Turn R. onto Broad St. The John Rutledge House is the 4th house on the right.

TEL. 803-723-7999; 800-476-9741; FAX 803-720-2615
116 Broad St.
Charleston, SC 29401
Richard Widman, Owner &
Linda Bishop, Innkeeper

THE RHETT HOUSE

10 Rooms, $125/$200 B&B/SC only 4-star B&B

Visa, MC

All Private Baths

Open Year-round

Appropriate for Children over 5; No Pets

Antiques, Historic Antibellum Mansions, Moss-draped Live Oaks, Fabulous Barrier Island Beaches, Tennis, Carriage and Sailboat Tours, Lovely Gardens, Golf

Breakfast, Afternoon tea; Picnic Lunch & Candlelit Dinners by Reservation, Wine & Liquor

Smoking–Verandas Only

Conference Facilities (40)

Wheelchair Access (3 rms., dining rm. & conf. fac.)

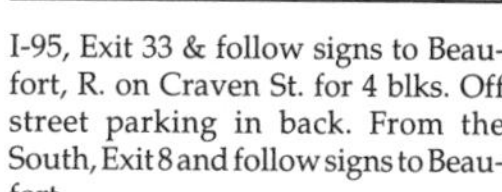
I-95, Exit 33 & follow signs to Beaufort, R. on Craven St. for 4 blks. Off street parking in back. From the South, Exit 8 and follow signs to Beaufort.

TEL 803-524-9030
FAX 803-524-1310
1009 Craven St.
Beaufort, SC 29902

Steve & Marianne Harrison, Innkeepers

Located in historic Beaufort by the bay, The Rhett House Inn is a beautifully restored 1820 plantation house. Furnished with English and American antiques, oriental rugs, fresh flowers, fireplaces and spacious verandahs. Romantic candlelit dinners featuring gourmet regional cuisine are graciously served with an extensive California wine list. Film site for *Forrest Gump, Prince of Tides, The Big Chill,* and several upcoming productions. History laden Beaufort, Charleston and Savannah offer rich exploring. (*Elegant, Greek Revival, In-Town, Inn. Member since 1991*)

TWO MEETING STREET INN

9 Rooms $120/$225 B&B

No Credit Cards

All Private Baths

Closed Christmas (3 days)

Appropriate for Children over 8 years; No Pets

Easy access to Shopping, Antiquing, World-class Golf, Tennis, Beaches, Plantations, Historic Houses, Museums, and Fine Dining

Continental Breakfast; Afternoon Tea and Sherry

No Smoking

N/A

From 26E, exit Meeting Street. Travel south - Located on corner of Meeting and South Battery at White Point Garden.

TEL. 803-723-7322
2 Meeting Street
Charleston, SC 29401

Pete and Jean Spell,
Karen Spell Shaw
Innkeepers

Given as a wedding gift by a bride's loving father, this Queen Anne mansion welcomes all who are romantic at heart. From Southern rockers on the beautiful arched piazza, guests overlook White Point Gardens at Charleston's historic Battery. Family antiques, oriental rugs, Tiffany windows, and four-poster canopy beds create a most charming atmosphere. Share Texas size homemade muffins in the courtyard and enjoy a relaxing afternoon with sherry and tea on the wide veranda. For 55 years, the Spell family has graciously welcomed guests.
(*Elegant, Victorian, In-Town, Breakfast Inn. Member since 1992*)

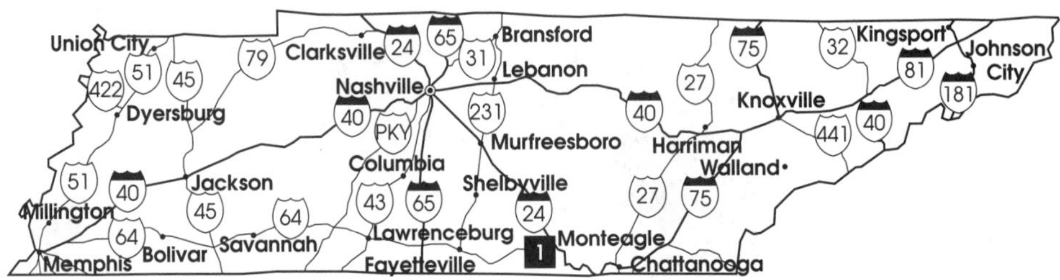

1. Adams Edgeworth Inn, Monteagle

ADAMS EDGEWORTH INN

13 Rooms $65/$115 B&B
1 Suites, $150/$175 B&B

Visa, MC, Amex

All Private Baths

Open Year-round

Children welcome by prior arrangement; No Pets, kennel nearby

TN Aquarium, Sewanne University, Sauna, Music, Theatre, Hike, Tennis, Swim, Bike, Chautauqua

Breakfast, picnics on request, Candlelight Dinners by reservation; BYOB

Smoking Restricted

Conference Facilities (20)

Wheelchair Access (1 rm., dining rm. & conf. fac.)

Nestled in a wilderness atop the Cumberland Mtns., Adams Edgeworth is an 1896 "Camelot" in a forest garden of brooks & tall trestle foot bridges. Come enjoy this National Register Inn featuring English manor decor, fine art, antiques, collector quilts, fireplaces and handmade mattresses on beautiful beds. Tour on bikes or our electric cart around the 150 Victorian cottages in our gated 96-acre private village. Fine candlelight dining by advance reservation. Musical & cultural events. Gift shop. Air conditioned. (*Traditional, Village, Inn. Member since 1992*)

I-24, Exit #134, R. 1/2 mi., L. under "Monteagle Assembly" archway. Thru stone gateway. Follow signs.

TEL. (615) 924-4000
FAX (615) 924-3236
Monteagle Assembly
Monteagle, TN 37356

Wendy & David Adams,
Innkeepers

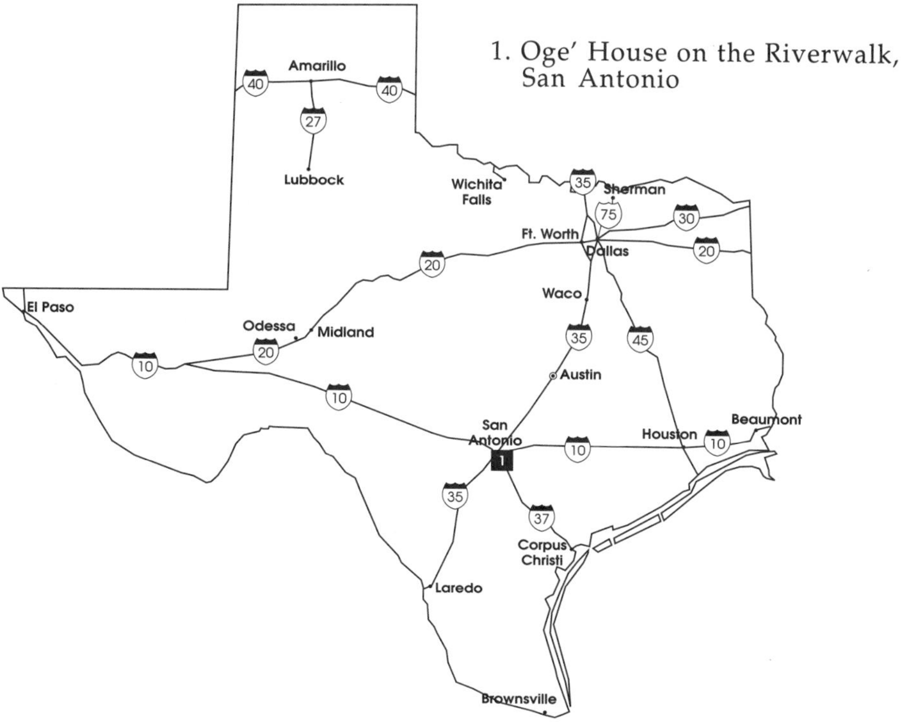

1. Oge' House on the Riverwalk, San Antonio

OGE' HOUSE ON THE RIVERWALK

 5 rooms, $110/$135 AP
4 Suite, $140/$195

 Visa, MC, Amex, Discovr, Diners

 All Private Baths

 Open Year-round

 No Facilities for children or pets

 Riverwalk, Alamo, Missions, Museums, Zoo, Botanical Gardens, 2 Theme Parks (Sea World), Fiesta Texas,Texas Convention Center, Golf, Tennis

 Breakfast

 Smoking outside only

 Conference Facilities (12)

N/A

From airport: Hwy. 37S to Durango Alamodome, exit R on Durango. Go thru 3 stop lights, turn L on Pancoast; Inn is 1st house on R with Black Historic marker at street.

TEL. 210-223-2353
1-800-242-2770
FAX. 210-226-5812
209 Washington St.
San Antonio, TX 78204
Sharrie & Patrick Magatagan, Innkeepers

Privately located on 1½ landscaped acres along the famous San Antonio Riverwalk in The King William Historic District. This 1857 Antebellum Mansion with its grand verandas is known for its elegance, quiet comfort and luxury. Furnished in European and American Antiques, all rooms have King or Queen beds, telephones, cable tv, hospitality refrigerators and some with fireplaces and verandas. Conveniently located downtown within 6 blocks of Alamo Convention Center. Alamodome shopping, dining and entertainment. Fax and PC hookups. (*Elegant, In-Town, Breakfast Inn. Member since 1994*)

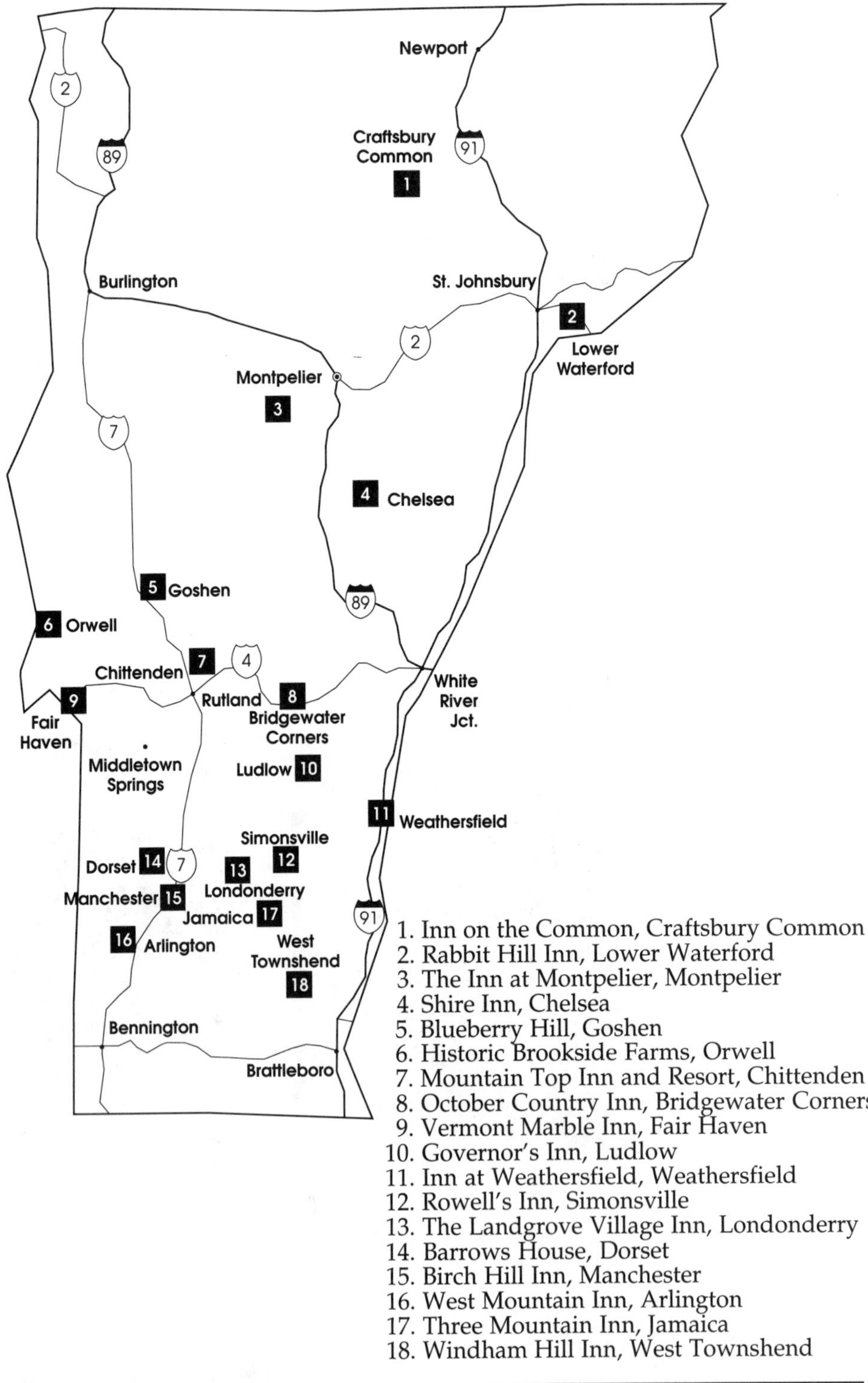

1. Inn on the Common, Craftsbury Common
2. Rabbit Hill Inn, Lower Waterford
3. The Inn at Montpelier, Montpelier
4. Shire Inn, Chelsea
5. Blueberry Hill, Goshen
6. Historic Brookside Farms, Orwell
7. Mountain Top Inn and Resort, Chittenden
8. October Country Inn, Bridgewater Corners
9. Vermont Marble Inn, Fair Haven
10. Governor's Inn, Ludlow
11. Inn at Weathersfield, Weathersfield
12. Rowell's Inn, Simonsville
13. The Landgrove Village Inn, Londonderry
14. Barrows House, Dorset
15. Birch Hill Inn, Manchester
16. West Mountain Inn, Arlington
17. Three Mountain Inn, Jamaica
18. Windham Hill Inn, West Townshend

BARROWS HOUSE

18 Rooms, $135/$230 MAP
10 Suites, $135/$230 MAP

Visa, MC, Amex, Discov

All Private Baths

Open Year-round

Children Welcome
Pets in 3 Cottages only

Heated Pool,Sauna, Tennis Courts, Bike, Skiing, Hiking, Historic & Fine Arts centers, Shopping, Game & Puzzle Room

Breakfast, Dinner, B&B available, Liquor & Wine available

Smoking Restrictions

Conference Facilities (20)

Wheelchair Access (1 rm., dining rm. & conf. fac.)

Manchester, Rte. 30 (N) 6 mi. to inn on R. Accessible from Vt. Rtes. 7, 4, 11, 30 and I-91 & 87.

TEL. 802-867-4455
800-639-1620 (Outside VT)
FAX 802-867-0132
Route 30
Dorset, VT 05251
Linda & Jim McGinnis, Innkeepers

The Barrows House is a collection of white clapboard buildings situated on 11 acres in the heart of a small picturebook Vermont town. Guests have a choice of 28 accommodations in eight different buildings, each with a history and style of its own. Dining at the Barrows House is an informal and delicious adventure in American regional cuisine. Whether with iced tea in the gazebo and English garden or mulled cider in front of a warm fire and historic stenciling, the Barrows House extends its welcome.
(Traditional, Federal, Village, Inn. Member since 1974)

BIRCH HILL INN

5 Rooms, $105/$130 B&B
1 Cottage, $115 B&B

Visa, MC, Amex

All Private Baths

Closed Nov. 1 - Dec. 26
Apr. 10 - May 30

Appropriate for Children over 6; No Pets

Pool, Trout Pond, Walking & XC Ski Trails, Antiquing, Summer Theatre

Breakfast & Tea; Dinner winter weekends only; BYOB

No Smoking

N/A

In Manchester Center, Junction of Rtes. 7A & 30, take Rte. 30 (N) for 2.7 mi. to Manchester West Rd. go L. (S) for 3/4 of mi.

TEL. 802-362-2761
Res. 800-372-2761
West Road, P.O. Box 346
Manchester, VT 05254

Pat & Jim Lee, Innkeepers

This inn has a spectacular location. On a back road away from busy village streets, among fabulous white birches, the inn has the feeling of a gracious home and quiet, peaceful retreat. Each cheerfully decorated room has views of surrounding mountains, farm and gardens. Hearty breakfasts and fine country dinners are among the pleasures to be found here.
(Traditional, Country, Breakfast Inn. Member since 1982)

VERMONT

BLUEBERRY HILL

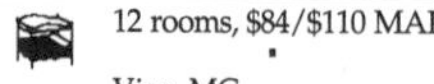

12 rooms, $84/$110 MAP

Visa, MC

All Private Baths

Year-round Except April

Children Welcome
No Pets

75 km. of groomed & tracked XC Ski Trails, Host of the 18th Annual American Ski Marathon every 1st Sun. in Feb., 30 mi hiking, Mountain Biking Trails in Summer

Breakfast, Lunch (Trail Bagged Lunch), Dinner; BYOB

No Smoking

Conference Facilities (40)

Wheelchair Access (1 rm., dining rm. & conf. fac.)

5 Located in the tranquility of the Green Mountain National Forest, the Inn is artistically fashioned with antiques and warm quilts. A greenhouse adjacent to the kitchen, with brick walkway and ever blooming plants, brings the outdoors inside even during the height of winter. Step out the door in Winter for some of the most scenic skiing in New England or in summer, bike or hike your way around Romance Mountain. Come share our special way of life. (*Colonial, Mountain, Inn. Member since 1994*)

From Brandon: Rte 73 East to Forest Road 32 on left, follow signs. From East Middlebury: Rte 125 East thru Ripton, to Forest Road 32 on right, follow signs.

TEL. 802-247-6735
FAX 802-247-3983
RD 3
Goshen, VT 05733
Tony Clark & Shari Brown, Innkeepers

THE GOVERNOR'S INN

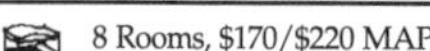

8 Rooms, $170/$220 MAP

Visa, MC, Pers. Checks

All Private Baths

Open Year-round

Not appropriate for young Children; No Pets

Downhill & XC Skiing, Antiquing, Golf, Boating, Fishing, Hiking, Winery, Summer Theater, Priory

Full Breakfast, Picnic Baskets, Dinner, Afternoon Tea, Wine & Liquor available

No Smoking

Conference Facilities (16)

N/A

10 Three times judged one of the Nation's Ten Best Inns and awarded ★★★★ by Mobil and ◆◆◆◆ by AAA, this may be the ultimate experience at a Victorian country inn. From potpourri scented air to soft strains of classical music, to beautifully kept heirlooms, attention is given to every detail insuring pleasure and comfort. Fifteen culinary awards, including "Vermont's Best Apple Pie," and recognition for excellence in innkeeping, service, and ambiance only add to the warm and generous hospitality intended to delight and surprise. (*Elegant, Victorian, Village, Inn. Member since 1987*)

Ludlow is located at junction of Rtes. 100 & 103. Inn is (S) on Rte. 103, just off village green.

TEL. 802-228-8830; 800-GOVERNOR (468-3766)
86 Main Street
Ludlow, VT 05149

Charlie & Deedy Marble, Innkeepers

HISTORIC BROOKSIDE FARMS

5 Rooms, $85/$150 B&B
1 Suite, $150/$185 B&B

No Credit Cards

Private & Shared Baths

Open Year-round

Children Welcome
No Pets

Hiking, XC Skiing, Boating, Fishing, Golf, Tennis, Horseback riding

Breakfast, Dinner including wine; Lunch by request

Smoking Restricted

Conference Facilities (50)

Wheelchair Access 1 Rm.

From I-87 (N), exit 20 (Glen Falls). L. on Rte. 9 to Rte. 149 (E) to Rte. 4 (E) to Rte. 22A (N) on 22A for 13 mi. From I-89 (N) exit White River Junction, Rte. 4 (W) to 22A (N).

TEL. 802-948-2727
FAX 802-948-2015

Route 22A
Orwell, VT 05760

Joan & Murray Korda, Innkeepers

This magnificent 200-year-old Greek Revival mansion is an architect's dream, where antique furnishings, paintings, and music abound. Skiers have only to step out the door to enjoy 300 acres of trails and meadow skiing. The farm provides wholesome food for the table, with beef, lamb and vegetable gardens. Three generations of innkeepers welcome guests to this elegant setting.
(Greek Revival, Country, Inn. Member since 1987)

THE INN AT MONTPELIER

19 Rooms, $99/$153 B&B (7 Deluxe)

Visa, MC, Amex, Diners, CB

All Private Baths

Open Year-round

Children Welcome
No Pets

Downhill Skiing, 25 miles. State Capitol, Shops, & 100 acre park a short walk.

Generous Continental Breakfast; Dinner daily; Restaurant closed Monday eves.
Wine & Liquor available

Smoking Accepted

Conference Facilities (16)

Wheelchair Access (dining rm. & conf. fac.)

I-89 to exit 8 Montpelier. Go to 4th light, turn L onto Main St. Inn approximately 3 blocks on right.

TEL. (802) 223-2727
FAX (802) 223-0722

147 Main St.
Montpelier, VT 05602

Maureen & Bill Russell, Innkeepers

An elegant, comfortable historic inn where fine dining and caring service are our specialties. Enjoy fireside dining or relax on Vermont's grandest porch. Each guest room is uniquely decorated with antiques, reproductions, fine art and many have fireplaces. Guest pantries offer at-home convenience and warmth with refreshments at any time. TV, telephone and air-conditioning. AAA ◆◆◆◆ for both the Inn and Restaurant, 1st of only three in the state.
(Elegant, Village, Inn. Member since 1992)

THE INN AT WEATHERSFIELD

9 Rooms, $175/$209 MAP
3 Suites, $190/$242 MAP

Visa, MC, Amex, Discov, CB, Diners

All Private Baths

Open Year-round

Appropriate for children over 8; Pets Accepted with Prior Notice

Golf, Skiing, Hiking, Biking, Fishing, Sleigh & Carriage Rides, Sauna, Aerobics Equipment

High Tea, Dinner & Breakfast included with stay; Wine & Liquor Available

Smoking Restricted

Conference Facilities (40)

Wheelchair Access (1 rm.)

Congeniality and caring have made this gracious "Colonial Sampler," woven with romance, tradition, music and poetry, one of America's "Ten Best Inns." The 21-acre Country Inn is nestled in the lap of Vermont history with skiing, golf, biking, swimming and horse-draw sleigh/carriage rides. Many of the twelve individually decorated suites and guest rooms feature canopy beds, fireplaces, and all have private baths. Award Winning Wine List, English high tea, five-course dinners with duo grand piano entertainment and bountiful breakfast buffet round out the ultimate inn experience. Mobil ★★★★ (*Traditional, Colonial, Mountain, Inn. Member since 1982*)

From I-91 (N), Exit 7 (Springfield), Rte. 11 (W) to Rte. 106 (N). Inn 5 mi. on left. From I-91 (S), Exit 8, Rte. 131 (W) to Rte. 106 (S). Inn is 4 mi. on right.

TEL. 802-263-9217; 800-477-4828; FAX 802-263-9219

Rt 106 (Nr Perkinsville), Bx 165
Weathersfield, VT 05151

Mary Louise & Ron Thorburn, Innkeepers

INN ON THE COMMON

14 Rooms, $190/$270 MAP
2 suites, $230/$270

Visa, MC

All Private Baths

Open Year-round

Children Accepted
Pets Accepted

Pool, Tennis Court, Gardens, XC Skiing, Golf, Lake, Trails

Breakfast & Dinner
Wine & Liquor available

No Smoking in Dining Room

Conference Facilities (20)

N/A

With the ambiance of a sophisticated country house hotel, this inn offers outstanding cuisine and an award-winning wine cellar. With beautiful gardens and wonderful views, the lovely and comfortable guest rooms elegantly decorated with antiques and artworks, some with fireplaces, are spread among a compound of 3 meticulously restored Federal houses. (AAA◆◆◆◆)

(*Elegant, Federal, Country, Inn. Member since 1976*)

From I-91 (N), Exit 21, Rte. 2 (W) to Rte. 15 (W),. In Hardwick, Rte. 14 (N) 7 mi. turn R., 3 mi. to inn. From I-91 (S) Exit 26, Rte. 58 (W). Rte. 14 (S) 12 mi. to marked L. turn.

TEL. 802-586-9619; RES. 800 521-2233; FAX 802-586-2249

Main Street
Craftsbury Common, VT 05827

Michael & Penny Schmitt, Innkeepers

THE LANDGROVE INN

16 Rooms, $85/$105 B&B
$60/$78 MAP

Visa, MC, Discov

All Private Baths

Closed Apr. 1-May 15
Nov. 1-Dec. 15

Children Welcome
No Pets

Tennis Courts, Heated Pool, Platform Tennis, Hay & Sleigh Rides, Golf, XC & Downhill Skiing, Stocked Pond

Breakfast & Dinner
Wine & Liquor available

No Smoking in Dining or Sleeping Rooms

Conference Facilities (40)

N/A

I-91 (N), Exit 2 (Brattleboro). Rte. 30 (N), R. onto Rte. 11. L. at signs for Village Inn, bear L. in village of Peru. From Rte. 7 (N), (E) in Manchester on Rte. 11. Continue as above.

TEL. 802-824-6673
800-669-8466
R.D. 1, Box 215, Landgrove
Landgrove, VT 05148
Jay & Kathy Snyder
Innkeepers

The principle of "Vermont continous architecture" extended this original 1840 farmhouse into the rambling inn it is today. It is in a true country inn setting, tucked into a valley in the mountains, with gravel roads and a town population of 200. There's candlelit, fireside dining, and a mix of activities and fun for all ages at this informal, engaging country inn. Three generations of the Snyder family define the meaning of "family run country inn." The kind of place where relaxation and recreation come together in a most idyllic and secluded setting.
(Colonial, Country, Inn. Member since 1977)

MOUNTAIN TOP INN AND RESORT

35 Rooms $104/300 B&B
22 Chalets $124/$326 B&B

Visa, MC, Amex

All Private Baths

Open Year-round

Children Welcome
No Pets—Kennels nearby

Full resort — XC Skiing, Skating, Horseback & Sleigh Rides, Swimming, Sailing, Boating, Golf, Tennis

Breakfast, Lunch, Dinner
Wine & Liquor available

No Smoking in dining room

Conference Facilities (180)

N/A

Chittenden is 10 mi. (NE) of Rutland. (N) on Rte. 7 or (E) on Rte. 4 from Rutland. Follow state signs to "Mountain Top Inn."

TEL 802-483-2311
or 800-445-2100
Mountain Top Rd.
Chittenden, VT 05737

William Wolfe, Innkeeper

Commanding a spectacular lake & mountain view on a 1,000-acre estate, this inn offers a complete resort experience. Included in the rates are tennis, heated pool, pitch 'n' putt golf, sailing, fishing, trap shooting, mountain biking, and fly fishing. Special horseback riding vacations with instructions in riding, jumping, dressage and introductory polo and golf school are available. In winter cross country skiing, horsedrawn sleigh rides, sledding, ice skating and winter horseback riding. Attractive, congenial surroundings, and fine dining complete the picture.
(Rustic, Mountain, Resort. Member since 1987)

VERMONT

OCTOBER COUNTRY INN

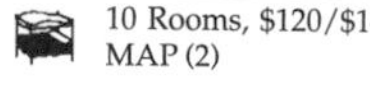 10 Rooms, $120/$149 MAP (2)

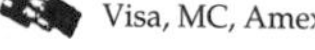 Visa, MC, Amex

Private and Shared Baths

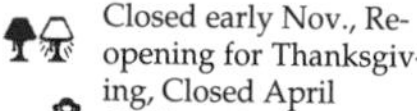 Closed early Nov., Reopening for Thanksgiving, Closed April

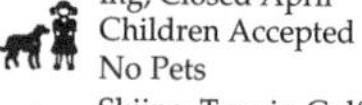 Children Accepted
No Pets

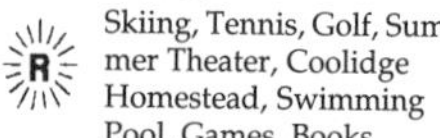 Skiing, Tennis, Golf, Summer Theater, Coolidge Homestead, Swimming Pool, Games, Books

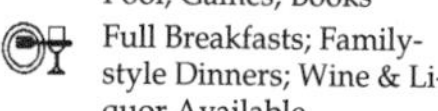 Full Breakfasts; Family-style Dinners; Wine & Liquor Available

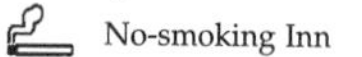 No-smoking Inn

 Conference Facility (18)

 N/A

8 Relaxed and comfortable, this converted 19th century farmhouse on five acres near Woodstock offers warmth and intimacy in the finest innkeeping tradition. The scents of baking breads, fresh herbs and homemade desserts fill the inn as Chef Patrick works magic in Mexican, Italian, French Country, Greek and American motifs. Swim in the pool, bicycle, hike, ski, shop, sightsee or simply relax by the fire—then dine by candlelight. Away from the crowds, yet close to Killington, Woodstock and Dartmouth.

(*Traditional, Country, Inn. Member since 1992*)

From Woodstock continue 8 miles west on Rte 4 to junction of Rte 100A. Continue on 4 for 200 yards. Take 1st rt. then rt. again.

TEL. 802-672-3412; 800-648-8421

Upper Road, P.O. Box 66
Bridgewater Corners, VT 05035

Richard Sims & Patrick Runkel, Innkeepers

RABBIT HILL INN

16 Rooms $169/$249 MAP
4 Suites $209/$249 MAP

 Visa, MC, Amex

All Private Baths

Closed April & Nov. 1-16

Appropriate for Children over 12; No Pets

Downhill & XC Skiing, Hiking, Canoeing, Iceskating, Swimming, Golf, Antiquing, Fishing, Lawn Games.

Full Breakfast, Dinner, Teatime, Picnics
Wine & Liquor available

No Smoking

Conference Facilities (20)

Wheelchair Access (1 rm., 1 dining rm. & conf. fac.)

2 Full of whimsical and charming surprises, this 1795 Federal-period inn has been lavished with love and attention. Many rooms with fireplaces, canopy beds, jacuzzis for 2. Candlelit 4-Diamond dining, unique turn-down service and a sense of pampered relaxation make this an enchanting hideaway. Set in a tiny hamlet that is an Historic District overlooking mountains, the Inn is elegantly stylish and romantic, renowned for exceptional service and detail; personal, caring touches above all! On of the nation's "10 Best Inns" 3 years in a row. AAA ◆◆◆◆ Inn.

(*Elegant, Country, Federal. Member since 1990*)

From I-91 (N or S), Exit 19 to I-93 (S). Exit 1 R. on Rte. 18 (S), 7 mi. to inn. From I-93 (N), Exit 44, L. on Rte. 18 (N), 2 mi. to inn.

TEL. 802-748-5168
Reserv. 800-76-BUNNY
FAX 802-748-8342

Route 18
Lower Waterford, VT 05848

John & Maureen Magee, Innkeepers

ROWELL'S INN

 5 Rooms, $140/$160 MAP

 Visa, MC, Personal Checks preferred

 All Private Baths

Closed Apr. & 1st 2 weeks of Nov.

 Appropriate for Children over 12; No Pets

 Skiing, Golf, Tennis, Fishing, Bicycling, Hiking

 Breakfast & Dinner for houseguests only; Wine & Beer available

 Smoking Restricted

N/A

The inn is on Rte. 11 (an east/west rte.) connecting Rtes. 7 & I-91. *The inn is 7 mi. (W) of Chester and 7 mi.* (E) of Londonderry.

TEL. 802-875-3658
RR #1, Box 267-D
Simonsville, VT 05143

Beth & Lee Davis
Innkeepers

12 This 1820 stagecoach stop (National Register of Historic Places) continues to welcome weary travelers with a brand of hospitality those early guests never enjoyed. With antiques & memorabilia, cozy fireplaces, an English-style pub, & a kitchen overflowing with enticing aromas, this inn offers guests hearty, scrumptious dishes, & casual, homey comfort in authentic period surroundings.
(*Traditional, Country, Inn. Member since 1985*)

SHIRE INN

 6 Rooms, $90/$130 B&B $150/$210 MAP

 Visa, MC, Discovr, Personal Checks

 All Private Baths

 Open Year-round

 Appropriate for Children over 6; No Pets

 XC & downhill Skiing, Skating, Sleigh Rides, Bicycling, Swimming, Canoeing, Antiquing, Lawn Games

Breakfast & Dinner
Wine & Beer available
Afternoon Tea

 No Smoking

Conference Facilities (10)

 Wheelchair Access (1 rm., dining rm. & conf. rm.)

I-89, Vt. Exit 2 (Sharon) L. for 300 yds., R. on Rte. 14 (N). R. onto Rte. 110 (N). 13 mi. to Chelsea. From I-91 Exit 14, L. onto Rte. 113 (N/W) to Chelsea.

TEL. 802-685-3031
800-441-6908
Main Street, Box 37
Chelsea, VT 05038

Jay & Karen Keller, Innkeepers

4 Centrally located for easy day trips to the best of rural and historic attractions in both Vermont and New Hampshire, this Inn and Chelsea Village (National Register) provide "just the kind of withdrawn New England atmosphere you hoped to find." (Norman Simpson) The traditional 1832 Adams-style brick and granite home on 25 acres offers large guest rooms with high ceilings, tall windows, canopied queen-sized beds and fireplaces. The antique laden parlor is well stocked with books, puzzles and games. Exceptional meals start and end a day of genial relaxation.
(*Traditional, Federal, Village, Inn. Member since 1986*)

VERMONT

THREE MOUNTAIN INN

14 Rooms, $80/$110 B&B
$130/$170 MAP
1 Suite, $200/$230 MAP
Amex, Visa, MC, Discov

All Private Baths

Closed April 1 — Mid May

Children over 6 welcome;
No Pets

Swimming pool, Hiking, Biking on premises, Tennis, Golf, Horseback riding, XC and Downhill Skiing nearby—10 minutes away

Breakfast & Dinner
Wine & Liquor available

Smoking restricted

Conference Facilities (40)

N/A

17 Capture the feeling of Vermont's past in this authentic 1790's inn where the innkeepers make the guests feel welcome. Relax, surrounded by mountain views in an unspoiled village. Rooms with canopied beds and fireplaces. Casual dining with a choice of the menu. Fireplaces in two romantic dining rooms with excellent reputation for pridefully prepared gourmet fare. Featured in *Gourmet*. Hike, bike, or x-ct ski to Jamaica State Park. Storage barn for bikes. Backroads maps available. Pub lounge. Specializing in small weddings, family gatherings and group functions.
(*Traditional, Village, Inn. Member since 1982*)

Jamaica is located on Rte. 30, 1/2 hr. (NW) of Brattleboro (I-91) Exit 2 and 1/2 hr. (E) of Manchester (Rte. 7N to Rt. 30/11).

TEL. 802-874-4140
FAX 802-874-4745
P.O. Box 180R
Jamaica, VT 05343

Charles & Elaine Murray,
Innkeepers

VERMONT MARBLE INN

8 Rooms, $145/$200 MAP
4 Suites, $210/$225 MAP

Visa, MC, Amex

All Private Baths

Open Year-round

Children over 12
No Pets

Water sports, Skiing, Golf, Tennis, Bicycling, Horseback Riding, Hiking

Breakfast, Dinner, Afternoon Tea; Wine & Liquor available

Smoking restrictions

Conference Facilities (20)

N/A

9 This totally restored Victorian marble mansion with its hand-carved, working fireplaces and high ceilings offers an elegant and romantic intimacy. The candlelit breakfast is truly a banquet, and the award-winning cuisine has earned rave reviews. The warm hospitality of the innkeepers is legend. Judged one of the nation's "10 Best Inns." Rated sublimely romantic, Vermont's only AAA ◆◆◆◆ and MOBIL★★★★ country inn, with a AAA ◆◆◆◆ restaurant.
(*Elegant, Victorian, Village, Inn. Member since 1990*)

I-87, Exit 20. L to Rte. 149 (E) to Rte. 4 (N). Exit 2 in Vt., R off ramp. Straight down street to Park. Inn faces center of Park.

TEL. 802-265-8383
800-535-2814
FAX 802-265-4226
On the Town Green
Fair Haven, VT 05743
Bea & Richard Taube, Shirley Stein, Innkeepers

WEST MOUNTAIN INN

12 Rooms $139/$172 MAP
6 Suites, $184/$214 MAP
Cottages, $139/$152
Visa, MC, Amex, Discov
All Private Baths
Open Year-round
Children Welcome
No Pets
Hiking, Canoeing, Tubing, Flyfishing, Wilderness X-Country Skiing, Sledding, Skating and Golf and Tennis nearby. Downhill Skiing also nearby.
Breakfast & Dinner; Lunch by special arrangement
Wine & Liquor available
No Smoking
Conference Facilities (40)
Wheelchair Access (1 rm., dining rm. & conf. fac.)

Rt. 7 (N), Exit 3. Take access road to end, R. on Rte. 7A into Arlington. L. on Rte. 313 for .5 mi. L. on River Rd. to inn.

TEL. 802-375-6516
FAX 802-375-6553
Box 481, Rte. 313 & River Rd.
Arlington, VT 05250

Mary Ann & Wes Carlson, Innkeepers

16 Llamas and African violets are only two of the delightful surprises at this happy, relaxed country inn, nestled on a mountainside overlooking the Battenkill River. In addition to Wes Carlson's herd of treking llamas and the custom of presenting guests with a lovely African violet, there are cheerful rooms and a rich outdoor world to explore. Miles of trails for hiking or wilderness x-country skiing, and river sport opportunities abound. Guests dine on exceptional New England country cuisine in an atmosphere filled with a spirit of genuine warmth and hospitality.
(Traditional, Country, Inn. Member since 1984)

WINDHAM HILL INN

15 Rooms, $160/$210 MAP
Visa, MC, Amex, Discovr, DC
All Private Baths
Closed Apr. to mid-May, early Nov.
Appropriate for Children over 12; No Pets
XC Ski Learning Center, floodlit Skating pond, Downhill Skiing, Hiking, Day Tripping, nearby Tennis, Swimming & Golf.
Breakfast & Dinner
Non-smoking Inn
Conference Facilities (30)
Wheelchair access (1 rm.)

I-91 (N). Exit 2 (Brattleboro Rte. 30 (N) for 21.5 mi. R. on Windham Rd. 1.5 mi. to inn.

TEL. 802-874-4080
800-944-4080
R.R. 1, Box 44
West Townshend, VT 05359

Grigs & Pat Markham
Innkeepers

18 On 160 acres at the end of a country road, threaded by rock walls and magnificent views across the hills. Friendly innkeepers and staff welcome guests to this peaceful, secluded retreat with its sparkling rooms, memorable six-course gourmet meals, award-winning ambiance, and closeness to nature. Extensive onsite trail network for hiking and cross country skiing. Designated an "Inn of Distinction" having been judged one of the nation's ten best inns for a third year.
(Traditional, Country, Inn. Member since 1989)

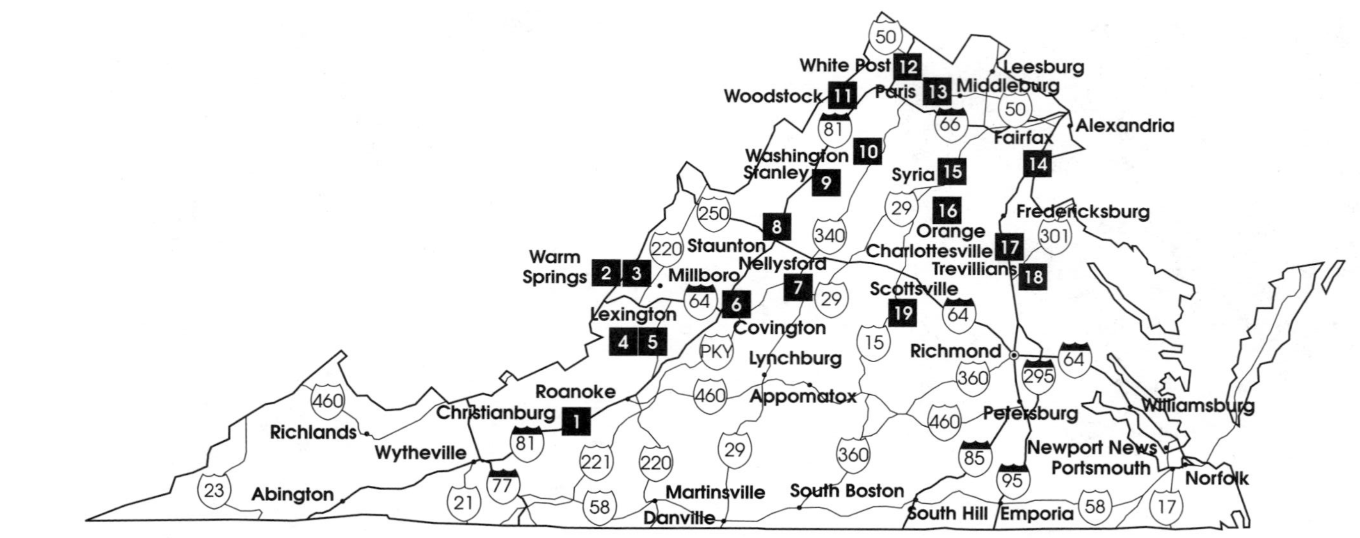

1. The Oaks Bed & Breakfast Inn, Christianburg
2. Inn at Gristmill Square, Warm Springs
3. Meadow Lane Lodge, Warm Springs
4. Alexander Withrow House/McCampbell Inn, Lexington
5. Maple Hall, Lexington
6. Fort Lewis Lodge, Millboro
7. Trillium House, Nellysford
8. The Belle Grae Inn, Staunton
9. Jordan Hollow Farm Inn, Stanley
10. Inn at Little Washington, Washington
11. Inn at Narrow Passage, Woodstock
12. L'Auberge Provencale, White Post
13. Ashby Inn, Paris
14 The Bailiwick Inn, Fairfax
15. Graves' Mountain Lodge, Syria
16. The Hidden Inn, Orange
17. Silver Thatch Inn, Charlottesville
18. Prospect Hill, Trevilians
19. High Meadows, Scottsville

ALEXANDER-WITHROW HOUSE/ McCAMPBELL INN

14 Rooms, $95/$110 B&B
8 Suites, $130/$150 B&B

MC, Visa, Discov

All Private Baths

Open Year-round

Children Welcome
No Pets - Kennels available

Historic Buildings, Museums, Fishing, Canoeing, Tennis, Pool, Croquet

Breakfast for houseguests
Dinner at Maple Hall nightly

Limited Smoking

Conference Facilities (15)

N/A

I-81 or I-64, take either exit for Lexington and continue to town center, Main & Washington Sts. Inns across from Court House.

TEL. 703-463-2044
FAX 703-463-7262
11 No. Main Street
Lexington, VA 24450
The Peter Meredith Family, Owners;
Don Fredenburg, Innkeeper

4 In southwest Virginia, replete with impressive history and scenery, is the town of Lexington and two gracious and graceful inns, the Alexander-Withrow House, (ca. 1789) and McCampbell Inn (ca. 1809) of Historic Country Inns. Parents of VMI or W&L students as well as business or holiday travelers enjoy the comforts of these inns, within easy walking distance of all attractions. Each room interestingly furnished offers individual heating and cooling controls, TVs, phones & refreshment centers. Your needs and comfort are our main concern. (*Traditional, Town, Inn. Member since 1991*)

THE ASHBY INN

6 Rooms, $90/$150 B&B
4 suites, $175 B&B

Visa, MC

8 Private, 1/2 shared baths

Closed Jan. 1, July 4, Dec. 24 & 25

Appropriate for Children over 10; No Pets

Antiquing, Vineyards, Horseback Riding, Golf, Tennis, Hiking

Breakfast, Dinner Wed.–Sat.; Sun. Brunch
Wine & Liquor available

No Smoking in guest rms.

Conference Facilities (20)

N/A

From Wash. D.C. Rte 66 (W) to Exit 23 —Rte. 17 (N), 7.5 mi. L. on Rte. 701 for .5 mi. Or Rte. 50 (W) thru Middleburg; 3 mi. beyond Upperville. L. just after traffic light (Rte. 759).

TEL. 703-592-3900
FAX 703-592-3781
Rte. 1, Box 2A
Paris, VA 22130
John & Roma Sherman, Innkeepers

13 This 1829 inn finds its character in the small village of Paris and its heart in the kitchen. The views from guest rooms or dining patio are wonderful in every direction. The menu changes daily, ranging from home-cured salmon gravlaks or local wild mushrooms on toast to jumbo lump crabcakes or duckling with turnips.
(*Traditional, Colonial, Village, Inn. Member since 1988*)

THE BAILIWICK INN

13 Rooms, $130/$195 B&B
1 Suite $295 B&B
Bridal Suite, $275 B&B
Visa, MC, Amex
All Private Baths, 2 with Jacuzzis
Open Year round
Children Welcome
No Pets
Mt. Vernon, Gunston Hall, & Woodlawn Plantations. Convenient to Washington, D.C. by metro. Civil War battlefields. Vineyard tours and Antiquing.
Full Breakfast; Afternoon Tea; Candlelight Dinner
Wine & Beer available
No Smoking
Conference Facilities (20)
N/A

14 This luxurious National Historic Register Inn is located 15 miles from Washington, D.C. with convenient access by metrorail. The rooms are patterned after those of famous Virginians featuring antiques, queen size feather beds, fireplaces and jacuzzis. Candlelight dinners are available by reservation. The inn has monthly Winemaster Dinners and Murder Mystery Weekends.

(*Elegant, In-Town, Inn. Member since 1992*)

Route 123 (Chain Bridge Rd.) 1 mi. (S) of I-66, or via Rte. 50 from I-495 and I-95 to the (E) and (S). Midway National and Dulles International Airports.

TEL. 703-691-2266
800-366-7666
FAX 703-934-2112
4023 Chain Bridge Road
Fairfax, VA 22030
Bob & Annette Bradley, Innkeepers
Holly Snyder, Manager

THE BELLE GRAE INN

9 rooms, $69/$119 B&B
5 suites, $119/$139 B&B
Visa, MC, Amex
All Private Baths
Open Year-round
Well-behaved young adults 12 and above are welcome; No Pets
Hiking the Mountains, Touring 5 Historic Districts, Historic Museums; Woodrow Wilson Birthplace; Museum of American Frontier Culture; Statler Brothers Museum
Breakfast daily, 7:30-9:30 A.M.; Dinner daily, 6-9 P.M.; MAP Rates Available
Wine & Liquor Available
Smoking in Some Rooms
Conference Facilities (50)
Wheelchair Access (2 rms., dining rm. & conf. fac.)

8 With a wide veranda and wicker rockers for chatting and sipping, and graciously furnished rooms with fireplaces, canopied and 4-poster beds and antiques, this group of restored Victorian mansions is in the center of Historic Staunton, near the homes of 4 Presidents and numerous museums. Southern-flavored Continental cuisine is served in the Old Inn or in the courtyard cafe.

(*Traditional, Victorian, In-Town, Inn. Member since 1990*)

Exit 222 off I-81. Follow 250 west to center of Staunton. Left on Frederick St. to 515 W. Frederick St. Circle block for off-street parking.

TEL. 703-886-5151
FAX 703-886-6641
515 W. Frederick St.
Staunton, VA 24401

Michael Organ, Innkeeper

FORT LEWIS LODGE

9 Rooms, $120/$140 MAP
3 Family Suites, $150 MAP
2 Log Cabins, $180 MAP
Visa, MC

All Private Baths

Closed Jan. - Mar.

Children Welcome
Prior Approval for Pets

3 mi. private River Fishing, Hiking, Mtn. Biking, Horseback Riding, Swimming, Golf, Deer Watching

Breakfast, Dinner, Picnic Lunch available
Beer & Wine available

No Smoking in Guest Rooms

Conference Facilities (35)

N/A

From Staunton, Rte. 254 (W) to Buffalo Gap; Rte. 42 to Millboro Sprgs.; Rte. 39 (W) for 0.7 mi to R. onto Rte. 678, 10.8 mi. to L. onto Rte. 625, 0.2 mi. to lodge on L.

TEL. 703-925-2314
FAX 703-925-2352
HCR 3, Box 21A
Millboro, VA 24460
John & Caryl Cowden, Innkeepers

6 It's not just getting away, it's getting back. To a 3200-acre mountain farm where your companions are the earth, the sky, and the river. At the heart of it all is a truly unique country inn, decorated with wildlife art and locally hand-crafted furniture. A silo with 3 bedrooms "in the round" and two historic hand-hewn log cabins with stone fireplaces are ideal for a romantic getaway. Meals served in the restored Lewis Mill reflect a rare devotion to home cooking.

(*Rustic, Mountain, Retreat/Lodge. Member since 1990*)

GRAVES' MOUNTAIN LODGE

53 Rooms/Cottages
Hotel Rooms $75/$85 AP
Cottages, $95/$175
Visa, MC, Discovr

Private and Shared Baths

Open March 17, 1995 to Nov. 26, 1995

Children Accepted; Pets Accepted in some rooms

Swimming, Tennis, Nature Walks, Hiking, Fishing, Basketball, Horseback riding

Breakfast, Lunch, Dinner, Beer & Wine available

Smoking allowed in Designated areas

Conference Facilities (100)

Wheelchair Access (38 rooms)

From Madison, Va. U.S. Rt. 29, take Rt. 231 (N) for 7 mi. to L. at Greystone Service Sta. Turn L. on Rt. 670. Go 4 mi. to Syria Merchandise Store. Lodge 200 yds. past Syria on L.

TEL. (703) 923-4231
FAX (703)923-4312
General Delivery
Syria, VA 22743
Jim & Rachel Graves, Innkeepers

15 A tradition for five generations, the Graves' family continues to offer their own kind of Southern hospitality at this rustic retreat complete with motel rooms, cabins and cottages. Guests eat delicious country-cooked meals, served family style, three times a day while enjoying rest and relaxation. Trout streams and farm ponds are available for fishing. Hiking trails and horseback rides through the foothills of the beautiful Blue Ridge Mountains are also available for guests during their visit. Open mid-March through November.

(*Rustic, Country, Retreat/Lodge. Member since 1972*)

THE HIDDEN INN

8 Rooms $79/$129 B&B
2 Cottages $139/$159 B&B

Visa, MC, Amex

All Private Baths
4 Jacuzzis

Closed Christmas

Children Accepted
No Pets

Lawn games, Wineries, Antiquing, Historic Sites, Biking, Fishing, Boating

Full Breakfast & Afternoon Tea; Optional candlelight Picnic; Tues.-Sat. fixed price Dinner; Wine & Beer available

No Smoking

Conference Facilities (20)

N/A

16 Lace and fresh-cut flowers accent this romantic Victorian farmhouse, surrounded by seven wooded acres and gardens in the heart of historic Virginia's wine country. Enjoy a cup of tea before a crackling living room fire or sip lemonade on the veranda porch swing. A full country breakfast in the sunlit dining room starts the day, packed with fascinating things to do. Guests can visit Monticello, Montpelier, tour several wineries, shop at local shops & antique stores. Bicycling, horseback riding, golf and hiking are nearby.
(*Traditional, Victorian, Village, Inn. Member since 1991*)

From Wash., DC, I-66 (W) to Rte. 29 (S) at Gainesville to Rte. 15 (S), Orange exit, to Orange; inn on L. From Richmond, I-64 (W) to Rte. 15 (N), through Gordonsville to Orange; inn on R.

TEL. 703-672-3625; 800-841-1253; FAX 703-672-5029
249 Caroline St.
Orange, VA 22960
Ray & Barbara Lonick, Innkeepers

HIGH MEADOWS

7 Rooms, $85/$145 B&B
5 Suites, $110/$155 B&B

Visa, MC, Pers. Checks

All Private Baths

Closed Dec. 24 & 25

Appropriate for Children over 8; Prior Approval for Pets

Hiking, Wine-tasting, Croquet, Vineyard, Canoeing, Tubing, Fishing, History, Antiquing, Horseshoes, Monticello

Breakfast & Dinner; Twilight Wine-tasting; Sat. rates MAP, add $40 pp

Smoking restricted

Conference Facilities (20)

Wheelchair Access (1 rm.)

19 Choice accommodations and diversions as individual as you. Spacious and comfortable rooms & suites with fireplaces, porches, soaking and whirlpool tubs. Romantic flower gardens, relaxing walks on 50 tranquil acres of rolling meadows; spectacular mountain sunsets; European supper baskets at the pond, in the gazebo or the vineyard; Full country breakfasts on the terrace or by the fire; Fine candlelight dining after a twilight tradition of Virginia wine-tasting are a few of the pleasures that await you at this 19th-century inn (National Register of Historic Places).
(*Traditional, Country, Inn. Member since 1990*)

I-64 in Charlottesville, Exit 121 to Rte. 20 (S) for 17 mi. After intersection with Rte. 726, continue .3 mi. to L. at inn sign

TEL. 804-286-2218
800-232-1832
Route 20 S., Rte. 4, Box 6
Scottsville, VA 24590
Peter Sushka and Mary Jae Abbitt, Innkeepers

THE INN AT GRISTMILL SQUARE

8 Rooms, $80/$95 B&B
7 Suites, $85/$150 B&B

Visa, MC, Discov

All Private Baths

Open Year-round

Children Welcome; Pets not allowed

Swimming Pool, Tennis, Sauna, Golf, Horseback Riding, Hiking, Fishing, Skiing, Ice Skating

Continental Breakfast & Dinner; Sun. Brunch; MAP Available
Wine & Liquor available

Smoking Allowed

Conference Facilities (45)

N/A

From (N) on Rte. U.S. 220 turn R. (W) on Rte. 619 (Small state marker) for .3 mi. to inn on R. From (S) on Rte. 220, L. (W) on Rte. 619.

TEL. (703) 839-2231
FAX: 703-839-5770
P.O. Box 359
Warm Springs, VA 24484

The McWilliams Family, Innkeepers

On a designated historic site, a 1771 gristmill and a blacksmith's shop are among the cluster of restored 19th-century buildings comprising this handsome inn. Guest rooms are tastefully furnished in both traditional and contemporary decor; many have working fireplaces. Exceptional dining and the many attractions of the Allegheny Mountains & spa country draw visitors from afar.

(*Traditional,Village, Inn. Member since 1977*)

THE INN AT LITTLE WASHINGTON

9 Rooms, $240/$515 B&B
3 Suites, $390/$615 B&B

MC, Visa

All Private Baths

Open Year-round

Children by special arrangement; No Pets

Blue Ridge Mtns., Shenandoah Natl. Park, Luray Caverns, 1 1/2 hr. from Washington, D.C.

Breakfast for inn guests Dinner; Wine & Liquor available

Smoking Restrictions

Conference Facilities (20)

Wheelchair Access

From Wash., D.C., (1.5) hrs.) to I-66 (W) to Exit 43A (Gainesville) to Rte. 29 (S) to R. on Rte. 211 (W) (Warrenton). Continue 23 mi. to R. on Bus. Rte. 211 to Washington (W) for 0.5 mi. to inn on R.

TEL. 703-675-3800
FAX 703-675-3100
Middle and Main Streets,
Washington, VA 22747
Patrick O'Connell and Reinhardt Lynch, Innkeepers

In a sleepy village, America's 1st 5★ 5◆ inn offers luxurious guest rooms, lavishly furnished in imported English antiques and lush fabrics, some with balcony views of town and countryside. Chef Patrick O'Connell has captured international acclaim with his creative regional cuisine, which, along with the impeccable service, makes a visit here a memorable experience. The Inn At Little Washington has been named the nation's Restaurant of the Year by The James Beard Foundation.

(*Elegant, Victorian, Country Village, Inn. Member since 1988*)

INN AT NARROW PASSAGE

 12 Rooms, $85/$110

 Visa, MC

10 Private Baths

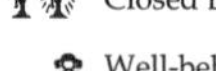 Closed Dec. 24 & 25

Well-behaved Children welcome; No Pets

 Fishing, Canoeing, Vineyards, Antiquing, Hiking, Skiing, Historic Sites, Caverns

 Full Breakfast
BYOB

No Smoking in guest rooms

 Conference Facilities (20)

N/A

11 This historic 1740 log inn with five acres on the Shenandoah River is a convenient place to relax and enjoy the beauty and history of the valley. In a country setting along the old Valley Pike, the inn's newer guest rooms open onto porches with views of the river and Massanutten Mountain. Early American antiques and reproductions, working fireplaces, queen-sized beds, original beams, exposed log walls, and pine floors create a comfortable Colonial atmosphere. Fine restaurants for lunch and dinner are nearby.
(*Rustic Colonial, Country, Breakfast Inn. Member since 1990*)

From Wash., D.C.; I-66 (W) to I-81 (S) to Exit 283 (Woodstock) and U.S. Rte. 11 (S) for 2 mi. The inn is at the corner of Rte. 11 and Rte. 672.

TEL. 703-459-8000
FAX 703-459-8001
U.S. 11 South,
Woodstock, VA 22664

Ellen & Ed Markel, Innkeepers

JORDAN HOLLOW FARM INN

21 Rooms $140/$180 MAP per couple

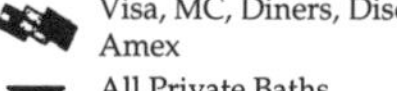 Visa, MC, Diners, Discov, Amex

All Private Baths
4 Whirlpools

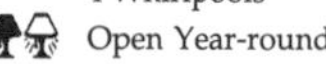 Open Year-round

Well-behaved Children Welcome; No Pets

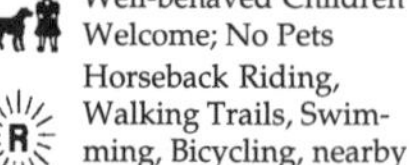 Horseback Riding, Walking Trails, Swimming, Bicycling, nearby hiking, fishing, caverns, historic battlefields

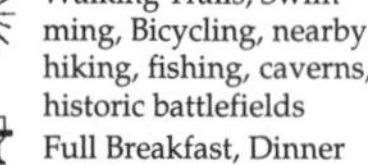 Full Breakfast, Dinner and Box Lunches
Wine & Liquor available

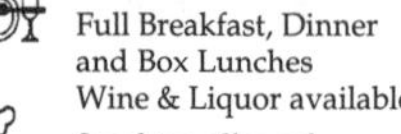 Smoking allowed

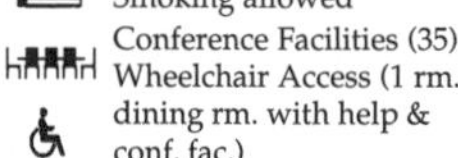 Conference Facilities (35)
Wheelchair Access (1 rm., dining rm. with help & conf. fac.)

9 A cozy 200-year-old restored Colonial horse farm with walking trails and spectacular views, located in the beautiful Shenandoah Valley. Guest rooms have sun porches, and rocking chairs, some have whirlpool baths and fireplaces. The restaurant serves a "country continental" menu. The stable offers trail rides daily and carriage lessons by appointment. Guests can bring their own horses. Located near Luray Caverns, Skyline Drive, New Market Battlefield Museum, antiquing. Two hours west of Washington, D.C.
(*Traditional, Country, Ranch. Member since 1985*)

Luray, Va. Rte. 340 Business (S) for 6 mi. to L. onto Rte. 624 L. on Rte. 689 over bridge & R. on Rte. 626 for .4 mi. to inn on R.

TEL. 703-778-2285
FAX 703-778-1759
Route 2, Box 375
Stanley, VA 22851

Marley & Jetze Beers, Innkeepers

L'AUBERGE PROVENÇALE

 9 Rooms, $145/$175 B&B; 1 Suite, $195 B&B

 Visa, MC, Amex, Diners, Discov

All Private Baths

Feb 1—Dec 31; closed Jan.

 Appropriate for Children over 10; No Pets

 Biking, Hiking, Horseback Riding, Antiquing, Canoeing, Skiing, Tennis, Museums, Golfing, Vineyard Tours, Outlet Shopping, Theatre

 Breakfast & Dinner; Sunday Brunch; Wine & Liquor available

Smoking not allowed in guest rms. or dining rms.

Conference Facilities (30)

Wheelchair Access (dining rm. & conf. fac.)

On Rte. 340 (S). 1 mi. (S) of Rte. 50; 20 mi. (W) of Middleburg, 9 mi. (E) of Winchester, VA

TEL. 703-837-1375
800-638-1702
FAX 703-837-2004
Route 340, P.O. Box 119
White Post, VA 22663

Celeste & Alain Borel, Innkeepers

12 A warm, "south of France" breath blows over this eclectic and sophisticated country inn, with its renowned "cuisine moderne Provençale" by French master- chef/owner Alain Borel, who grows his own vegetables, herbs and spices. Charming guest rooms and the bucolic setting in the hunt country of northern Virginia offer a special experience for discerning guests. 4 ◆◆◆◆ rated.
(*Elegant, Country, Inn. Member since 1988*)

MAPLE HALL

 16 Rooms, $95/ $110 B&B 5 Suites, $130/$150 B&B

 Visa, MC, Discov

 All Private Baths

 Open Year-round

 Children Welcome; No Pets—Kennel 1/4 mile

 Tennis, Pool, Croquet, Fishing, Walking Paths, Canoeing, Hiking, Museums, Historic Sites

 Breakfast, Houseguests Dinner daily; Wine & Liquor available

 Smoking somewhat restricted

 Conference Facilities (20)

 Wheelchair Access (1 Room)

I-81 Exit 195 to Rte. 11 (N). Inn is (E) of the Interstate.

TEL. 703-463-2044
FAX 703-463-6693
11 No. Main St.
Lexington, VA 24450

Peter Meredith Family, Owners Don Fredenburg, Innkeeper

5 A member of the Historic Inns of Lexington, this 1850 plantation home on 56 rolling acres offers guests a lovely place for recreation, exploring historic sites, or just relaxing. There are walking trails, a swimming pool, tennis and fishing. The new Pond House has lovely suites and many of the attractive guest rooms have fireplaces. Historic Lexington is just a short drive away. Convenience, comfort, quiet and service attract many private and corporate groups to select Maple Hall for their small business conferences from 4 to 40.
(*Elegant, Greek Revival, Country Inn. Member since 1987*)

MEADOW LANE LODGE

11 Rooms, $90/$115 B&B
3 Suites, $100/$145 B&B
3 Cottages, $100/$130 B&B
Visa, MC, Amex
All Private Baths
Open Year-round
Children over 5 accepted in some rooms with prior approval; No Pets
Tennis, Fishing, Hiking, Swimming, Mtn. Biking, Birding, Croquet, Camping, Canoeing, Golf, Horseback Riding, Sporting Clays, Skiing, Ice Skating
Full Breakfast daily; Picnic lunches available; Dinner Fri. & Sat. (Apr.—Oct.); Beer & Wine available; BYOB
No smoking
Conference Facilities (18)
N/A

3 With miles of hiking trails and two miles of scenic private trout and bass stream rippling through its 1,600 acres of mountain forests and meadows, this is one of the most unusual inns to be found anywhere. Guests enjoy working fireplaces, sunny porches, and roosters crowing wakeup calls to an unforgettable country breakfast. Wildflowers, wildlife, birdlife, and domestic animals galore add to the enjoyment of this beautiful, peaceful estate, a rarity in today's rapidly expanding world.
(*Traditional, Mountain, Retreat/Lodge. Member since 1978*)

From Staunton, Rte. 254 (W) to Buffalo Gap, Rte. 42 S. to Millboro Springs; Rte. 39 (W) to Rte. 220, continue Rte. 39 (W), 4.5 mi. to lodge on right.

TEL. 703-839-5959
HCR OI, Box 110
Warm Springs, VA 24484

Cheryl & Steve Hooley,
Innkeepers

THE OAKS BED & BREAKFAST INN

5 rooms, $75/$130 B&B
Visa, Mc, Amex, Disc
All Private Baths
Open Year-round
No Pets; Children over 12
Garden hot tub, Sauna for two, croquet court, library, TV/VCR, etc.
English-style breakfast
Smoking outside only
Conference Facilities (15–20)
N/A

1 Warm hospitality, comfortable, relaxed elegance and memorable breakfasts are the hallmark of The Oaks, a century-old Queen Anne Victorian; National Register of Historic Places. Set on Christiansburg's highest hill and located in the beautiful mountain highlands of southwest Virginia, The Oaks delights and welcomes leisure and business travelers from around the world. Surrounded by lawn, perennial gardens and 300-year-old oak trees, the inn faces Main Street, once part of the Wilderness Trail blazed by Daniel Boone and Davey Crockett. Mobil 3-star; AAA 3-diamond.
(*Elegant Victorian, Village, Breakfast Inn. Member since 1993*)

I-81 (exit 114) 2 miles. From Blue Ridge Parkway, (MP165) Route 8 west 24 miles to The Oaks.

TEL. 703-381-1500
311 East Main Street
Christiansburg, VA 24073

Margaret & Tom Ray,
Owners/Innkeepers

PROSPECT HILL PLANTATION INN

 10 Rooms, $200/$300 MAP
3 Suites, $300/$325 MAP

 Visa, MC, Discov

 All Private Baths
8 Jacuzzi tubs

Closed Dec. 24 & 25

 Children Accepted in some Rooms; No Pets

 Swimming Pool, Walking Paths, Hiking, Biking, Golf, Carriage Rides, Antiquing, Ballooning, Peace & quiet

 Breakfast & Dinner daily
Wine & Beer available

 Smoking not allowed in dining room

Conference Facilities (26)

N/A

Rte. 29 (S) to Rte. 15 (S) to Zion Crossroads & Rte. 250 (E) 1 mi. to L. on Hwy. 613 for 3 mi. to inn. (Inn is 15 mi. (E) of Charlottesville via Rte. 250; 98 mi. (SW) of D.C.)

TEL. 800-277-0844
703-967-0844
FAX 703-967-0102
Route 3 (Hwy. 613) Box 430
Trevilians, VA 23093
The Sheehan Family, Innkeepers

18 Prospect Hill is a 1732 plantation just 15 miles east of Charlottesville, Virginia. Lodgings are in the manor house and renovated outbuildings featuring working fireplaces, verandahs, Jacuzzis, and breakfast-in-bed. Continental candlelight dinners served daily by reservation. Please accept our invitation to arrive early enough to enjoy afternoon tea and relax before dinner. AAA◆◆◆◆; Winner Uncle Ben's Best Inn of the Year 1992–93.
(*Traditional, Country, Inn. Member since 1979*)

SILVER THATCH INN

 7 Rooms, $110/$150 B&B

 Visa, MC, Amex, DC, CB

 All Private Baths

 Open Year-round exc. Dec. 24–25

 Well-behaved Children over 5 welcome; No Pets

 Swimming, Tennis. Nearby—Golf, Horseback Riding, Jogging, Hiking, Biking, Blue Ridge Mtns., Monticello, U. of Va.

 Breakfast, houseguests
Dinner Tues.-Sat.
Wine & Liquor available

 No Smoking

Conference Facilities (20)

 N/A

From (N); U.S. Rte. 29 (S) 1 mi. (S) of Airport Rd. to L. on Rte. 1520 to inn. From(S): U.S. 250 (W) Bypass to U.S. Rte. 29 (N) 5 mi. to R. on Rte. 1520 to inn.

TEL. 804-978-4686
FAX: 804-973-6156
3001 Hollymead Dr.
Charlottesville, VA 22901
Rita & Vince Scoffone, Innkeepers

17 This historic inn began life as a barracks built by captured Hessian soldiers during the Revolutionary War. It now provides gracious accommodations in antique-filled guest rooms and elegant candlelit dining. The restaurant features modern American cuisine, which changes with the seasons, and a wine list that won the Wine Spectator Award of Excellence.
(*Traditional, Country, Inn. Member since 1986*)

TRILLIUM HOUSE

 10 Rooms, $90/$105 B&B
2 Suites, $120/$150 B&B

 Visa, MC

 All Private Baths
Closed Dec. 24 & 25

 Well-behaved Children with Responsible Parents Welcome; No Pets

 Skiing, Golf, Tennis, Swimming, Hiking, Fishing, Horseback Riding, Canoeing, Antiquing

 Breakfast; single entree fixed-price Dinner Fri. & Sat.; Reservation required
Wine & Liquor available

 Smoking Restrictions

 Conference Facilities (25)

Wheelchair access (1 rm., dining rm. & conf. fac.)

7 One of the newer country inns, designed and built in 1983 to meet today's standards while retaining the charm of yesteryear. Outstanding common areas, library and sunroom. In the heart of Wintergreen's Devil's Knob Village, a year-round 11,000-acre resort, with an assortment of recreational activities available to guests at preferred rates, includes indoor swimming across the road. Mountain country, with trees, birds and a golf course seen from the dining room. Motorcycle restrictions.
(*Traditional, Mountain Resort, Inn. Member since 1985*)

(S) of I-64; (E) of I-81; (W) of Rte. 29. On Rte. 664, which connects Rte. 151 with Blue Ridge Pkwy, between Mile Posts 13 & 14.

TEL. 804-325-9126
RES. 800-325-9126
FAX 804-325-1099
Wintergreen Dr., Box 280
Nellysford, VA 22958
Ed & Betty Dinwiddie, Innkeepers

Country Inn Cuisine

For a number of Country Inns, dining becomes the raison detre; the inn being established as a showcase for the chef/owner's self expression. At Chef-owned Inns, the diner can be assured that each meal will be an individually created masterpiece (or nearly so) prepared especially for him. Since the quality and design of the comestibles from such a kitchen carry with them the reputation and perhaps even livelihood of their creator, guests are treated to outstanding, sometimes innovative examples of what man can create for the palate. The cuisine will often be the first thing mentioned in the guest's bragging about this Inn.

Many, many people in America are "meat and potatoes" kinds of folks. They prefer comfortable, delicious everyday fare. The pot roast, recently enjoyed by this author, which was cooked on a wood burning kitchen stove at a farmhouse Inn in New Hampshire should not be missed by such a connoisseur. And the honest to goodness home cooking and farm fresh vegetables served from an abundant Lazy- Susan table on a mountain top in North Carolina is reason enough to go there.

Perhaps the more typical Country Inn cuisine for Independent Innkeepers' Association members is created by a talented chef working hand in hand with the innkeeper to complete the total hospitality experience for the guests of the Inn. Often he is well trained and widely experienced. Sometimes he has worked up through the ranks in the kitchen "learning from the school of hard knocks." Some Country Inn chefs formerly worked at larger hotels but simply do not enjoy impersonally produced cuisine. Whatever the route, Country Inn chefs usually feel they have finally found their niche.

It is the feeling of most Innkeepers that hospitality includes providing sustenance to meet their guests' needs. Whether this means hot cider in the parlor, the ever-ready coffee/hot chocolate pot, home-baked cookies, gourmet breakfast, a picnic lunch, or candlelit dinner in an intimate dining room, the cuisine at a country inn is usually given very careful consideration.

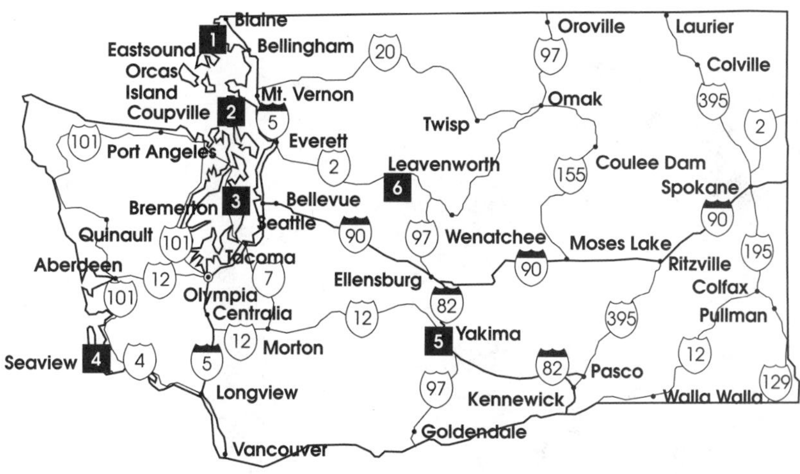

1. Turtleback Farm Inn, Eastsound
2. Captain Whidbey Inn, Coupeville
3. Willcox House Country Inn, Bremerton
4. Shelburne Inn, Seaview
5. Birchfield Manor, Yakima
6. Haus Rohrbach, Leavenworth

BIRCHFIELD MANOR

Call for directions.
TEL. 509-452-1960
2018 Birchfield Road
Yakima, WA 98901

Wil & Sandy Massett, Innkeepers

5 This award-winning restaurant and country inn is in the casual, relaxed atmosphere of a gracious home. Park-like grounds surround the outdoor swimming pool, and there is also an indoor spa open year-round. On the edge of sunny Washington Wine Country. We can personalize a wine tour just for you! Mobil ★★★
(Traditional, Country, Inn. Member since 1993)

THE CAPTAIN WHIDBEY INN

23 Rooms, $85/$125;
2 Suites & 7 other, $145/ $195 B&B (Full)
Visa, MC, Amex, Discov, Diners
Private & Shared Baths
Open Year-round
Children Welcome in some Rooms; No pets (off-premises boarding avail.)
Beach, Library, Boats, Bikes, Horseshoes, Walking Trails, Historic Town, Sailing, Charters avail.
Breakfast (Full), Lunch (avail. daily July-Sept; wknds. Oct-June); Dinner daily; Wine & Liquor available
Non-Smoking areas
Conference Facilities (30, Lagoon Lib.; 40, Cove Cottage)

2 This romantic, rustic log inn dates from 1907 and overlooks the waters of Penn Cove. Feather beds, antiques and artwork in every room and superb Northwest coastal cuisine and wines are enjoyed by guests. Spot eagles and herons, or sail the cove on a day-cruise available with our innkeeper. A gracious welcome and profound relaxation await you.

(Rustic, Country, Inn. Member since 1973)

From north: I-5 (S) Exit 230 & Hwy. 20 to Coupeville. Turn on Madrona. From (S): I-5 (N) Exit 189, Mukilteo Ferry, Hwy. 525. Hwy. 20. From west: Keystone Ferry, Hwy. 20.

TEL. 360-678-4097
800-366-4097
FAX 360-678-4110

2072 W. Captain Whidbey Inn Rd.
Coupeville, WA 98239
Capt. John Colby Stone, Innkeeper

HAUS ROHRBACH PENSION

9 Rooms, $85/$125 B&B
3 Suites, $150/$160 B&B
Visa, MC, Amex, Discov, DC
8 Private Baths
Open Year-round; Closed Weekdays in Nov, Thanksgiving Day, Dec. 23-25
Children Welcome; No pets
Hiking, Biking, Skiing, Horseback Riding, Hay Rides, Sleigh Rides, Shopping, Art Galleries, Jogging, Rafting, Golf, nearby. Swimming, Hot Tub, Sledding on Site
Picnic Lunch & Dinner Available for Conference Groups
Non-Smoking
Conference Facilities (12-24)
Wheelchair Access (2 rms., dining rm. and conf. fac.)

6 Hugging a mountainside in the foothills of the Cascades, Haus Rohrbach, fashioned after the pensions of Europe, offers guests the experience of "gemutlichkeit" meaning coziness, joviality and kindness. The inn enjoys spectacular valley views. Close-up the fragrant flower boxes and well maintained gardens soothe the soul. Guests are pampered with a welcoming common area, suites designed for romance, down comforters, homemade desserts and a standard of cleanliness to put you at ease. Whatever your whim—shopping, outdoor recreation or peaceful relaxation—the richness of our four seasons makes your stay a time to remember.

(Rustic, Mountain, Breakfast Inn. Member since 1994)

From Seattle: I-5 N to Everett; Hwy 2/ Wenatchee-Stevens Pass Exit. Stay on Hwy 2 to Leavenworth. Turn L on to Ski Hill Drive for 1/2 mi. Turn left on Ranger Rd to end of road.

TEL. 509-548-7024
800-548-4477
FAX 509-548-5038

12882 Ranger Rd.
Leavenworth, WA. 98821
Robert & Kathryn Harrild, Innkeepers

SHELBURNE INN

 13 Rooms, $89/$125 B&B
2 Suites, $160/$165 B&B

 Visa, MC, Amex

 All Private Baths

 Open Year-round

 Quiet, well-supervised Children; No Pets

 Beachcombing, Bicycling, Golf, Horseback Riding

Breakfast, Lunch, Dinner
Wine & Liquor available

Smoking restricted

Conference Facilities (35)

Wheelchair Access
(1 Room)

From Seattle, I-5 (S) to Olympia Hwy. 8 & 12 to Montesano & Hwy. 101 (S) to Seaview. From OR coast, U.S. 101 across Astoria Bridge L. to Liwaco (N) 2 mi. to Seaview.

TEL. 360-642-2442
FAX 360-642-8904
Box 250, 4415 Pacific Way
Seaview, WA 98644
David Campiche & Laurie Anderson, Innkeepers

4 An unspoiled 28-mile stretch of wild Pacific seacoast is just a 10-minute walk through rolling sand dunes from this inviting country inn, built in 1896. Restoration and refurbishing of the award-winning inn has included the addition of Art Nouveau stained glass windows, along with antique furnishings and fine art. A sumptuous breakfast featuring the best of the northwest is complimentary with your room. Innovative cuisine has brought national recognition to the outstanding restaurant and pub, where lunch and dinner are served. The Shelburne has been named one of the "Top 25 inns worldwide." (*Traditional, Village, Inn. Member since 1988*)

TURTLEBACK FARM INN

7 Rooms, $80/$160 B&B

Visa, MC

All Private Baths

Open Year-round

Appropriate for children over 8; Pets not allowed

Hiking, Salt & Fresh-water Fishing, Sea Kayaking, Golf, Bicycling, Boating, Local Crafts

Full Breakfast, Beverages any time, Sherry and Fruit BYOB

No Smoking

Conference Facilities (15)

Wheelchair Access
(3 Rooms)

From Orcas ferry landing, follow Horseshoe Hwy. (N) to first intersection (2.9 mi.). Turn L. to first R. (0.9 mi.). Continue on Crow Valley Rd. 2.4 mi. (N) to inn.

TEL 206-376-4914
Crow Valley Rd., Route 1
Box 650, Eastsound,
Orcas Island, WA 98245
William & Susan C. Fletcher, Innkeepers

1 A country farmhouse located on Orcas Island, the loveliest of the San Juan Islands which dot Puget Sound. This graceful and comfortable inn is considered one of the most romantic places in the country (*L.A. Times, USA Today*). Turtleback is noted for its spectacular setting, detail-perfect restoration and expansion, spotless maintenance & award-winning breakfasts. A haven for those who enjoy breathtaking scenery, varied outdoor activities, unique shopping and superb food, Turtleback Farm Inn provides a perfect destination for the discriminating traveler.
(*Traditional, Country, Inn. Member since 1991*)

WILLCOX HOUSE COUNTRY INN

4 rooms, $110/$175 B&B
1 suite, $110 B&B

Visa, MC

All Private Baths
(2 with Jacuzzi)

Open year-round

Children over 15; No pets

Private beach & pier, Floating dock, Row boat & Peddle boat, Hiking, Golf courses in area, Antiquing

Breakfast, Lunch, Dinner Afternoon wine & cheese hour; breakfast included, prix fixe; lunch and dinner by reservation; wine list; Wine available

Smoking outdoors only

Conference Facilities (10)

Wheelchair access (1 rm., dining rm.)

Overlooking Hood Canal, this historic 1930's Country House Inn is situated in a forest setting between Seattle and the Olympic peninsula. The mansion estate offers park-like grounds, private saltwater beach and spectacular views. Comfortable period pieces and antiques are featured in guest rooms and the great room, billiard room, pub, library, and view dining room. *Country Inns Magazine* award: one of the top twelve inns in North America in 1993.
(*Elegant, Waterside, Inn. Member since 1993*)

17 mi. east of Bremerton on Hood Canal, near Holly. Call for directions.

TEL. 360-830-4492
FAX 360-830-0506
(call first)
2390 Tekiu Rd.
Bremerton, WA 98312

Cecilia & Phillip Hughes,
Innkeepers

Rates are quoted for 2 people for 1 night and do not necessarily include service charges and state taxes. An asterisk after the rates indicates a per-person rate for AP and MAP plans. For more detailed information, ask the inns for their brochures.

AP — American Plan (3 meals included in room rate)

MAP — Modified American Plan (breakfast & dinner included in room rate)

EP — European Plan (meals not included in room rate)

B&B — Bed & Breakfast (breakfast included in room rate)

R — Represents recreational facilities and diversions either on the premises of an inn or nearby

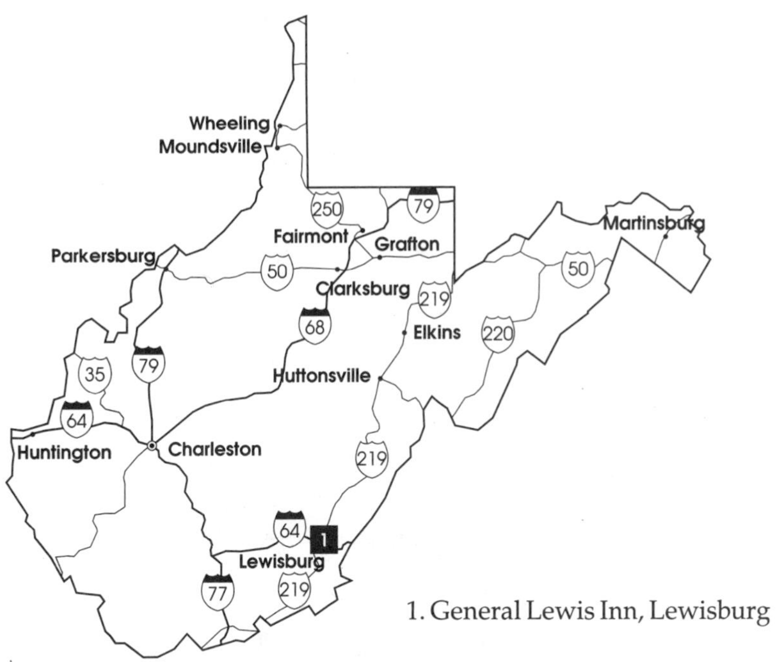

1. General Lewis Inn, Lewisburg

THE GENERAL LEWIS

23 Rooms, $60/$108 EP
2 Suite, $88/$106 EP

Visa, MC, Amex

All Private Baths

Open Year-round
Children Welcome
Pets Allowed

Garden, National Historic District, Golf, Tennis (all seasons), Hiking Trails, Biking, Horseback Riding, Carriage Ride, Swimming (all seasons), Fishing, Canoeing, White Water Rafting, Antiquing, Theater, Caverns

Breakfast, Lunch, Dinner
Wine & Liquor available
No Smoking

Wheelchair Access (1 rm. & dining rm.)

I-64, Lewisburg Exit 169 & Rte. 219 (S) for 1.5 mi. to Rte. 60 (E) for .3 mi. to inn on R.

TEL. 304-645-2600
800-628-4454
FAX: 304-645-2600
301 E. Washington St.
Lewisburg, WV 24901

Mary Noel Hock &
Jim Morgan, Innkeepers

Come rock in a chair on the veranda of the General Lewis Inn. See passengers alight from a horse-drawn carriage. On chilly days dream by the fireplace, solve one of the puzzles, or play a fascinating game. Don't miss Memory Hall's display of old tools for home and farm. Antiques furnish every room, including comfortable canopy, spool and poster beds. The dining room in the 1834 wing features Southern cooking. Nestled in beautiful Greenbrier Valley, the Inn offers nearby walking tours. Explore the Lewisburg district and browse the antique shops. AAA ◆◆◆ Mobil ★★★
(Traditional, Village, Inn. Member since 1973)

1. Old Rittenhouse Inn, Bayfield
2. White Gull Inn, Fish Creek
3. Inn at Cedar Crossing, Sturgeon Bay
4. White Lace Inn, Sturgeon Bay
5. The Creamery, Downsville

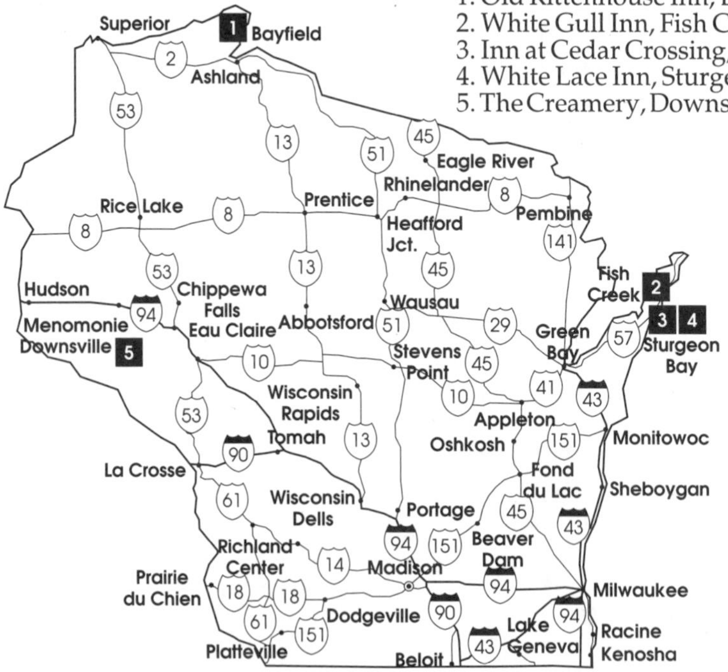

THE CREAMERY RESTAURANT & INN

3 Rooms, $100/$115 B&B
1 Suite, $130 B&B

Visa, MC

All Private Baths

Closed Jan.-March

Children - Yes
Pets Discouraged

Dunn Co. Pottery & Gallery, Red Cedar St. Park, Hiking, Biking, Skiing Historical Museums

Breakfast daily for guests; Lunch, Dinner Tues.-Sun., Sun. Brunch; Wine & Liquor available

Smoking not encouraged

N/A

5 This remodeled turn-of-the-century creamery in the hills of western Wisconsin contains four large guest quarters with cherry woodwork, handmade tiles, pottery lamps and concealed TVs. Its sweeping views of the Red Cedar River Valley and hills along with a reputation for exceptional cuisine and fine wines has made this family-run inn well known from Chicago to Minneapolis. Dunn County Pottery studio and showrooms adjacent to the restaurant. (*Contemporary, Village, Breakfast Inn. Member since 1991*)

From I-94, Exit 41 at Menomonie; Hwy. 25(S) 10 mi., L. at CTH "C," 1/3 mi. on R. (75 mi. E. of St. Paul, MN.)

TEL.715-664-8354
P.O. Box 22
Downsville, WI 54735

Richard, David, John Thomas; Jane Thomas De Florin, Innkeepers

INN AT CEDAR CROSSING

 9 Rooms, $59/$138 B&B

 Visa, MC, Discov

 All Private Baths
5 Whirlpools

Open Year-round exc. Dec. 25

 Older Children Welcome
No Pets

 Sailing, Hiking, Skiing, Beaches, 5 State Parks, Galleries, Shops, Summer Theater, Golf, Tennis

 Breakfast, Lunch, Dinner, Evening Refreshments
Wine & Liquor available

 Smoking Restricted

 Conference Facilities (26–off season)

Wheelchair access (dining rm. & conf. fac.)

Hwy. 42 or 57 (N) to Sturgeon Bay. Bus. Rte. 42/57 into town across old bridge. L. on 4th Ave. 1 blk., then L. on Louisiana St. to inn.

TEL. 414-743-4200 (lodg.)
414-743-4249 (dining)
336 Louisiana St.
Sturgeon Bay, WI 54235

Terry Wulf, Innkeeper

Warm hospitality, elegant antique-filled guestrooms, and creative regional cuisine are tradition at this most intimate Door County inn (National Register of Historic Places). Lovingly restored, you'll find cozy fireplaces, room service, and evening refreshments await pampered travelers. Guestrooms are exceptionally furnished—oversized canopied beds, double whirlpool tubs, private porches, inviting fireplaces. Exquisite dining features fresh ingredients, enticingly prepared entrees, sinful desserts, and casual pub, set in the beauty and culture of Wisconsin's Door Peninsula.
(*Traditional, In-Town, Inn. Member since 1990*)

OLD RITTENHOUSE INN

 17 Rooms, $99/$129 B&B
4 Suites, $129/$199 B&B

 Visa, MC

 All Private Baths
5 Whirlpools

 Open Year-round; inquire for Winter weekdays

 Children Accepted

 Sailing, Biking, Skiing, Tennis, Swimming (indoor year-round)

 Breakfast/Dinner/Sun. Brunch open to public
Wine available

 No Smoking in Dining Rooms

 Conference Facilities (15)

Wheelchair Access (2 rms., dining rm.)

Duluth Hwy. 2 (E) for 60 mi. to L. on Hwy. 13 (N) (just outside Ashland) for 20 mi. to Bayfield

TEL. 715-779-5111
301 Rittenhouse Ave., P.O. Box 584
Bayfield, WI 54814

Jerry & Mary Phillips, Innkeepers

Three turn-of-the-century homes make up this Victorian inn where hospitality, superior dining, and music blend into a joyous whole. Mary and Jerry Phillips share in the creation of wonderful meals, lovely dinner concerts and other events. Guest rooms are handsomely outfitted with antiques, working fireplaces and the entire inn offers a delightful sojourn.
(*Elegant, Victorian, Village, Inn. Member since 1980*)

THE WHITE GULL INN

14 Rooms, $85/$160 EP
5 Cottages, $140/$225 EP

Visa, MC, Amex, Discov, Diners

14 Private Baths

Open Year-round exc. Thanksgiving Day, Dec. 24–25

Children Welcome in suitable rooms; No Pets

Golf, Tennis, Swimming, Sailing, Hiking, Biking, XC Skiing, Summer Stock Theatre, Music Festival, Antique Shops, Art Galleries

Breakfast, Lunch, Dinner, Wine & Beer available

No Smoking

Wheelchair Access (dining room)

2 Established in 1896, this white clapboard inn is tucked away in the scenic bayside village of Fish Creek, on Wisconsin's Door Peninsula. The turn-of-the-century antiques and fireplaces give the inn rooms and surrounding cottages a warm, comfortably hospitable atmosphere. Famous for hearty breakfasts and lunches and quiet candlelight dinners, the inn is renowned for the unique, traditional Door County fish boils, featuring locally caught whitefish cooked outside over an open fire.
(*Traditional, Village, Inn. Member since 1979*)

Milwaukee I-43 for 98 mi. to Green Bay, then R. on Rte. 57 (N) for 39 mi. to Sturgeon Bay; (N) on Rte. 42 for 25 mi. to Fish Creek. L. at stop sign for 3 blks. to inn.

TEL. 414-868-3517
FAX 414-868-2367
4225 Main St., P.O. Box 160
Fish Creek, WI 54212

Andy & Jan Coulson, Innkeepers

WHITE LACE INN

14 Rooms (10 with fireplaces), $48/$165 B&B
1 Suite, $140/$165 B&B

Visa, MC, Discover

All Private Baths
7 Whirlpools

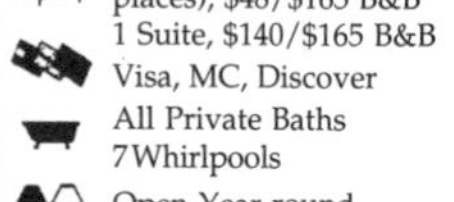

Open Year-round

Older Children welcome
No Pets

Gardens, Beaches, Sailing, Shopping, XC Skiing, Hiking, Golf

Breakfast & Snacks

No smoking

Wheelchair Access (1 Room)

4 Romance begins as you follow a winding garden pathway that links this charming inn's 3 historic homes. Guest rooms are furnished with exceptional comforts, period antiques, oversized whirlpool tubs, and inviting fireplaces. A warm welcome awaits as guests are greeted with lemonade or hot chocolate. Located in the resort area of Door County, the inn is close to many delights.
(*Traditional, Village, Breakfast Inn. Member since 1988*)

Hwy. 57 (N) to Sturgeon Bay & Bus. Rte. 42-57 into town. Cross downtown bridge to L. on 5th Ave.

TEL. 414-743-1105
16 No. 5th Ave.
Sturgeon Bay, WI 54235

Dennis & Bonnie Statz, Innkeepers

INTERNATIONAL HOSPITALITY

We are proud to feature in this *Register* a fine array of accommodations in Canada and Great Britain. The increase in number over those listed in previous editions reflects our recent Association emphasis in assisting the international traveler.

Now, more than ever before, guests who enjoy IIA Inns in the United States are also traveling across the borders and across the oceans seeking similar kinds of hospitality there. Certainly international travelers who are accustomed to depending on the quality of the Independent Innkeepers' Association in the continental United States will be looking for assurance of corresponding hospitality experiences wherever they travel in other countries. Conversely, IIA member Inns in the United States would like very much to show the foreign traveler our place in the world of hospitality.

Whether in the United States, Canada, England, Scotland, or Wales, the Independent Innkeepers' Association includes hospitality establishments of the finest quality. These select establishments include country house hotels, manor houses, historic homes, traditional inns, farmhouses, and small hotels. They are located in the countryside, in towns, along seashores, on mountain tops, and in other locations, all worth a visit.

To stay with any of our international number is to discover the finest innkeeper care and hospitality in comfortable, unique and well maintained facilities which you will want to brag about when you return home.

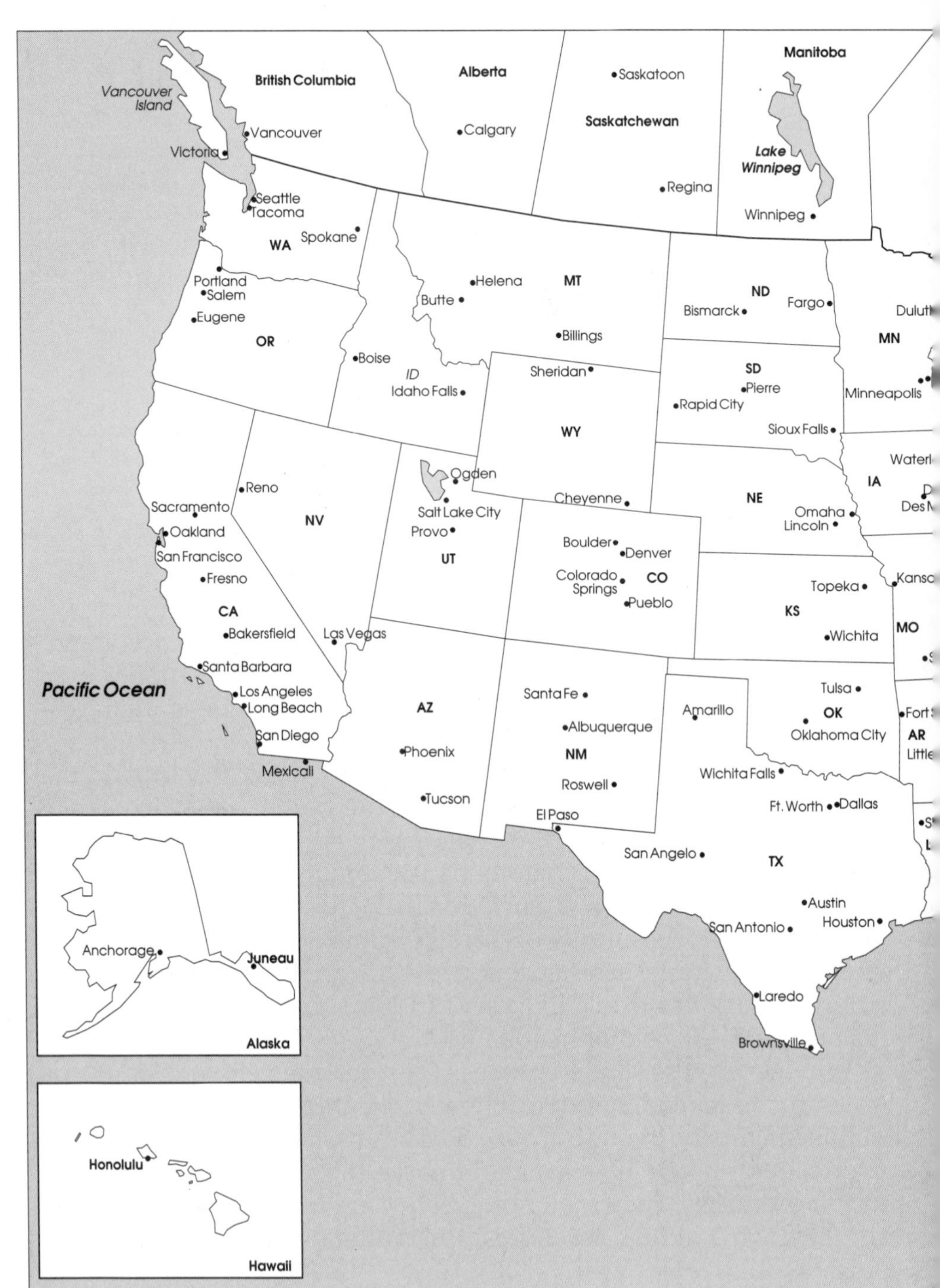

British Columbia
Alberta
Saskatoon
Saskatchewan
Manitoba
Vancouver Island
Vancouver
Victoria
Calgary
Regina
Lake Winnipeg
Winnipeg
Seattle
Tacoma
Spokane
WA
Portland
Salem
Eugene
OR
Boise
ID
Idaho Falls
Helena
Butte
MT
Billings
ND
Bismarck
Fargo
MN
SD
Pierre
Rapid City
Sioux Falls
Minneapolis
Sheridan
WY
Ogden
Salt Lake City
Provo
UT
Reno
NV
Sacramento
Oakland
San Francisco
Fresno
CA
Bakersfield
Las Vegas
Santa Barbara
Los Angeles
Long Beach
San Diego
Mexicali
Pacific Ocean
Cheyenne
NE
Omaha
Lincoln
IA
Boulder
Denver
Colorado Springs
CO
Pueblo
Topeka
KS
Wichita
MO
AZ
Phoenix
Tucson
Santa Fe
Albuquerque
NM
Roswell
El Paso
Amarillo
Tulsa
OK
Oklahoma City
AR
Wichita Falls
Ft. Worth
Dallas
San Angelo
TX
Austin
Houston
San Antonio
Laredo
Brownsville
Anchorage
Juneau
Alaska
Honolulu
Hawaii

Canada

United States

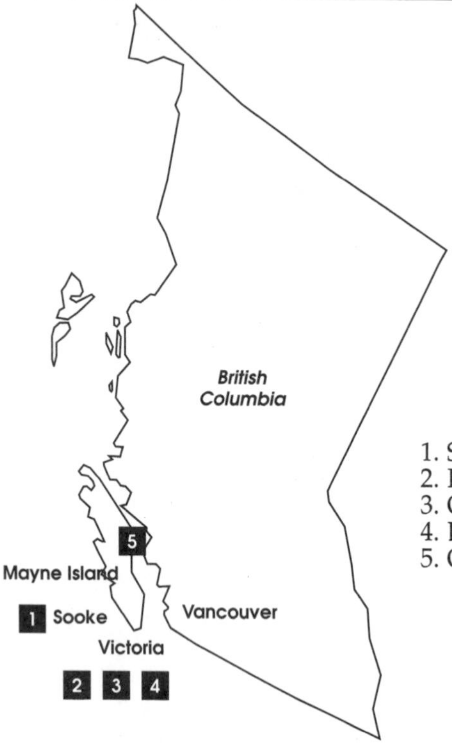

British Columbia

5 Mayne Island

1 Sooke

Vancouver

Victoria

2 3 4

1. Sooke Harbour House, Sooke
2. Holland House, Victoria
3. Oak Bay Beach Hotel, Victoria
4. Beaconsfield Inn, Victoria
5. Oceanwood Country Inn, Mayne Island

BEACONSFIELD INN

4 An Award-winning Heritage restoration, this 1905 Edwardian Manor set in an English cottage garden is a luxurious retreat in the residential heart of Victoria. Finely chosen amenities include original oak wainscotting and mahogany floors, English antiques, oriental carpets, stained glass windows, down comforters, eleven fireplaces, six jacuzzi tubs. A gourmet breakfast in the Dining Room or Sunroom, Afternoon tea and evening Sherry Hour in the Library is included. Four blocks to oceanfront/downtown. (*Elegant, In-Town, Breakfast Inn. Member since 1994*)

From North: Hwy 17 to City Centre; L. on Humboldt St. From Inner Harbor: Government St. N to Humboldt St. Turn R. for 4 blocks.

TEL. 604-384-4044
FAX: 604-721-2442
998 Humboldt St.
Victoria, B.C. V8V 2Z8
Con & Judi Sollid
Innkeepers/Owners

HOLLAND HOUSE INN

10 Rooms, $80/$145-$120/$225 Can. B&B
$80/$145 Off Season
$115/$210 On Season
Visa, MC, Amex, Diners
All Private Baths

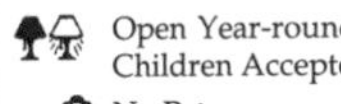
Open Year-round
Children Accepted;
No Pets
Golf, Fishing, Cycling, British High Tea, Butchart Gardens, Royal B.C. Mus-eum, Antiques, Beacon Hill Park
Full Gourmet Breakfast
Beverages at any time.
Wine Available; BYOB
Non-Smoking Environment
Conference Facilities (20)
Wheelchair Access (1 Room)

From Hwy. 17; (S) to Belleville St., L. on Government St. for 2 blocks (S) to corner of Government & Michigan.

TEL. 604-384-6644
FAX 604-384-6117
595 Michigan St.
Victoria, B.C. Canada
V8V1S7

Lance Austin-Olsen & Robin Birsner, Innkeepers

2 This unique small hotel, where fine art and unequalled comfort are combined, creates an atmosphere of casual elegance — luxurious rooms, some fireplaces, queen-size beds, goose-down duvets, antique furnishings and delightful small balconies. The Gallery Lounge, where you may relax by the fire or browse in the art library, showcases original works by premier artists of Victoria.
(*Traditional, Inn-Town, Breakfast Inn. Member since 1990*)

OAK BAY BEACH HOTEL

47 Rooms, $78/$226 Can. B&B; 4 Suites, $248/$385 Can. B&B
Visa, MC, Amex, Diners
All Private Baths
Open Year-round
Children Welcome
No Pets
Yacht Excursions, Fishing, Whale Watching, Lunch/Dinner Cruises, Jogging. Also: Golf, Tennis, Pool. Recreation Center nearby.
Breakfast, High Tea or Lunch
Cruise Included; Dinner, High Tea Daily; Wine & Liquor avail.
Some Non-Smoking rms.
Conference Facilities (150)
Wheelchair Access (3 rms., dining rm. & conf. fac.)

South on Hwy. 17 Left on Hillside (E), which becomes Lansdowne. Right on Beach Dr. to Hotel.

TEL. 604-598-4556
800-668-7758
FAX 604-598-4556
1175 Beach Dr.
Victoria, B.C. Canada
V8S 2N2
Kevin & Bruce Walker, Innkeeper

3 Beautiful seaside location, warm and gracious hospitality, crackling fireplaces, first-class accommodations in an atmosphere of old world charm. This prestigious family-owned hotel in the residential area of Oak Bay is a significant part of the history and heritage of the city of Victoria. Magnificent lawns and gardens rolling to the ocean, islands, mountains in the distance, provide wonderful views. The Tudor-style architecture is complemented by antiques and period pieces. Meals, service and hospitality are the best. Rates incl. lunch cruise or High Tea AAA ◆◆◆◆ award. (*Victorian, Waterside, Resort. Member since 1979*)

OCEANWOOD COUNTRY INN

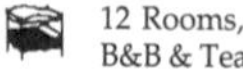

12 Rooms, $120/$295 B&B & Tea

Visa, MC

All Private Baths

Open March–Nov.

No Children under 16; No Pets

Sauna, Hot Tub, Bicycles, Hiking, Tennis, Ocean Kayaking

Breakfast, Lunch, Dinner, Afternoon Tea; Wine & Liquor Available

Smoking restrictions; Library & Outside only

Conference Facilities (12)

(1 rm., Dining rm. & conf. fac.)

5 On the waterfront in Canada's spectacularly beautiful Gulf Islands, Oceanwood is like a cozy and civilized English country house. Twelve individually-decorated guest rooms, all with private bath, many with fireplaces. Comfortable living room, well-stocked library, bright, plant-filled garden room and cozy games room. Charming dining room, overlooking Navy Channel, features Pacific Northwest cuisine and West Coast wines. Island activities include ocean kayaking, cycling, tennis, country walks and the infinite pleasure of peace and quiet. (*Traditional, Country, Inn. Member since 1994*)

BC Ferries from either Tsawwassen or Swartz Bay; arrive at Village Bay on Mayne Island; Turn R. out of terminal onto Dalton Dr.; R on Mariners Way; L. on Dinner Bay Road & follow it until you see Oceanwood Sign on L.—630 Dinner Bay Rd.

TEL. 604-539-5074
FAX: 604-539-3002
630 Dinner Bay Rd.
Mayne Island, B.C. V0N 2J0
Marilyn & Jonathan Chilvers, Owners

SOOKE HARBOUR HOUSE INN

13 Rooms, $145/$205–$165/205 B&BL (includes lunch)

Visa, MC, Amex, Enroute

All Private Baths
7 Jacuzzis

Open Year-round; some restrictions during the week Nov-March

Children Welcome; Pets Accepted, charge of $20 per day

World Class Fishing, Golfing, Whale Watching, Gardens, Biking & Hiking Trails and Beaches, etc.

Breakfast & Lunch for Houseguests; Dinner for Public; Wine & Liquor Available

No Smoking

Conference Facilities (30)

Wheelchair Access (1 Rm., dining rm. & conf. fac.)

1 Cozy and homelike, consistently rated one of Canada's top ten restaurants which has become known as a leader in West Coast Canadian cuisine. The restaurant uses only fresh, organic ingredients which are grown in the inn's gardens, by nearby organic farms or harvested in the wilds from around Sooke. The inn offers secluded, romantic rooms with fabulous views of the ocean and mountains. Each room features fireplaces, jacuzzi and antique furnishings and art pieces.
(*Waterside, Retreat/Inn. Member since 1988*)

Victoria, B.C., Hwy. 1 (W) to Hwy. 14 & Sooke Village. Through Stoplights, 1 mi. to L. on Whiffen Spit Rd. for .5 mi. to inn.

TEL. 604-642-3421
FAX: 604-642-6988
1528 Whiffen Spit Rd.
R.R. #4, **Sooke, B.C., Canada**
V0S 1N0
Fredrica & Sinclair Philip, Innkeepers

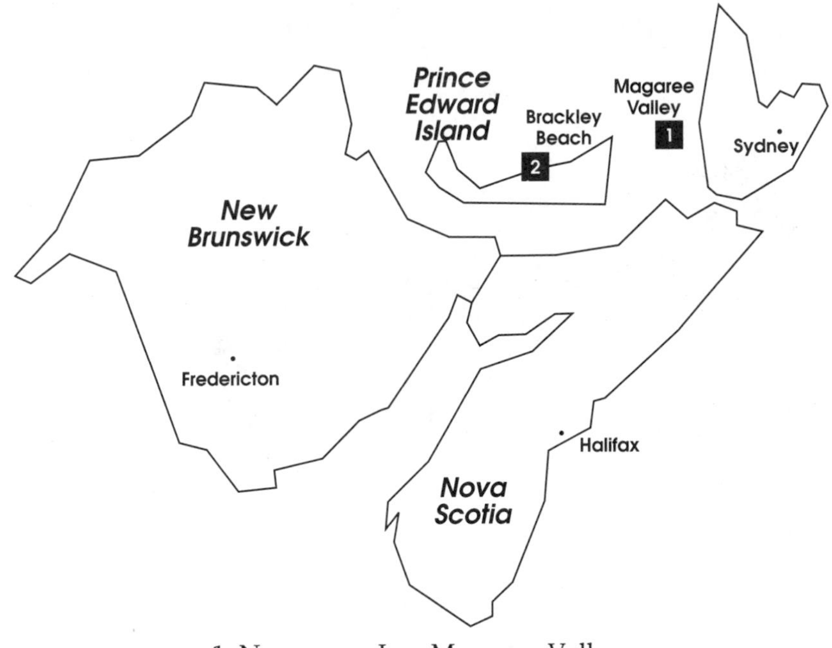

1. Normaway Inn, Margaree Valley
2. Shaw's Hotel, Brackley Beach

NORMAWAY INN

9 Rooms, $159/$199* Can. B&B; 5 (1pers., $117)
19 Cabins, $184/$199* Can. B&B
Visa, MC
All Private Baths
Open June 16 to Oct. 15
Children Accepted; Pets by prior Arrangement
Tennis, Hiking, Biking, Lawn Games, Fiddle Concerts/Barn Dances, Canoeing, Salmon Fishing, Whale Cruises
Breakfast & Dinner; Packed Lunches; Wine & Liquor Available
No Smoking in Dining Room
Conference Facilities (50)
Wheelchair Access (2 Rooms)

STrans Canada Hwy. Jct. 7 at Nyanza (N) on Cabot Trail. 17 mi. Between Lake O'Law and N.E. Margaree turn at Egypt Rd. 2 mi. to inn.

TEL. 800-565-9463
or 902-248-2987
FAX902-248-2600
Box 138, Margaree Valley.
VN.S. Canada BOE 2C0
David M. MacDonald, Innkeeper

Nestled in the hills of the Cape Breton Highlands, near the beginning of the spectacular Cabot Trail, this 250-acre property offers a 1920's inn and cabins, most with woodstove fireplaces and some with jacuzzis. Enjoy superb food, service, and choice wines. Guests often relax by the fire after dinner and enjoy films of traditional entertainment. *(Traditional, Country, Inn. Member since 1972)*

SHAW'S HOTEL

We are the oldest family operated Inn in Canada. The Shaw's family continues the tradition which began in 1860. Shaw's Hotel is located on a 75 acre pennisula overlooking glistening Brackley Bay. It provides an ideal setting for its 17 antique furnished rooms and suites plus its 18 charming cottages ranging in size from 1 to 4 bedrooms. Our 7 deluxe chalets featuring sauna & whirlpools are open yearly. Shaw's Hotel provides superb meals in their rates. We provide many recreational activities and are located 600 yards from Brackley Beach. (*Traditional, Ocean Side, Resort. Member since 1975*)

Take ferry or plane to P.E.I. Trans Canada Hwy. (Rte.1) to Charlottetown. Follow signs to airport and Rte. 15 for 10 mi. to Brackley Beach.

TEL. 902-672-2022
FAX 902-672-3000
Brackley Beach
Prince Edward Island, Canada C1E 1Z3
Robbie and Pam Shaw, Innkps.

THE STAFF AT A COUNTRY INN - PERSONAL INTEREST AND SERVICE

It doesn't take many visits along the Country Inn circuit to realize that a key ingredient for any hospitality recipe is the staff who "keep it all together". Since the size of most Inns limits the number of employees needed, the sometimes cumbersome employer/employee structure is usually not necessary. Staff members take personal interest in what they do, thereby losing that "employee" aura.

Many innkeepers very quickly and proudly introduce staff members to guests since they are often considered members of the Inn family. Sometimes they actually are members of the innkeeper's family. Besides the expected mother/father/offspring team found at many Inns, guests are sometimes surprised to have the innkeeper introduce the dishwasher or desk clerk as his mother. One very successful innkeeper employs his mother-in-law as a housekeeper; in another inn a retired gentleman is employed by his niece as a waiter.

Because Inns are usually very highly respected businesses in a community, they are often considered prestigious places to work. I recall overhearing one staff member tell her friend, "My friends *have* to work at other establishments in town. I *get* to work at the Inn." It is very difficult to hide this attitude from guests.

Every staff member from the lawn boy to the desk person to the housekeeper has an important role in providing consummate hospitality for every guest. The personal interest and service of staff members at an Inn is a big measure of what brings guests to enjoy their visits. Fortunately, in our Inns it is easy for staff to feel the importance of their contribution. Certainly, guests perceive this Inn-family teamwork, and that makes all the difference . . . for everyone.

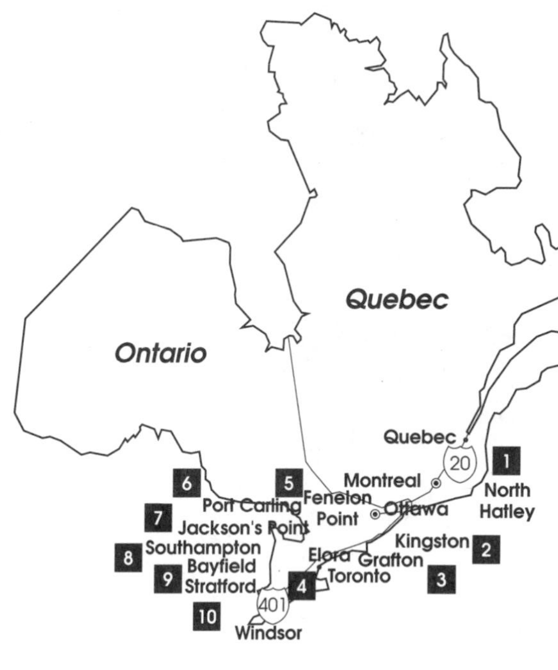

1. Hovey Manor, North Hatley
2. Rosemount Inn, Kingston
3. Ste. Anne's, Grafton
4. Elora Mill Inn, Elora
5. Eganridge Inn, Fenelon Falls
6. Sherwood Inn, Port Carling
7. The Briars, Jackson Point
8. Chantry House Inn, Southampton
9. Little Inn of Bayfield, Bayfield
10. Stone Maiden Inn, Stratford

THE BRIARS

46 Rooms, $170/$220 U.S. MAP; 4 Suites & Cott., $178/$278 U.S. MAP
Visa, MC, Amex
All Private Baths
Open Year-round
Fun-filled Children's program (in season)
Pet Kennels nearby
Golf, Tennis, Swimming, Boating, Summer Theatre, Nature Trails, Fireplaces, Solarium Pool, Whirlpool, Sauna & Game Rooms.
Breakfast, Lunch, Dinner
Wine & Liquor available
No pipes/cigars in dining room
Conference Facilities (75)
Wheelchair access (14 rms.)

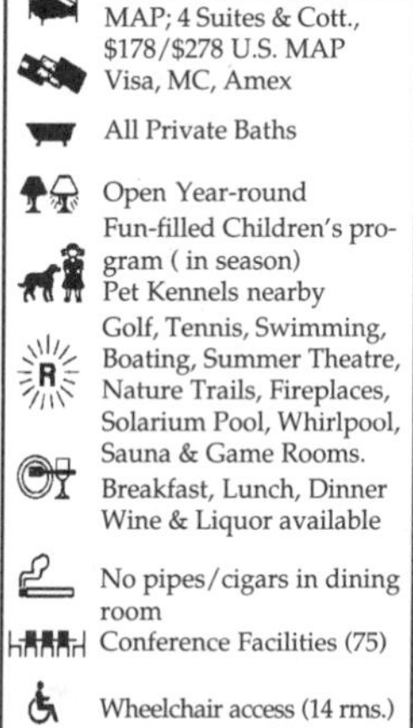

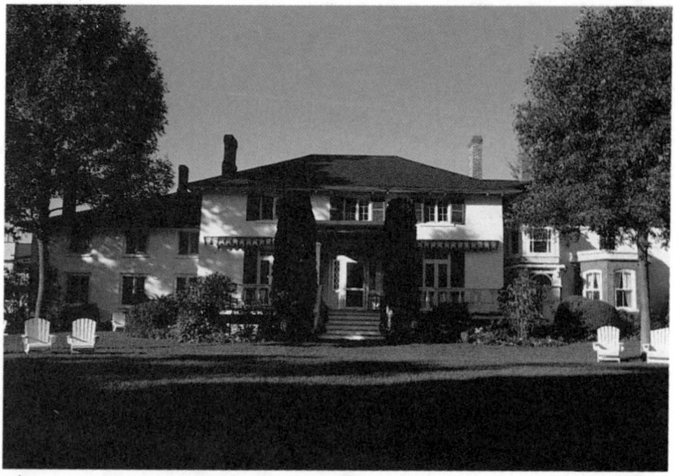

Toronto Hwy 404 (N) to Davis; R (E) to Woodbine; L (N) 20 mi. on hwy to Sutton; L (N) on Dalton to Jackson's Pt; R (E) on Lake Drive .6 mi to Hedge Rd & Briars.

TEL 800-465-2376
FAX 905-722-9698
55 Hedge Rd., R.R. #1
Jackson's Point, Ontario, Can. LOE 1LO
John & Barbara Sibbald & family, Innkeepers

7 The resort that feels like a Country Inn tantalizes the senses, and restores the soul amid genuine old world charm. Guests recount how this 200-acre estate elevates relaxation to an artform and provides the amenities and dining that one would expect in a AAA/CAA Four Diamond luxury resort. It boasts a Scottish woodlands style golf course, lush lawns with vast gardens, and invites exploration of a variety of natural habitats. The estate nestles on the shores of sparkling Lake Simcoe, where guests are accommodated in the 150 year old Manor House, its adjoining wings, and lakeside cottages. The Briars is located just an hour north of Toronto.
(*Traditional, Waterside, Resort. Member since 1980*)

CHANTRY HOUSE INN

4 Rooms, $150/$75 (for 2) Can. MAP; 3 Suites, $175/$200 Can. MAP
MC, Visa
All Private Baths
Open Year-round
Well-supervised Children
Kennel for Pets nearby
Birds, Boardwalk & Beaches, Lake Huron, Golf, Tennis XC Skiing, Bird Sanctuary, Historic Lighthouses
Breakfast for houseguests
Dinner by reservation
Wine & Liquor Available
No Smoking
Conference Facilities (20)
N/A

8 Chantry House Inn is the "Finale" of David Snyders' Revelation Lights and Virgil Foxs' Heavy Organ Production which toured the United States and Canada in the 1960's and 1970's.

Diane and David have together created the Inn, so guests can enjoy wonderful meals, dinner concerts and reminiscing. The Inn is comfortably ecclectic and filled with special things for special people.

(*Traditional, Village, Inn. Member since 1991*)

Turn West off Hwy 21 (scenic Bluewater Rte.) 2 blks. toward Lake Huron at the only stoplight in Southhampton.

TEL. 1-519-797-2646
IF BUSY 1- 519-797-5538
118 High Street
Southampton, Ontario, Canada NOH 2LO
Diane & David Snyder, Innkps.

EGANRIDGE INN & COUNTRY CLUB

5 Cotts., $140/$175 Can. B&B; 6 Suites, $120/$190 Can. B&B
Visa, MC, Amex
All Private Baths
Closed Nov.–Apr.
Children Accepted
No Pets – Kennels nearby
Private Golf, Tennis, Beach, Boating, Theater, Antiquing, Galleries, Shopping
Lunch, Dinner, Room Service; MAP Rates available
Wine & Liquor available
Some Non-smoking areas
Conference Facilities (45)
Wheelchair Access (4 Rms.)

5 Overlooking a spectacular vista across Sturgeon Lake, in a setting of pine and stone, this inn includes Dunsford House, one of North America's finest preserved examples of 2-story, hand-hewn log home architecture, built in 1837. Challenging golf, award-winning continental cuisine, and the ultimate in luxurious accommodations fulfill guests' highest expectations.

(*Elegant, Georgian, Waterside, Inn. Member since 1991*)

From Toronto, (E) on Hwy. 401 to Exit 436. Hwy. 35. R. on Hwy. 121 to Fenelon Falls. R. on County Rd. 8 for 9 km to inn signs.

TEL. 705-738-5111
RR#3, **Fenelon Falls Ontario, Canada, K0M IN0**
John & Patricia Egan, Innkeepers

ELORA MILL INN

29 Rooms, $95/$200 Can. B&B; 3 Suites, $170/$200 Can. B&B

Visa, MC, Amex En Route

All Private Baths

Open Year-round

Children Welcome
No Pets
Golf, Tennis, Squash, Hiking, XC Skiing, Canoeing, Crafts & Antiques Shopping, Mennonite tours, Music & Highland Fest.
All Meals
MAP Rates available

Wine & Liquor available
Non-smoking Dining Rm.
Conference Facilities (120)
Wheelchair Access (dining rm. & conf. fac.)

From Hwy. 401, Exit 295 (N) on Hwy. 6 (Guelph Bypass) for 2 mi. (N) of Guelph. Turn L. on Elora Rd. for 9 mi. to flashing light. Turn R. & follow signs to Elora center.

TEL. 519-846-5356
FAX 519-846-9180
77 Mill St. West
Elora, Ontario, Canada N0B 1S0
Timothy & Kathy Taylor, Innkeepers

4 This converted 19th-century grist mill is perched on the spectacular Grand River Falls in the quaint village of Elora. With heritage guest rooms and a fireside dining room and lounge, the historic country inn serves Canadian specialties with a Continental flair. Guests can enjoy the diversions of Ontario festival country or while away the hours in the inn's out-of-the-way nooks.
(*Traditional, Village, Inn. Member since 1991*)

THE LITTLE INN OF BAYFIELD

19 Rms, $90/$165 Can. EP; 12 Sts, $150/$195 Can. EP; 10% disc. w/ theatre fest. tickets
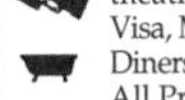
Visa, MC, Amex, EnRoute, Diners
All Private Baths
Open Year-round
Children Welcome
Pets by prior arrangement
Beaches, Boating, Birds, Cycling, Hiking, Riding, Golfing, XC SKiing, Skating, Shopping, Museums and Art Galleries, Cooking Weekends, Winetastings, Traditional Holiday Calibrations

All Meals, afternoon Tea; Sun. Brunch; MAP avail.;
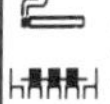
Wine & Liquor available
Non-smoking dining area
Conference Facilities (65)
Wheelchair access (5 rms., dining rm. & conf. fac.)

From Port Huron, MI. Hwy. 402(E) to Hwy. 21(N) to Bayfield. From Toronto, Hwy. 401(W) to Hwy. 8(W) to Seaforth; follow signs to Bayfield.

TEL 519-565-2611
1-800-565-1832
FAX 519-565-5474
Main Street, **Bayfield**
Ontario, Canada N0M1G0
Patrick & Gayle Waters, Innkeepers

9 Originally a stagecoach stop, this inn has welcomed guests to the picturesque lakeside village of Bayfield since the 1830's. This designated heritage Inn is replete with fireplaces, ensuite whirlpools, books and games, sauna, games and books. Fine dining has long been a tradition with superb meals and imaginative menus. Guests have a perfect base to explore the countryside and attend the Stratford and Blyth Festivals. There is much to do any time of the year.
(*Traditional, Village, Inn. Member since 1991*)

ROSEMOUNT INN

8 rooms, $79/$139 Can. B&B

Visa, MC, Amex

All Private Baths

Open mid-Jan.–mid-Dec.

Not suitable for children under 13; No pets

Historic Tours, Stage Productions, Farmers' Market, Auction Sales, Antique Market, 4 Blocks to Waterfront, Parks & Marina, Boutiques & Fine Dining

Full Gourmet Breakfast

No smoking

Conference Facilities (16)

N/A

2 Step through the old iron gates into the quiet charm of an 1850 limestone Tuscany Villa in the heart of historic Kingston. Let us pamper you . . . your room is exquisitely appointed with Victorian antiques, fine linens and down duvets. In the morning, be awakened by the aroma of Holly's "just baked" muffins or perhaps by John's "Welsh Toast" with a s-c-r-u-m-m-y berry sauce and local maple syrup. A short stroll will take you to the historic sites, antique market, fine dining and specialty boutiques.

(*Traditional, Victorian, In-Town, Breakfast Inn. Member since 1993*)

U.S.: 1000 Island Pkwy. to Hwy. #2 to Kingston; R on Brock; 4 blocks; L at Sydenham; Can: Hwy. 401 to exit #615; South 5 km.; L at Johnson; 2 km. R at Sydenham St.

TEL. 613-531-8844
FAX. 613-531-9722
46 Sydenham St. South
Kingston, Ontario K7L 3H1

Holly Doughty & John Edwards, Innkeepers

STONE MAIDEN INN

14 rooms, $85/$175 Can. B&B

Visa, MC, Personal checks

All Private Baths

Open mid-April–late Dec.

Not suitable for young children; No pets

Tennis, Swimming nearby; Lots of Local Galleries, Bookstores and Antique Shops; Historic Walking Tours; Shakespearean Theatre Festival May through October.

Breakfast (full breakfast buffet)

Smoking restricted

Conference Facilities (25)

N/A

10 Named after the stone maiden-heads which grace our front hallway, we offer quiet Victorian elegance with superior accommodations and the utmost in personal service. Hand-made quilts, ensuite bathrooms and handsome antiques grace our 14 air-conditioned rooms. Some rooms have canopy beds, fireplaces and whirlpool tubs. Afternoon refreshments and our generous breakfasts are complimentary. Visit Stratford during May to October for our world-renown Shakesperean Festival. Located close to city-centre and our 3 theatres. Call for theatre info.

(*Victorian, In-Town, Breakfast Inn. Member since 1993*)

From Detroit: Hwy. 401 E., Exit 222 N. to Stratford.From Toronto: Hwy 401 to Hwy. 8 W. to Stratford. From Buffalo: Hwy. Q.E.W. to Hwy. 403 at Hamilton; W. to Hwy. 2 at Brantford; Hwy. 403 W. to Hwy. 401 W. to Exit 222; N. to Stratford.

TEL. 519-271-7129
123 Church Street
Stratford, Ontario N5A 2R3

Barb & Len Woodward, Innkps.

SHERWOOD INN

28 Rooms, $85/$143* MAP - $99 B&B
2 Suites, 9 Cottages, $124/ $212* MAP
Visa, MC, Amex, Diners, Enroute
Private & Shared Baths
Open year-round
Children Welcome: No Pets
Tennis, Water Skiing, Windsurfing, Boating, Sailing, Canoeing, Fishing, Volleyball, Badminton, Shuffleboard, XC Skiing, Skating, Ice Fishing, Dog-Sledding, Golf nearby.
Breakfast & Lunch, Dinner available
Wine & Liquor available
Smoking Restricted
Conference Facilities (90)
Wheelchair Access (dining rm. & conf. fac.)

Hwy. 400 N to Hwy. 69 N to Foat's Bay. Turn R on Hwy. 169 S, Travel 10 km S to Sherwood Rd. Turn L on Sherwood Rd, follow to end.

TEL. 705-765-3131
800-461-4233
FAX 705-765-6668
PO Box 400, Lake Joseph
Port Carling, ONT P0B IJ0
John & Eva Heineck, Innkps.

Set amongst towering pines on the edge of Lake Joseph, tranquil Sherwood Inn offers atmosphere, impeccable service and gastronomic excellence, complimented by an outstanding wine cellar. Attentive staff anticipate guests' needs with quiet efficiency and genuine friendliness. Most of all, Sherwood is a place where guests may relax and rediscover the finer qualities of life. Received the Four Diamond Award from AAA for the past 17 years.
(*Elegant, Country, Inn. Member since 1992*)

STE. ANNE'S COUNTRY INN & SPA

7 Rooms, $150/$200 (Can.)
3 Suites, 1 Cottage, $365/ $385 AP (Can.) (includes $50 credit in the spa)
Visa, MC, Amex, Enroute
All Private Baths

Open Year-round

Not suitable for Children
No Pets

Tennis, Swimming Pool, Hot Tub, Walking Trails, Victoria Hall, The Northumberland Players, Antique Hunting, Full Spa
Breakfast, Lunch & Dinner available for guests; BYOB

No Smoking Throughout

Conference Facilities (10)

N/A

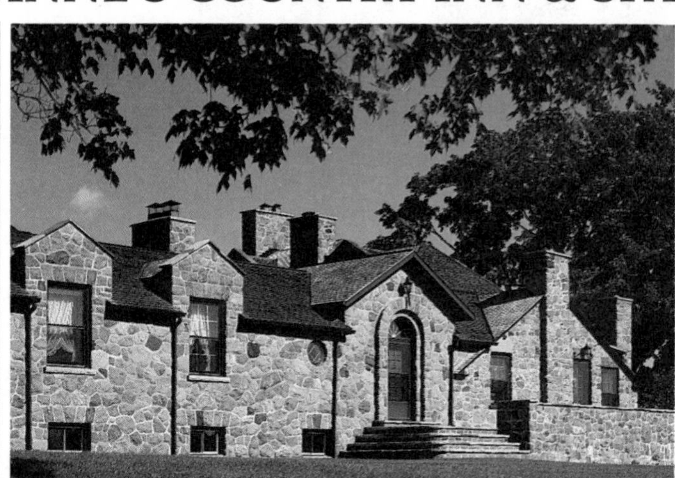

Hwy. 401 to Grafton. Exit @ 487. N towards Centreton on Aird St. for 1.5 km, to Academy Hill Rd. 1.5 km, L. to stone wall.

TEL. 800-263-2663
FAX 905-349-3106
Massey Road, R.R. 1
Grafton, Ontario, Canada K0K 2G0
Jim Corcoran and Anne Harris, Innkeepers

Rest, relax, rejuvenate... savor the sweet smell of fresh country air, drink pure spring water, enjoy a candle lit dinner. Pamper yourself with a massage, or maybe a facial. All this can be found in this English style "Castle" nestled on 560 acres in the hills of Northumberland County, one hour from Toronto. Exclusive spa packages mix the finest elements of a country inn ambiance with pampering and/or invigorating treatments to ensure the ultimate in relaxation and rest. Come for the day by train on the "Stress Express" from Toronto or Kingston.
(*Traditional, Country, Inn. Member since 1992*)

HOVEY MANOR

40 Rooms, $75/$145 US MAP (gratuities included)
Visa, MC, Amex, Diners, EnRoute
All Private Baths, 14 Jacuzzis; 24 Fireplaces
Open Year-round
Young Children and Babies Discouraged; No Pets
On site: Beaches, All Water Sports, Tennis, Touring Bikes, XC-Ski Trails, Skating Rink, Snowshoes, Ice-Fishing, Massage Room, Games Room, and Exercise Room on Site. Alpine Skiing, Golf, Riding nearby.
Breakfast, Lunch, Dinner Wine & Liquor available
Smoking restrictions; Many non-smoking rooms
Conference Facilities (2 rms.)
Wheelchair Access (2 rms., dining rm. & conf. fac.)

Formerly a private estate modeled on Mt. Vernon, this gracious manor abounds with antiques and flowers in a romantic, lakeside setting. Most of the individually decorated rooms offer combinations of fireplaces, jacuzzis, canopy beds and private balconies with superb views of the lake and English gardens. Acclaimed contemporary French cuisine and a full range of year-round recreational facilities on site and included in our rates make this resort inn a destination in itself, only 20 minutes from Vermont and convenient to Montreal, Quebec City and Ottawa. (*Elegant, Waterside, Resort. Member since 1973*)

VT. I-91 (N) to border. Continue on Rte. 55N for 29 kms. to No. Hatley Exit 29 & Rte. 108 (E) for 9 kms. to No. Hatley & Hovey Manor signs.

TEL. 819-842-2421
Res. 1-800-661-2421
FAX 819-842-2248
Hovey Rd., P.O. Box 60,
No. Hatley, Quebec, Canada
J0B 2C0
Steve & Kathy Stafford, Innkeepers

I WOULD LIKE TO MAKE A RESERVATION PLEASE

Any time a place of business can accommodate only a limited number of people at a given time, some system must be worked out to schedule those people in an orderly fashion. We're all familiar with the "take a number" system at the ice cream store, and the appointment secretary at the dentist's office and the beauty parlor. Today, it seems everything from service for your car to grooming for your pet requires a reservation. And for every kind of reservation system that exists, some sort of program must be put into place to mitigate interruption of continuous service when one of the reservations can not be kept. For some systems the cancellation of a reservation causes such a minor flurry it is hardly perceivable. For others, of course, major changes in schedules, quantities, and/or physical arrangements must be made.

Various methods are employed by businesses to insure that when reservations can not be kept, the reservationist is notified. This is important especially when loss of business/income would result. Usually a cash deposit, payment in full, ticket, or credit card number is required to make sure that cancellation, should that be necessary, takes place in time to make the proper adjustments.

Businesses with limited space and capacity, such as Country Inns and their dining rooms, understand more than anyone how very important proper cancellation notification can be. Innkeepers' hospitable nature, as well as their business sense, makes them ever sensitive to the trust placed on them when a reservation is made, and to their obligation to refund a deposit when that reservation must be canceled. Receiving and accommodating friends and strangers with kindness and fairness *is* the Country Inn business. All with proper reservations of course.

Great Britain

1. Knockie Lodge
   Invernesshire, Scotland
2. Druimnacroish
   Isle of Mull, Scotland
3. Invercreran Country House
   Argyll, Scotland
4. Kildrummy Castle Hotel
   Aberdeenshire, Scotland
5. Ballathie House Hotel
   Perthshire, Scotland
6. Cromlix House
   Perthshire, Scotland
7. Philipburn House Hotel
   Scottish Borders, Scotland
8. The Mill Hotel
   Cumbria, England
9. Pheasant Inn
   Cumbria, England
10. White Moss House
    Cumbria, England
11. Bilbrough Manor
    York, England
12. Hotel Maes-y-Neuadd
    Gwynedd, Wales
13. Ynyshir Hall
    Powys, Wales
14. The Old Vicarage House
    Shropshire, England
15. Cottage in the Woods
    Worcestershire, England
16. Church Farm
    Worcestershire, England
17. Orton Hall Hotel
    Cambridgeshire, England
18. Knight's Hill Hotel
    Norfolk, England
19. Congham Hall
    Norfolk, England
20. LeStrange Arms Hotel
    Norfolk, England
21. The Rising Sun Hotel
    Devon, England
22. Calcot Manor
    Gloucestershire, England
23. Fosse Manor Hotel
    Gloucestershire, England
24. Petty France Hotel
    Avon, England
25. Royal Oak Hotel
    Somerset, England
26. The Crown Hotel
    Somerset, England
27. Langley House Hotel
    Somerset, England
28. Chedington Court
    Dorset, England
29. Woolley Grange Hotel
    Wiltshire, England
30. Somerset House
    Avon, England
31. Esseborne Manor
    Hampshire, England
32. Fifehead Manor
    Hampshire, England
33. Langshott Manor
    Surrey, England
34. The Beaufort
    London, England
35. Maison Talbooth &
    LeTalbooth Restaurant
    Essex, England

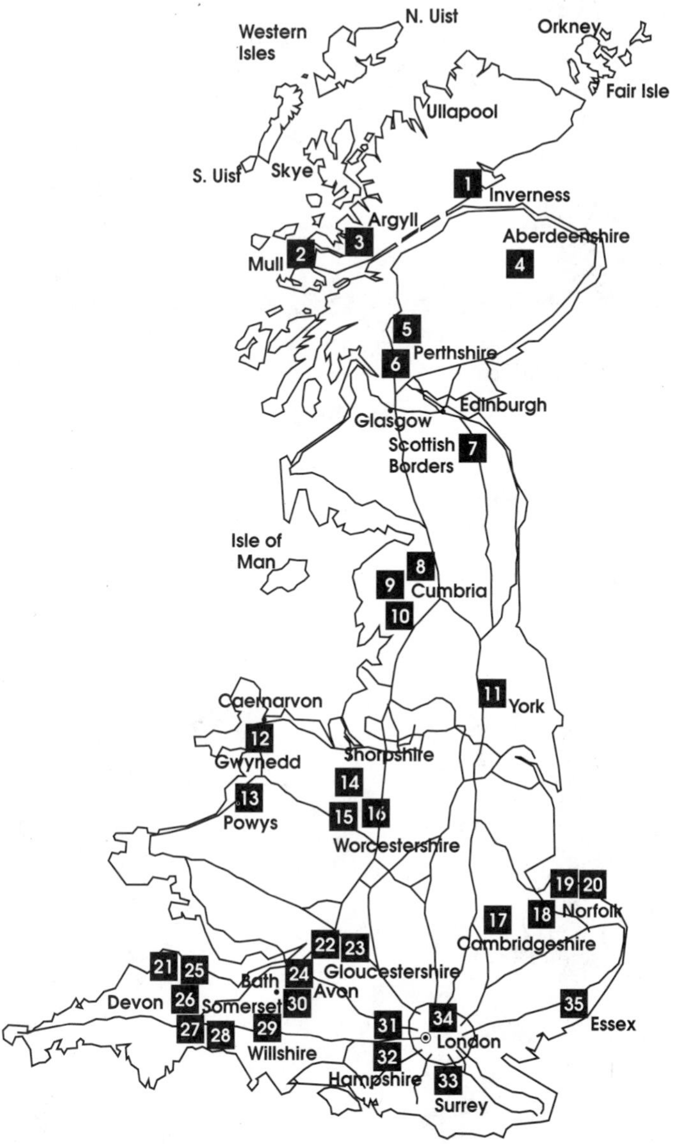

Western Isles
N. Uist
Orkney
Fair Isle
Ullapool
S. Uist
Skye
1 Inverness
Argyll
Aberdeenshire
4
3
Mull 2
5
Perthshire
6
Edinburgh
Glasgow
Scottish Borders 7
Isle of Man
8
9 Cumbria
10
11 York
Caernarvon
12
Gwynedd
Shropshire
14
13
Powys
15 16
Worcestershire
19 20
18 Norfolk
17
Cambridgeshire
22 23
21 25
Bath 24
Gloucestershire
Avon
Devon 26
Somerset 30
35
Essex
27 28 29
Willshire
31
34
London
32
Hampshire
33
Surrey

Members of the Independent Innkeepers' Association

The Shining Light in Hospitality

THE CROWN HOTEL

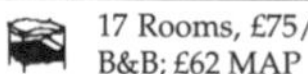
17 Rooms, £75/£90; £80 B&B; £62 MAP

Visa, MC, Access, Amex

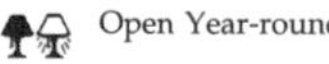
All Private Baths

Open Year-round

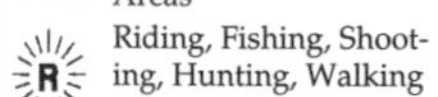
Children Welcome; Dogs Welcome but not in Publc Areas

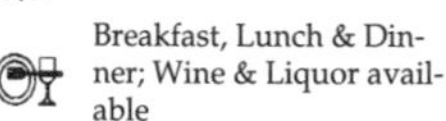
Riding, Fishing, Shooting, Hunting, Walking

Breakfast, Lunch & Dinner; Wine & Liquor available

Smoking permitted

Wheelchair access (dining room)

26 The Crown is a 17th century Coaching Inn which has 20th century comforts. Elegant cosy log fired lounge and spacious relaxing dining room where our French Chef Rene serves superlative food using fresh produce mainly from the region. The bedrooms are all en Suite and furnished to a very high standard and provide comfort and warmth. To top it all the hotel is situated in the middle of the beautiful Exmoor National Park in Somerset.

WEST COUNTRY

From M5 Motorway turn off at Junction 27 and take A361 at First Island take A396 to Wheddon cross. Turn left at Wheddon Cross onto the B3224 for Exford.

TEL. 0164 383554/5

FAX 0164 383665

Exford,
Somerset, TA247QP
Michael Bradley & John Atkin

LANGLEY HOUSE HOTEL & RESTAURANT

8 Rooms, £98/£110 B&B

Visa, MC, Amex

All Private Baths

Open Year-round

Children & Pets accepted

Croquet & Tennis on site. Golf-8 miles-special arrangement with club. Fish-3 miles- special arrangement Game Shooting Nov.-Jan

Breakfast & Dinner Wine & Liquor available

No Smoking

Wheelchair access (dining room)

27 Small Country House Hotel dating back to 15th century but alterations in 1720 give the house a Georgian influence. Hotel winner of Wedgwood Interior Design Award. Resident Chef/ Proprietor cooks in modern English style and the restaurant has been honoured with Michelin Red 'M' and Good Food Guide 'Country Restaurant of the Year' award. Set in 4 acres of landscaped gardens on edge of Exmoor National Park yet only 10 miles from Motorway (M5-exit 25) and about 2 3/4 hours from London.

WEST COUNTRY

B3227 Taunton to Wiveliscombe, turn right at Wiveliscombe town centre (sign posted Langley Marsh) Hotel is 1/2 mi. out of town on right.

TEL. 01984 623318

FAX 01984 624573

Wiveliscombe,
Somerset, TA42UF
Peter & Anne Wilson

RISING SUN HOTEL

 15 Rooms, £79/£99 B&B
1 Suite, £120 B&B

 Visa, MC, Amex, DC

 All Private Baths

 Open Year-round

 Children over 5; Pets by arrangement

 Riding, Walking, Fishing for Salmon & Sea Trout in Inn's private stretch of river

 Breakfast, Lunch, Dinner Wine & Liquor available

 Smoking restricted in restaurant

N/A

WEST COUNTRY

Leave M 5 at Junction 23 (signposted Minehead) and follow A39 to Lynmouth. The Inn is situated on the harbourside.

TEL. 0598 53223
FAX 0598 53484
Lynmouth, Devon EX35 6EQ
Hugo Jeune

21 An award winning 14th Century thatched smugglers inn overlooking a tiny picturesque harbour and Lynmouth Bay with its stunning backdrop of the highest cliffs in England. The Inn is steeped in history with oak panelling, crooked ceilings and creaky uneven floorboards. It was here that R.D. Blackmore wrote several chapters of his West Country classic 'Lorna Doone' and the romantic poet P.B. Shelley spent his honeymoon with his child bride Harriet at the Inn's Cottage in 1812.

THE ROYAL OAK INN

8 Rooms, £60/£72 B&B; £56 MAP 1 Person

Visa, MC, Amex, DC

All Private Baths

Open Year-round

Children over 10; Pets Welcome

Riding, Hunting, Shooting, Fishing, Walking

Breakfast, Lunch, Dinner Wine & Liquor available

Smoking permitted

 Wheelchair access (dining room)

WEST COUNTRY

From M5 Motorway turn off at Junction 27 and take A361 at sign for North Molton turn right go through North Molton then onto Withypool

TEL. 0164 383506/7
FAX 0164 383659
Withypool,
Somerset TA247QP
Michael Bradley

25 The Royal Oak is a 17th century village inn with beamed ceilings and open log fires. The bedrooms which have private bathrooms are all individually furnished and decorated. Our chef Peter produces food with imagination and flair and has gained many awards. The village of Withypool with the River Barle running through it is steeped in Norman history.

SOMERSET HOUSE

10 Rooms, £25/£31 B&B
£41/£49 MAP, 1 person

Visa, MC, Amex

All Private Baths

Open Year-round

Children and Small Pets Welcome (2/3 rate for children 10–13)

Large Garden (over 1 acre), Miniature Railway (not always in operation), Parlor Games, Piano

Breakfast & Dinner daily
Wine & Beer available

No Smoking

Conference Facilities (25-30 if non-residential)

N/A

30 Somerset House is an elegant Georgian town house from which guests may enjoy views across the city of Bath as well as walks into the adjacent National Trust fields. The city centre (Abbey and Roman Baths) is only twelve minutes walk away (3/4 of a mile). To convey the emphasis we place on the food, we describe Somerset House as a restaurant with rooms. We want our guests to enjoy the freshness of the best of local produce. (*Traditional, Georgian, In-Town, Inn*)

WEST COUNTRY

Off A36 (Pulteney Rd.) at St. Mary-the-Virgin-Church on rd. to Bath University.

TEL. 01225 466451
FAX 01225 317188
35 Bathwick Hill,
Bath BA2 6LD
Jean, Malcolm & Jonathan Seymour

WOOLLEY GRANGE HOTEL

18 Rooms, £150/£250 B&B
2 Suites, £200/£300 B&B

Visa, Amex, Access, Diners

All Private Baths

Open Year-round

Children and Dogs

Grass Tennis Courts, Croquet, Badminton, Heated Outdoor Swimming Pool, Children's Garden, Indoor Games Room, Large Victorian Vegetable Garden (walled).

All meals daily
Wine & Liquor available

Smoking except in dining room

Conference Facilities (35)

Wheelchair Access (1 rm. & dining rm.)

29 The home of the Baskerville family for two centuries, Woolley Grange is a stone manor house built in 1610 on the rural fringe of the Saxon Hillside Woolen town of Bradford-on-Avon. The hotel is renowned for the warmth of our welcome, the stylish but relaxed atmosphere, the quality of our food, much of which we grow or comes from local farms, and our genuine welcome for families. We offer the Woolley Bears Den, a manned nursery from 10 AM to 6 PM every day. (*Traditional, Country, Inn*)

WEST COUNTRY

Eight miles from Bath on B3109, 1/2 mile NE of the town of Bradford-on-Avon.

TEL. 01225 864705
FAX 01225 864059
1-800-848-7721
Woolley Green, Wiltshire
BA15 1TX England
Nigel & Heather Chapman

THE BEAUFORT

 23 Rooms & 5 Junior Suites, £250 B&B

 All Credit Cards

 25 Private Baths

 Open Dec. 28–Dec. 18

 Children & Pets by arrangement

 Complimentary health club membership, tennis nearby

 Wine & Liquor available

Smoking restricted in some rooms

 Conference facilities nearby

N/A

LONDON/SOUTH/SOUTHEAST

100 yards from Harrods.

TEL. 01715 845252
FAX 01715 892834

33 Beaufort Gardens,
London SW3 1PP

Diana Wallis

34 Owned by Diana Wallis, we're 150 yards from Harrods in a peaceful Knightsbridge Square, and have 28 bedrooms. The Beaufort is outstanding value—low room rates include *all* drinks, including champagne, all light snacks, a delicious continental breakfast, health club membership, service and VAT. All rooms are air-conditioned, personal Fax/answerphones are available (all calls are charged at cost), and we have a closed front door for additional security. Rated by Zagat as London's top hotel for service. (*Elegant, Victorian, In-Town, Breakfast Inn*)

CHEDINGTON COURT

10 Rooms, £89/£129 B&B; £72/£92* MAP

Visa, MC, Access, Amex

All Private Baths

Closed Jan. 2–Feb. 2

Children & Pets accepted (with restrictions)

Golf Course, Billiards & Snooker, Croquet, Putting

Breakfast, Snacks, Dinner Wine & Liquor available

Some smoking restrictions

Conference Facilities (16)

Wheelchair Access (dining rm. & conf. fac.)

WEST DORSET

Just off the A356. Crewkerne to Dorchester Road 4 1/2 miles SE of Crewkerne at Winyards Gap.

Tel. 01935 891265
FAX 01935 891442

Chedington, Nr. Beaminster,
Dorset DT8 3HY

Philip & Hilary Chapman

28 Jacobean style manor. Renowned for food and wine. One of the most spectacular views in Southern England. Splendid 10 acre gardens, massive sculptured yew hedge, grotto, water garden, ponds, lawns, terraces. Welcoming interior, fine Persian rugs, antiques, stone fireplaces, atmosphere of distinctive informality and relaxation. 9–Hole par 74 golf course on beautiful parkland. Excellent center for seeing Dorset, Devon, Somerset and many country houses and gardens, antique shops, and Thomas Hardy country. (*Traditional, Victorian, Country, Inn*)

ESSEBORNE MANOR

12 Rooms £95/£120* B&B

Visa, MC, Amex, Diners

All Private Baths

Open Year-round

Children over 12
No pets

Tennis Court Outdoor; all Weather Surface

Breakfast, Lunch, Dinner
Wine & Liquor available

Smoking restricted

Conference Facilities (12)

Wheelchair Access (1 rm., dining rm. & conf. fac.)

31 The Hotel is a small, unpretentious yet stylish Country House perfectly placed for those who wish to visit and explore this enchanting area of England designated one of outstanding natural beauty. Aptly described as "invitingly snug," Esseborne has spacious and comfortable bedrooms, furnished to a very high standard, with views over the gardens and rich farmland beyond.The pretty dining room reflects the importance the owners place on their cuisine and service.
(*Traditional, Country, Inn*)

SOUTH/SOUTHEAST

One mi. N of Hurstbourne Tarrant on A343.

TEL. 01264 736444
FAX 01264 736473
Hurstbourne Tarrant
NR Andover
Hants SP11 OER
Michael & Frieda Yeo

FIFEHEAD MANOR

16 Rooms, £80/£110 B&B

Visa, Amex, Access

All Private Baths

Open Year-round

Children & Pets Welcome

Croquet

Breakfast, Lunch, Dinner
Wine & Liquor available

Smoking permitted

Conference Facilities (20)

Wheelchair Access (2 rms., dining rm. & conf. fac.)

32 A friendly family atmosphere attracts guests regularly to this convenient hotel managed by Margaret Van Veelen, who speaks French, German and Dutch. Our chef, Mark Robertson, creates some wonderful dishes. The oldest part of the house is 11th century but modern large bedrooms look out onto the attractive garden. Convenient, on main route west from London airports. (*Traditional, Village, Inn*)

SOUTH/SOUTHEAST

On A34S between Andover & Salisbury (after crossroads 5th house on left).

TEL. 0264 781565
FAX 0264 781400
Middle Wallop, Stockbridge,
Hampshire SO20 8EG

Mrs. Margaret Van Veelen

LANGSHOTT MANOR

7 Rooms, £106/£124 EP
Cont. Brkfst., £5 each;
Full Eng. Brkfst., £8 each

Visa, MC, Amex, Diners
All Private Baths

Open Year-round
Babes in arms & over 12 when possible; No pets

Croquet; Golf nearby

Breakfast, Lunch, Dinner
Wine & Liquor available

Smoking restricted

Conference Facilities (12)
Wheelchair Access (Dining & 1 rm.)

SOUTH/SOUTHEAST

From A23 at Horley take Ladbroke Rd. (Chequers Hotel roundabout) to Langshottt. The Manor is 3/4 mile down road.

TEL. 01293 786680
FAX 01293 783905
Gatwick (Horley)
Surrey, RH6 9LN
Geoff, Patricia & Christopher Noble

33 A beautifully restored Grade II Elizabethan manor house, tucked away down a quiet country lane, offering the warmest welcome and old-fashioned hospitality. Log fires, excellent, hearty food . . . a resting place, a perfect stopover for Gatwick Airport, 8 minutes away. Jaguar courtesy car to airport and rental car depots, an ideal base from which to explore London and the southeast of England.
(*Elizabethan, Country, Inn*)

PETTY FRANCE HOTEL

20 Rooms, £285/£295 B&B
Visa, MC, Amex, DC
All Private Baths
Open Year-round
Children & Pets Welcome
Croquet, Walking, Riding, Shooting, Golf, Biking
Breakfast, Lunch, Dinner
Wine & Liquor available
No Smoking
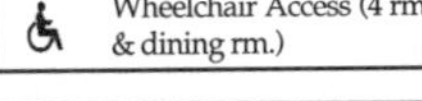
Conference Facilities (25)
Wheelchair Access (4 rms. & dining rm.)

SOUTH/SOUTHWEST

5 mi N of M4 (Exit 18) on A46

TEL. 01454 238361
FAX 01454 238768
Dunkirk, Badminton
Avon GL91AF
Bill Fraser

24 Petty France Hotel is a small Georgian and Regency house set in extensive private gardens located at the edge of the Cotswolds and run by the owners in an informal manner. Modern French and English food is served in the light and airy Regency dining room. A large lounge and small cosy bar both with fireplaces offer guests a place to meet and relax. Twelve rooms which are built in the old stables offer unusual charm.

CALCOT MANOR

22 This lovely Cotswold Manor House was originally a farmhouse, and its beautiful barns and stables, now converted into superb bedrooms, include a 14th-century tithe barn that is among the oldest in Britain. A recent conversion also provides 4 family suites. Located on the edge of the Cotswolds, Calcot is within 2 hours drive from Heathrow and makes an ideal base for visiting Bath, Cirencester, and Tetbury, famous for its antiques.

CENTRAL/EASTERN

From Junction 18 on M4: Travel north on A46. Turn right on A4135. Calcot on left. 4 miles west of Tetbury on A4135.

TEL. 01666 890391
FAX 01666 890394
Near Tetbury
Gloucestershire GL8 8YJ

Richard Ball

CHURCH FARM

16 On 230 acres of rolling Worcestershire countryside, Church Farm offers visitors comfort and privacy with the enjoyment of a warm welcome. Spacious rooms give a good setting for fine family furniture and fresh flowers. The cathedral city of Worcester is 6 miles away and many attractions of the midlands are in easy reach.
(*Elegant, Victorian, Country, Breakfast Inn*)

CENTRAL/EASTERN

From MS Jct 6 (Worcester North) A4538 toward Droitwich for 400 yds. Turn R at sign for Smite. Follow past Pear Tree Inn and turn R. Soon after T Jct turn L and then R after 40 yds. Church Farm is 1/3 mi on R.

TEL. 01905 772387
FAX 01905 772387
Oddingley, Droitwich
Worcestershire, WR9 7NE

Anne Dean

CONGHAM HALL

 12 Rooms, £99/£125 B&B
2 Suites, £160/£180 B&B

 Visa, Amex, Diners, Access

 13 Private Baths

 Open Year-round
No children under 12

 No pets in hotel; outside dog kennels

 Sandringham Royal Estate, Historic & National Trust Properties, Coastal Beaches, Golf Courses, Bird Sanctuaries, Race Courses

Breakfast, Lunch, Dinner
Wine & Liquor available

No smoking in restaurant

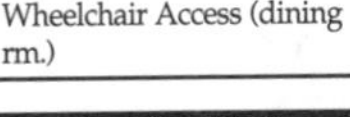 Conference Facilities (12)

Wheelchair Access (dining rm.)

CENTRAL/EASTERN

Go to the A149/A148 interchange NE of Kings Lynn. Follow the A148 to Sandringham Fakenham/Cromer for 100 yards then turn right to Grimston. Hotel is 2 1/2 miles on left-hand side.

TEL. 01485 600250
FAX 01485 601191
Lynn Rd., Grimston, Kings Lynn
Norfolk PE32 1AH
T.C. Forecast

19 In forty acres of parkland, yet only six miles from Kings Lynn, Congham Hall offers its guests complete relaxation. With its paddocks, orchards and gardens, visitors can unwind and enjoy their holiday in an atmosphere of complete tranquility. Built as a Georgian Manor House in the mid-eighteenth century, Congham Hall was converted into a luxury hotel in 1982. The owners have retained the family atmosphere and a welcoming warmth that is evident in all they and their staff do for you. (*Elegant, Georgian, Country, Inn*)

THE COTTAGE IN THE WOOD

 20 Rooms, £97/£135 B&B (English) Bargain Breaks Available

 Visa, MC, Amex, Access, Barclay Card

 All Private Baths

 Open Year-round

 Children & pets accepted

 Walking on 9-mile Malvern Hill Range. 18-hole golf, 1 mi. Squash, 1/2 mi. Clay pigeon shooting can be arranged.

 Breakfast, Lunch, Dinner
Wine & Liquor available

 No smoking in restaurant

 Conference Facilities (14)

N/A

CENTRAL/EASTERN

3 miles south of Great Malvern off A449 turning opposite Jet Gas Station. Signposted from main road.

TEL. 01684 575859
FAX 01684 560662
Holywell Road, Malvern Wells,
Worcester WR14 4LG

John and Sue Pattin, Proprietor

15 A family owned and run hotel, famed for both its magnificent position high on the Malvern Hills, commanding a 30-mile view to the Cotswold Hills, and for its cuisine for which an AA red rosette has been awarded. Small charming hotel guide also awarded a coveted Cèsar in 1992. The London Daily Mail entitled the view "the best view in England." An ideal touring base for the Cotswolds, Stratford upon Avon, Wye Valley, and the cathedral cities of Worcester, Gloucester, and Hereford.

THE FOSSE MANOR HOTEL

Rurally located in the heart of the Cotswold countryside an ideal base from which to explore the historic towns and antique centres. This old manor house is set in six acres of manicured gardens. Family owned and operated with an excellent reputation for friendly efficient service, all rooms are individually and tastefully decorated in keeping with the country house style. The elegant restaurant provides the very best of traditional English and Continental Cuisine.

CENTRAL/EASTERN ENGLAND

1 mi. S. of Stow-on-the-Wold on the A429 Warwick to Cirencester Rd.

TEL. 01451 830354
FAX 01451 832486
Stow-on-the-Wold
Gloucester, GL54 1JX

Mr. & Mrs. Johnston

KNIGHTS HILL HOTEL

With its origins firmly rooted in history—growing from a hunting lodge in the King's Chase to large working farm and hub of the local community—Knights Hill has evolved, through sympathetic renovation into a well-appointed, three-star hotel with a choice of bedroom styles, restaurants, a traditional country pub and extensive leisure center. Close to the royal estate at Sandringham, guests have a comfortable base from which to explore the coastal and rural beauty of West Norfolk. (*Traditional, Country, Hotel*)

CENTRAL/EASTERN

At junction of A148/A149 on King's Lynn ring road.

TEL. 01533 675566
FAX 01533 675568
South Wootton
Kings Lynn
Norfolk PE30 3HQ

Bernard Ducker &
Howard Darking

LE STRANGE ARMS HOTEL

 37 Rooms, 1 Suite £65/£75 B&B

 Visa, MC, Amex, Diners

 All Private Baths

 Open Year-round

 Children Welcome
Pets at Management's Discretion

 Tennis Court (grass), Children's Play Area, Snooker Room

 Breakfast, Lunch, Dinner
Wine & Liquor Available

 Smoking Restricted

 Conference Facility (150)
Wheelchair Access (dining rm. & conf. fac.)

CENTRAL/EASTERN

One mile north Hunstanton. Just off the A149 coastal road.

TEL. 01485 534411
FAX 01485 534 534724
Old Hunstanton
Norfolk PE36 6JJ

Robert & Anne Wyllie

20 A Victorian building located on the North West Norfolk coastline with lawns sweeping down to the beach. Near to many wildlife reserves and places of historical interest, such as Royal Sandringham, Houghton and Holkham Halls. The hotel has a wide range of accommodations, including four-poster rooms and family suites. The hotel's Restaurant has a reputation for fine food and friendly, yet professional service.

MAISON TALBOOTH & LE TALBOOTH RESTAURANT

 10 Rooms, £105/£140 B&B

 Visa, MC, Amex

 All Private Baths

 Open Year-round

 Children Welcome
No Pets

 Constable Country, Sailing & Golf by Arrangement

 Breakfast, Lunch, Dinner
Wine & Liquor Available

 Smoking Permitted

 Conference Facility (24)
Wheelchair Access (dining rm.)

CENTRAL/EASTERN

6 miles north of Colchester off A12.

TEL. 0206 322367
FAX 0206 322752
Dedham
Colchester, Essex C07 6HN

Gerald, Diana & Paul Milsom

35 John Constable country, with this unique combination of a hotel and restaurant 10 minutes walk apart. Gerald Milsom started this business nearly 40 years ago and has achieved fame with Pride of Britain Hotels, which he started. Maison Talbooth is elegant with luxurious bedrooms, some quite glamorous. Le Talbooth is very attractive with Tudor white and black half-timbers overlooking the garden and river Stour, with an appropriate high standard of food. (*Elegant, Country, Inn*)

THE OLD VICARAGE HOTEL

13 Rooms, £85/£100 B&B; £59.50 any 2 or more nights (supplement for luxury) MAP; 1 Suite, £100*
Visa, MC, Amex, Diners, Access
All Private Baths
Open Year-round
Children & dogs accepted
Half-price golf available at nearby golf course. Croquet on lawn.
Breakfast, Lunch, Dinner Wine & Liquor Available
6 no-smoking bedrooms; no-smoking bar; no-smoking dining room
Conference Facilities
Wheelchair Access (2 rms., dining rm. & conf. fac.)

14 Standing in 2 acres of grounds on the edge of Worfield, The Old Vicarage offers its visitors an opportunity to enjoy a peaceful retreat in the Shropshire countryside. An imaginative menu features the best of local produce with a wide range of British cheeses. Over 200 fine wines are kept in the cellar and a good selection of malt whiskies is available. Local attractions include the Ironbridge Gorge Museum Complex and the Severn Valley Steam Railway. Close to Birmingham and Manchester airports. (*Elegant, Victorian, Village, Inn*)

CENTRAL/EASTERN

8 miles west of Wolverhampton, 1 mile off A454; 8 miles south of Junction 4 of M54.

TEL. 01746 716497
FAX 01746 716552
Worfield, Nr. Bridgnorth
Shropshire WV15 5JZ

Peter & Christine Iles

ORTON HALL HOTEL

50 Rooms, £69/£112–£130 Special Wknd F.S.S. £57 DBB PP
Visa, MC, Amex, Diners
All Private Baths
Open Year-round
Children Yes; Pets by Arrangement
On site Croquet; within 1 mi. 2 Golf Courses, Sailing, Windsurfing, Front and Coarse Fishing, Swimming, Gym, Horse Riding, Nene Park, River Trips
Breakfast, Lunch, Dinner Wine & Liquor Available
Smoking Restricted
Conference Facilities (120)
Wheelchair Access (4 rms., dining rm. & conf. fac.)

17 A former stately home, this magnificent 17th Century building is one of Peterborough's finest Hotel and Conference Centres, set in twenty acres of glorious mature parkland in the heart of the conservation village of Orton Longueville, Peterborough. Excellent base from which to visit the rich assortment of local culture and history, in Peterborough, Cambridge, Oundle and Stamford—the set for the BBC's acclaimed period drama of George Eliot's "Middlemarch," with Burghley House close-by.

CENTRAL/EASTERN

From the A1 take A1139; then follow Nene Park signs, then Orton Longueville signs or A605 from city centre.

TEL. 01733 391111
FAX 01733 231912
The Village, Orton Longueville
Peterborough PE2 0DN
Barry Harpham

BILBROUGH MANOR

12 Rooms, £42.50/£75 B&B & VAT; £62.50/£95* B&B, dinner, & VAT

Visa, Amex, Diners, Access

All Private Baths

Closed Dec. 25–29

Children over 10 accepted; No pets

Croquet, Walking, Riding, Golf arranged

Breakfast, Lunch, Afternoon Tea, Dinner & Bar Lunches

No smoking in restaurant

Conference Facilities (30 theatre style; 12 boardroom style)

Wheelchair Access (restaurant)

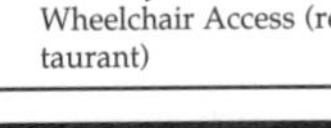

NORTH COUNTRY

Just off A64 York-Leeds road. Turn opposite Happy Eater.

TEL. 01937 834002
FAX 01937 834724
Bilbrough, York Y02 3PH

Colin & Sue Bell

18 Bilbrough Manor is the ancestral home of the Fairfax family dating back to 1086 and was converted into a Country House Hotel in 1986 by the present owners. Situated in 100 acres of pasture land on the edge of the rustic conservation village of Bilbrough, the House exudes warmth, charm and roaring log fires in chilly weather. Renowned for its good food, friendly and excellent service, this little gem is already a firm favourite with American visitors. Recommended in all Main Guides and is the Best Yorkshire Hotel in 1993.

THE MILL HOTEL

8 Rooms, £39/£55 MAP*
1 Suite, £48/£55 MAP*

None

7 Private Baths

Open Feb.–Nov.

Children and Dogs Welcome

Lake District National Park, Hiking, Fishing, Horseback Riding, Golf, Canoeing, Birding, Historic Sights, Bicycling

Breakfast & Dinner; Wine & Liquor Available

No smoking in restaurant

N/A

NORTH COUNTRY

Exit 40 on M6. A66 8 miles toward Keswick. Take sign right to Mungrisdale Village. Hotel next door to Inn.

TEL. 01768 779659
Mungrisdale, Penrith
Cumbria CA11 OXR

Richard & Eleanor Quinlan

8 At the foot of the Skiddaw Range in the Lake District is a charming white house by a stream. Here Richard & Eleanor Quinlan have established a good reputation for individual hospitality. Homemade bread and a mouth-watering range of puddings are featured alongside main courses which include vegetarian dishes as well as game, beef and lamb. Most people return again and again. The cluster of farms and the church nearby with the great fells towering around never cease to appeal. (*Traditional, Mountain, Hotel*)

PHEASANT INN

20 Rooms, £70/£94 B&B & VAT & service

Visa, Access

All Private Baths

Open Year-round

Reduction for children if sharing a room; Dogs allowed in lounges; not in bedrooms

Hill walking; Motoring around Lakes and to Roman Wall; Enjoying peace and quiet of our gardens and grounds

Breakfast, Lunch, Dinner Wine & liquor available

No smoking in dining room and 1 of 3 lounges

Wheelchair Access (1 rm., dining rm.)

9 Tranquil, traditional Lake District inn close to Bassenthwaite Lake. Surrounding gardens and woodland provide a wealth of wildlife. Three lounges feature antiques, open fires, beams, and fresh flowers. Commended by Major Guides for high quality English food and service. 20 individually decorated bedrooms all with private facilities. (*Traditional, Country, Inn*)

NORTH COUNTRY

7 miles west of Keswick; Just off A66 23 miles from Motorway M6.

TEL. 01768 776234
FAX 01768 776002
Bassenthwaite Lake
Near Cockermouth
Cumbria CA13 9YE

Barry & Mary Wilson

WHITE MOSS HOUSE

6 Rooms, £64/£86 MAP

Visa, MC

All Private Baths

Open Mar.–Nov.

Older Children Welcome No Pets

Fell (mountain & lake) walking from doorstep, Dove Cottage & Rydal Manor 1 mi. away. Free Fishing. Free use of local leisure club.

Breakfast, Dinner; Wine & Liquor Available

Smoking RestricteD

N/A

10 Wordsworth once owned this attractive house overlooking Rydal Water. A very intimate atmosphere has been created by Susan and Peter Dixon, that has so many comforts and good food. The reputation of the restaurant is well deserved and one should stay for at least two nights in this central area of the Lake District, with so much to see and such excellent walking in every direction.

NORTH COUNTRY

A 591 at Rydal Water halfway between Ambleside & Grasmere.

TEL. 01539 435295
Rydal Water, **Grasmere**
Cumbria LA229SE

Susan & Peter Dixon

BALLATHIE HOUSE HOTEL

 28 Rooms, £115/£155 B&B
1 Suite, £160/£200 B&B

 Visa, MC, Amex, Diners, J.C.B.

 All Private Baths

 Open Year-round Closed Dec. 24–26

 No restrictions on children; dogs in rooms

 Fishing (Salmon), Shooting, Tennis, Golf nearby, Walking,Touring

 Breakfast, Lunch, Dinner, Afternoon Tea. Wine & Liquor Available

 No Smoking in Dining Room

 Conference Facilites (20)

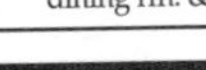 Wheelchair Access (2 rms., dining rm. & conf. fac.)

SCOTLAND

Take A9 N. of Perth to 1st exit (Stanley); take R. fork 1 mi. N. of Stanley. Hotel off B 9099.

TEL. 01250 883268
FAX 01250 883396
(Nr. Perth) Kinclaven, by Stanley
Perthshire PH1 4QN
Christopher J. Longden

5 Situated in its own estate overlooking the River Tay, Ballathie House offers Scottish hospitality in a house of character and distinction dating from 1850. The original public rooms are elegantly furnished and spacious premier bedrooms retain antique furniture and period bathrooms with all modern facilities. Standard rooms are cozy and charmingly decorated. On the ground floor there are rooms suitable for disabled guests and a suite opening out on to the lawns which incline to the river. Food is local with Tay Salmon, Beef, Lamb and West Coast seafood. (*Elegant, Country, Inn*)

CROMLIX HOUSE

 6 Rooms, £120/£170 B&B
8 Suites, £160/£240, B&B

 Visa, MC, Amex, Diners

 All Private Baths

 Open Feb. 3–2 Jan.

 Children welcome if supervised

 3 Trout Lochs: Salmon fishing: Sportings: Walking: Nearby: Golf, Horseriding, Stirling Castle, Scone Palace

 Breakfast, Lunch, Dinner Wine & Liquor Available

 No smoking in dining rooms

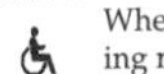 Conference Facilities (30)

Wheelchair Access (dining room, 3 steps)

SCOTLAND

Off A9, 1 mile north of Dunblane, through Kinbuck village. 2nd left after narrow bridge or on B8033 from Crieff.

TEL. 01786 822125
FAX 01786 825450
Kinbuck, by Dunblane
NR. Stirling FK159JT
Perthshire, Scotland
David & Ailsa Assenti

6 "To experience Cromlix is a taste of serenity." 1 hr. from Edinburgh. 40 mins. from Glasgow & Perth. Built in 1874 within its own 5,000-acre estate, Cromlix retains the feeling of a well-loved home where you are a most cherished guest. Original features. Antiques and fine furnishings throughout. Very spacious suites. Open fires. Peaceful & relaxed! A unique house!! Prestigious hospitality, quality & cuisine awards. Reduced rates October–March. Min. 2 nights. Truly an excellent touring base. Impressive private chapel for weddings (max. 40). Exclusive use available. (*Elegant, Victorian, Country, Mansion/Castle*)

SCOTLAND

DRUIMNACROISH

6 Rooms, £178 B&B

Visa, Access, Amex, DC

All Private Baths

Open Mid Apr. to Mid Oct.

Children over 12. Pets in room

Walking, Sailing, Fishing, Golf

Breakfast & Dinner
Wine & Liquor Available

Smoking restrictions

N/A

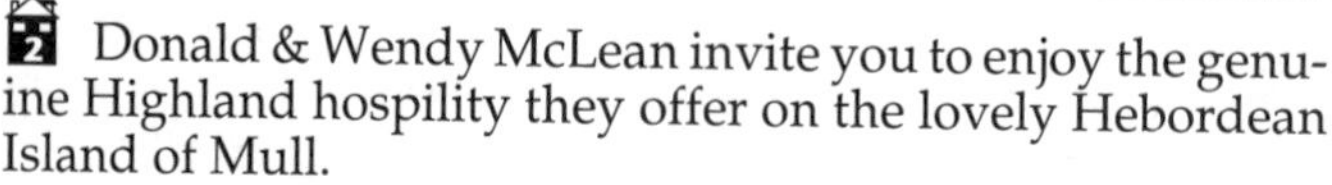

Donald & Wendy McLean invite you to enjoy the genuine Highland hospility they offer on the lovely Hebordean Island of Mull.

The comfort & elegance of our home with good food & fine wines create an atmosphere of indulgence. Ideal for active or relaxing Holidays.

SCOTLAND

Take Ferry from Oban N to Dervaig Via Salen. At Aros left fork to Dervaig; 8 mi., 3 cattle grids; 1 mi. after 3rd cattle grid; Druimnacroish on left.

TEL. 06884 274
FAX 06884 311
Dervaig, Isle of Mull,
Argyll, Scotland
Donald & Wendy McLean

INVERCRERAN COUNTRY HOUSE HOTEL

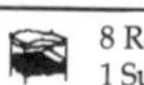 8 Rooms, £90/£124 B&B
1 Suite, £124/£140 B&B

 Visa, Access

 All Private Baths

 Open Mar. 1-Oct. 31, 1995

 Children over 5 No Pets

 All Sports can be Catered for in the Locality, Walking, Sightseeing

 Breakfast, Lunch, Dinner
Wine & Liquor Available

 No smoking in dining room

 Wheelchair Access (1 rm. & dining rm.)

"Deluxe" Invercreran enjoys a location of idyllic beauty, set within a magnificent highland glen. A uniquely styled mansion house luxuriously appointed. Superlatives are often over-used, but not here. Three generations of the Kersley Family are your hosts and are involved in all aspects of what is truly a family hotel. Invercreran is a haven for peace and tranquility, ideal base for exploring beautiful Argyll and the West Highlands only 2/3 hours from Glasgow, Inverness or Edinburgh.

SCOTLAND

From Glasgow Airport take the A82, at Tyndrum the A85 to Connel, cross the bridge onto the A828 which leads to Invercreran.

TEL. 0631 73414
FAX 0631 73532
Appin, Argyll,
Scotland PA38 4BJ
Kersley Family

KILDRUMMY CASTLE HOTEL

 15 Rooms, £110/£140 B&B

 Visa, MC, Amex

 All Private Baths

 Open Feb.–Dec.

 Children & Dogs Welcome

 Fishing, Golf, Horse Riding

Breakfast, Lunch, Dinner Wine & Liquor Available

Non-smoking Restaurant

N/A

SCOTLAND

Off A97 Huntly/Ballater Rd. 35 miles west of Aberdeen.

TEL. 01975 571288
FAX 01975 571288

Kildrummy by Alford
Aberdeenshire AB33 8RA

Thomas & Mary Hanna

4 A converted country mansion house set amidst acres of planted gardens, in the heart of the Grampian Highlands, 35 miles west of Aberdeen and close to the royal family's Scottish retreat—Balmoral Castle. All the facilities of a modern first-class hotel with the original turn-of-the-century interior—carved oak paneling, wall tapestries, oak ceilings—the perfect base from which to explore Scotland's Castle Trail, discover the Malt Whiskey Trail, and enjoy the northeast's fine natural produce.
(Elegant, Country, Inn)

KNOCKIE LODGE

 10 Rooms, £90/£150 B&B (4 dbl., 4 twin, 2 sgl.)

 Visa, MC, Amex, Diners

 All Private Baths

 Open May–October

 No children under 10 Dogs welcome

 Fishing, Deer stalking, Hiking, Sailing, Bird watching, Golf nearby

 Breakfast, Dinner Wine & Liquor Available

 No smoking in dining room

 Conference Facilities (10–12)

 N/A

SCOTLAND

Take A9N to Daviot or A82N to Fort Augustus. Then B862/851 to Whitebridge.

TEL. 01456 486276
FAX 01456 486389

Whitebridge
Inverness-shire IV1 2UP

Ian N. Milward

1 Situated 800 feet above Loch Ness few places can enjoy quite such a rare feeling of timelessness and perfect peace and quiet. The atmosphere at Knockie is cozy, friendly and extremely relaxed. It is essentially the home of Ian and Brenda Milward with its beautifully proportioned rooms filled with antique furniture, paintings and other personal belongings. Although remote, it is extremely accessible and provides an excellent base for exploring a wide area of the Northern Highlands.
(Traditional, Country, Lodge)

PHILIPBURN HOUSE HOTEL

4 Rooms, £77/£90 B&B
12 Suites, £77/£99 B&B

Visa, MC

All Private Baths

Open Year-round

Children Welcome
Pets by arrangement

Outdoor heated pool, Badminton Court, Table tennis, Games machines, Children's play area

Breakfast, Lunch, Dinner
Wine & Liquor Available

Smoking Restricted

Conference Facilities small

Wheelchair Access (1 rm., dining rm. & conf. fac.)

7 Philipburn, built in 1751, lies within beautifully tranquil lawns and flowers. The Hill Family fell in love with Philipburn twenty one years ago, and have since sensitively fashioned Philipburn into the Border's most sought after place to stay. Charming country house bedrooms, mellow pine, flowers and chintz flow into the restaurants overlooking the gardens and pool where after a preprandial drink in the bar you can dine on the finest Border beef, fish and game.

SCOTLAND

45 min. from Edinburgh; less than 90 from Glasgow. If driving South A1 & M6

TEL. 0750 20747
FAX 0750 21690
Selkirk
Scottish Borders TD7 5LS
Scotland
Jim Hill & Family

Hospitality

In the late '40's and early '50's as people began to explore the world of hotels and motels, the desire for sequestered namelessness and guaranteed decor during a night away from home was customary. Travelers were comforted by the assurance of not having to deal with an untested, off-brand accommodation. Certainly the last thing that concerned the traveler was the hospitality of the hotel/motel owner. For a quarter century chain hotels and motels reigned supreme. They were new, standardized, plentiful, and everyone was happy.

The needs and desires of the traveling public in the last twenty-five years, however, accompanied by the natural growth and development of the accommodations industry as a whole, have brought about a new emphasis in overnight accommodations. The '80's and 90's have brought a hue and cry for Hospitality from the now-experienced traveler, and he has discovered that this ingredient is the essence of the *Country Inn.*

Today's traveler, arriving in his late-model luxury sedan at a present day accommodation for an overnight or weekend, is looking *for an actual person whose purpose in life is to receive and entertain friends or strangers with kindness and generosity.* He wants first and foremost an *experience of Hospitality* in a quality establishment. Listen to what travelers in America brag about after their trips today. The hospitality of the innkeeper and the quality of the accommodation will always be mentioned first.

As the overnight accommodations industry has developed, *Country Inns and Hospitality,* through a natural process, have become good bedfellows: exactly what today's overnight traveler is looking for.

HOTEL MAES-Y-NEUADD

16 Rooms, £57.50/£98 B&B

Visa, MC, Amex, Diners, JCB

All Private Baths

Open Year-round

Children charged for meals only in parents' room; Dogs by arrangement

Royal St. Davids Golf Club nearby; Walking, Mountains, Historic Castle, Lakes, Beaches

Breakfast, Lunch, Dinner
Wine & Liquor Available

No smoking in dining room

Conference Facilities (14)

Wheelchair Access (3 rms., dining rm.)

WALES

3 miles north of Harlech off B4573.

TEL. 01766 780200
FAX 01766 780211
FAX TOLL FREE USA
1 800 653 3602
Talsarnau Nr. Harlech
Gwynedd, North Wales
LL476YA
June & Mike Slatter
Olive & Malcolm Horsfall

12 Maes-y-Neuadd, an ancient, part 14th-century granite built manor house, nestling into the mountains of Snowdonia, surrounded by some of the most spectacular scenery in Britain. All modern comforts have been blended into the historic fabric of the old beamed bar, charming lounge and gracious Georgian dining room. Delicious local produce for which the area is famous form the basis of the restaurant menus. (*Traditional, Country, Inn*)

YNYSHIR HALL

9 Rooms, £95/£130 B&B
3 Suites, £110/£130 B&B
(dinner priced separately)

Visa, MC, Amex, Diners, Access

All Private Baths

Open Year-round

Children over 9 welcome
Pets by prior arrangement in some rooms

Bird-watching, Golf, Walking, Fishing, Boating, Shooting, Riding, Castles & Museums

Breakfast, Lunch, Dinner
Wine & Liquor Available

No smoking in restaurant & in certain bedrooms

Conference Facilities (20)

N/A

WALES

About 3 hrs. from Manchester or Birmingham airport. Situated off the A487 6 miles from Macuynlletu & 11 miles from Aberystwytu.

TEL. 01654 781209
FAX 01654 781366
Eglwysfach, Machynlleth
Powys SY20 8TA, Wales

Rob & Joan Reen

13 Once owned by Queen Victoria and situated in 12 acres of glorious landscaped grounds on the edge of the Dyfi Estuary. Furnished with antiques and original paintings. Highly acclaimed cuisine and fine wines help make this one of Wales' best deluxe hotels. Ideally placed for exploring Wales and its beautiful countryside. An oasis of peace and tranquility.

A VISITOR'S GUIDE TO COUNTRY HOUSE HOTELS

Maison Talbooth

Ynyshir Hall

Woolley Grange

Calcot Manor

Esseborne Manor

Cromlix House

Langshot Manor

Congham Hall

Knockie Lodge

Maes-y-Neuadd